Photoshop creative collection

Imagine Publishing Ltd
Richmond House
33 Richmond Hill
Bournemouth
Dorset BH2 6EZ
☎ +44 (0) 1202 586200
Website: www.imagine-publishing.co.uk
Thank you for supporting Imagine Publishing – an independent specialist magazine publisher where quality, innovation and excellence are paramount.

Compiled by
Jo Cole

Designed by
Lora Sykes
Caroline Owen
Lawrence Donald
Emma Benham

Proofed by
Lesley Billen, Julie Easton

Printed by
William Gibbons, 26 Planetary Road, Willenhall, West Midlands, WV13 3XT

Photoshop creative collection

Welcome

The creative potential offered by Photoshop really is phenomenal, and this publication aims to show you how to use the program to its full capacity. Split into three chapters – photo editing, artistic, and techniques – you will learn new skills and pick up inspirational ideas to use in your own projects.

We kick things off with the photo-editing chapter. In here you'll find tutorials that explain common tools and functions needed to edit your images to perfection, whether it's cloning unwanted objects or boosting colour. But in addition to routine improvements, you'll also discover ways to meddle, mould and manipulate humble photos into something altogether different. From square fruit to changing weather to merging text and photos, there's plenty of inspiration.

"You will learn new skills and pick up inspirational ideas to use in your own projects in the future"

One area that tends to get overlooked is the artistic side of Photoshop. The various brushes mean you can create images that are just as good as if you painted them using traditional paints. If you don't believe us, see our collection of tutorials that re-create famous paintings.

Our final chapter deals with techniques. In here you will learn how to tame Photoshop's tools as well as how to sort out any problems.

We hope you have fun with these tutorials and that they help you get closer to being a Photoshop master!

Chapters

Transform an object's shape
page 42

Artistic

Try your hand at digital painting and illustration

Using Smart Objects
page 194

Photo editing

Tutorials for editing and manipulating photos

Create a Monet masterpiece
page 170

Techniques

Get to grips with Photoshop's tools

contents

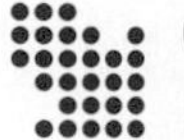

photo editing

Chapter One
Photo editing

artistic

Chapter two
Artistic

On the CD

Stock photos • Tutorial files • Resources

techniques

Chapter three
Techniques

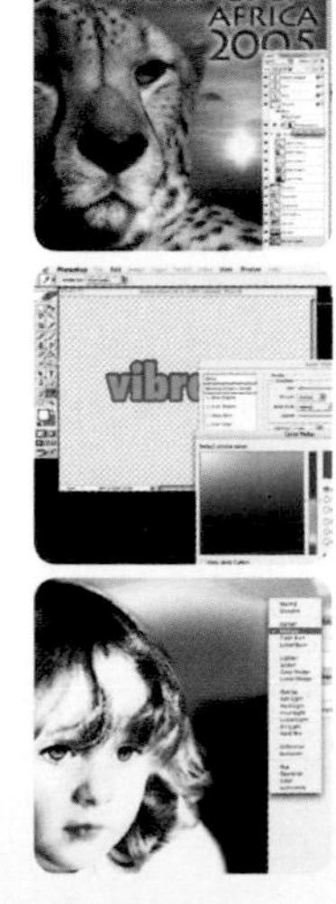

Photo editing

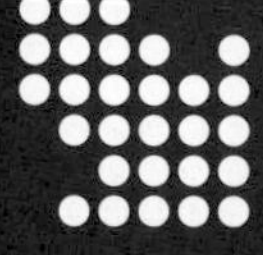

It's no overstatement to say that Photoshop has revolutionised the world of photography. Now users can preen and tweak photos until they shine with perfection. From sorting out colour issues to removing unwanted objects, Photoshop's tools will help elevate an okay image into one that shines with greatness.

In this section you'll find tutorials dedicated to editing and manipulating photos. In addition to techniques for enhancing photos or emulating traditional photographic effects, you will also learn about tweaking photos to give new effects or add mood to a scene.

Contents

A quick trip online can reveal a mountain of first-class creative resources that also happen to be free. Here are some of the best…

Imagine a world where you could access vast banks of images at the drop of a hat, where all the third party plug-ins in your copy of Photoshop were of a professional standard, where you could use unlimited fonts and where you weren't limited to Adobe's basic brushes. How much would you expect to pay to enter this creative nirvana? Thousands? No way. Hundreds? You must be joking. You can find all the above without once putting your hand into your wallet – ladies and gentlemen, we present the world of free resources.

Now we know what you must be thinking – that only low-quality resources, penned by non-experts are available for free. But that simply isn't the case. There's a whole community of image-sharers out there desperate for you to use their products in your own creations. We've found free Photoshop plug-ins that easily rival anything you could spend money on, not to mention brushes that'll open the door to image heaven in no time at all. And as for fonts – well, if your system isn't bulging with typefaces by the time you've read this article, then we'll be damned.

Through a mixture of community spirit, where the sentiment is the more the merrier, and commercial sense, where you're offered freebies in an attempt to persuade you to buy a paid-for resource, the world has never been rosier for Photoshop users. Over the next few pages you will be directed to some of the best free resource sites on the web. These people all offer ridiculously-good content for nothing more than a thank-you kindly. So put your credit card back in your wallet, and get ready to access the huge selection of online freebies.

Plug-ins

FREE for all!

If you love Photoshop so much that using it only makes you hungry for more, then plug-ins should be your first step to artistic nirvana. Every plug-in has a different purpose, and bolts an extra feature onto the software. Building up a collection of plug-ins means that you expand Photoshop's – and therefore your own – creative potential.

In some circles, plug-ins have a bad reputation, and are associated with silly effects that serious artists wouldn't be interested in. But this isn't always the case, as Peter from OptikVerveLabs (**www.optikvervelabs.com**) explains, "We created VirtualPhotographer to have a quick way to get cool professional film-like effects in our digital shots. We don't like crazy effects, just the things that you could have taken originally with the camera, or done in the darkroom." So, whether you seek the subtle or chase the crazy; there is a plug-in out there for you.

> "Once you've found the plug-ins that are right for you then you'll be surprised at how integrated they become in your workflow"

And of course, there's no need to part with any money, as there are various ways to get free plug-ins online. There are trial versions of commercial plug-in sets, so you try before you buy, for instance, the sets from FlamingPear (**www.flamingpear.com**), and the Eye Candy 4000 from Alienskin (**www.alienskin.com**). Alternatively, there are totally free plug-ins to be found on commercial sites, like Graphicxtras (**www.graphicxtras.com**). Andrew Buckle, the creator of this site and also Andrew's Filters, explains: "I don't feel I am just giving them away… they are there as samplers."

Andrew's Filters are tremendously popular, despite some of them having been around since 1996. **Cybia.co.uk** and **Thepluginsite.com** also offer creatives a whole load of great choices, so make sure you explore them. The crucial thing with the bigger sites is to check back regularly, because they are updated in just the same way as software. Buckle assures us that "with each release cycle, I go through all the plug-ins and add one or two new features to all 180 or so plug-ins in the collection."

Once you've found the plug-ins that are right for you – the ones that really enhance your creativity – then you'll be surprised how integrated they can become into your workflow. VirtualPhotographer from OptikVerveLabs is a great example of a plug-in that, although free, is used by professional photographers as far afield as Iraq and Mongolia. Wedding photographers are also fond of them, as Peter from OptikVerveLabs explains, "instead of showing clients a bunch of different shots, they will show less shots but with different effects… we hear over and over that they had throw-away shots that now look artistic and have turned into keepers."

There are over five million copies of VirtualPhotographer in existence, and it's a growing number because of the site's generous attitude. "We don't charge money because we can use it," says Peter, "and anyone else can use it too, but that doesn't impact the value we get from it, so why not have everyone be able to get the same effects easily and enjoy their photography?" It's the ethos of free resources in a nutshell, with Peter adding: "You can use it for anything you wish, but please don't charge others money for it."

Installing plug-ins

PC users: Head to your Program Files on the C drive. Access the Photoshop folder, then find the folder named Plug-ins. Drop your plug-in .exe in. Restart and you'll find your plug-in under the Filters menu.

Mac users: Go to Applications> Photoshop and drop the plug-in into the Plug-ins folder. Restart and look under Filters.

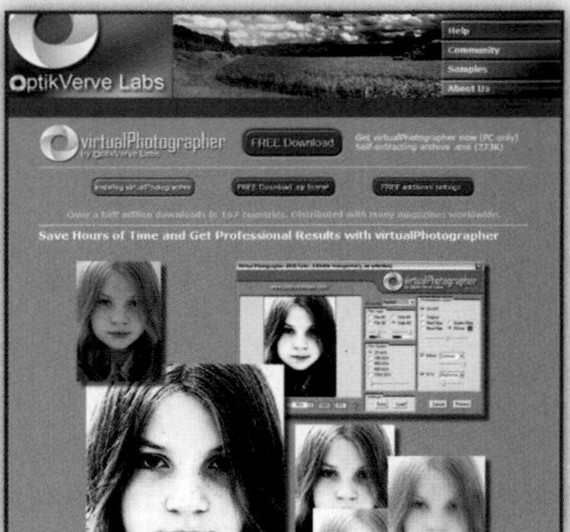

TOP: One of the best Photoshop plug-ins around, VirtualPhotographer boasts five million users

MIDDLE: The Graphicxtras site is jam-packed with not only the finest in plug-ins, but also a barrage of brushes, fonts and shapes

*BOTTOM: The free resources on Auto FX (**www.autofx.com**) are intended as tasters for the company's commercial products*

Pete Bailey – Xero Graphics

Pete Bailey runs Xero Graphics, a site containing freeware and commercial plug-ins

When did you start creating plug-ins?
I started about four years ago. I've been a keen amateur photographer for many years, and as I'm also a programmer by profession it seemed like a natural progression to put the two interests together.

I very quickly got hooked on plug-ins; image processing is a fascinating subject – although it may be that I'm just a sad geek who's easily amused, I suppose!

How long does it take to create a plug-in?
Most of the freeware plug-ins were written in about half a day; but then most of them were tinkered with for a couple of weeks before they were ready for release.

Why do you give away so many plug-ins?
When I first started the Xero site (**www.xero-graphics.co.uk**), I still considered myself a rank amateur; so the thought of asking users for money never even occurred to me. I had absolutely no idea of how popular plug-ins are, though.

About 12 months ago, when I suddenly found myself unexpectedly out of work, I decided to produce a commercial product, and 'Quasar' was born; now, when anyone writes to ask how they can make a donation, I just suggest that they buy Quasar. That way, they actually get something extra for their money!

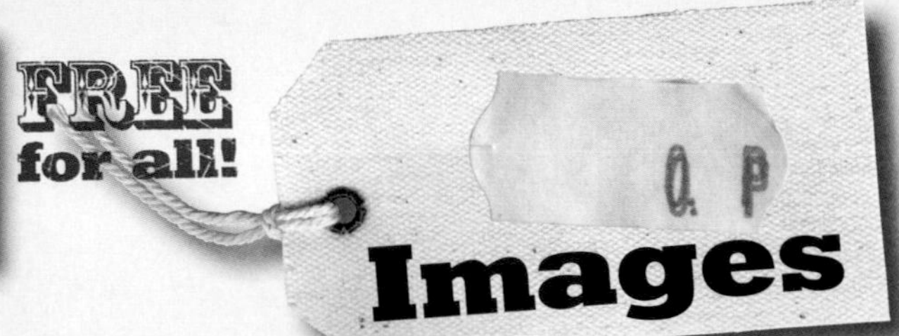

FREE for all! Images

Get great images from David Niblack at ImageBase (davidniblack.com/imagebase/)

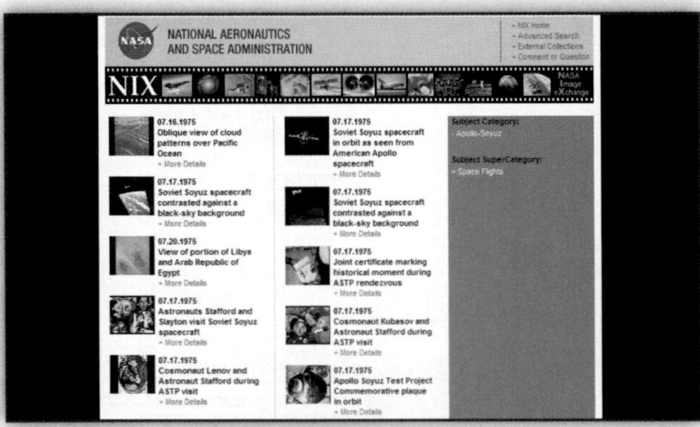

Think outside of the box and locate free images in unusual locations, like NASA

With global photographers, MorgueFile should be on every Photoshop user's list

Finding free photos online should be a doddle. After all, you have the world's most powerful search engine on your side, so it should surely be a case of typing 'free photos' into Google and basking in image heaven. Alas, what you'll actually end up with is a series of links to royalty-free photos, which may be very high quality, but will see you parting with cash for the privilege. Like so much of the web, the best things come to those who know exactly where to look.

One thing you should always look out for when searching for photos online is resolution. Many sites will appear resplendent with images, but if you see the word 'web' anywhere, it's probably best to depart quickly. Sure, web images are naturally smaller than their print equivalent, but even web designers like to start with images larger than 640x480. Also, a little lateral thinking could yield impressive and unexpected results. It's not common knowledge, but NASA has an impressive collection of mission photos on its site (at **nix.nasa.gov**). Instead of finding a photo site and searching for an image to suit, it can sometimes be more effective to go hunting for the image you want in unusual places.

You can roughly split the umpteen totally free photo libraries into two categories: in-house collections and collaboration sites. Sites like FreeImages (**www.freeimages.co.uk**), GeekPhilosopher (**geekphilosopher.com**) and ImageBase (**davidniblack.com/imagebase/index.htm**) all offer a number of decent, high-quality images. What's more, they're even split into categories to make your image-hunting tasks a whole lot easier. Image*After (**www.imageafter.com**) boasts a massive 12,000 free photos that you can plunder, ranging in subject from architecture to vehicles.

> "Instead of searching for an image to suit, it can sometimes be more effective to hunt for the image you want in unusual places"

Started in 1997, Image*After was born out of the frustration of sites that begin by offering free images, but then start charging later on. Every image on the site is taken on Nikon cameras by Tristan and Stefan, the dynamic duo who have been adding at least 50 photos a week for the last nine years. The site doesn't make a profit, but Google ads and sponsored banners at least cover server costs. Looking to the future, Lex Biesenbeek, the programmer at Image*After, says: "We want to increase the possibilities for user interaction, the long-term goal being to allow people to upload their own photos and add them to the collection."

This is no surprise, as image collaboration sites are becoming increasingly popular. Sites such as SXC (**www.sxc.hu**), MorgueFile (**www.morguefile.com**), Unprofound (**www.unprofound.com**), OpenPhoto (**openphoto.net**) and Photo Case (**www.photocase.com**) are all teeming with free images, uploaded by Photoshop users like you across the world. While all the images are gratis, it pays to read the small print. Each image on SXC has its own licence, for example, informing you what you can and cannot do with the photo. The easy-going rules on SXC state that you can use images for practically any purpose except pornography, and you cannot sell or redistribute. Many sites are more Draconian in their licensing, however, so it's vital that you make sure you know what you're letting yourself in for.

Michael Connors – MorgueFile

Michael Connors, the creator of MorgueFile, explains why he developed a free images site

What was the thinking behind MorgueFile?
I wanted to create a morgue file, which is basically a picture dictionary designed for artists and illustrators so they can see what something actually looks like and be able to use it free of copyright concerns. When I was in art school and just beginning my career as a designer, I spent a lot of time sifting through huge books of stock photos and then a little later on the internet. If you found the correct photo, most of the time it was a tiny preview with a big watermark on it. Certainly a lot has changed since then, but I always felt most stock photo places historically were too concerned with sales, royalties and beautiful artistic pictures.

What pleases you most about MorgueFile?
Seeing the work being produced and ideas coming to life. A lot of the contributors provide the photos so they can build a portfolio and get some kind of feedback on their photos.

What is the most popular image on the site?
Usually it's a woman, the more risqué – the more views. We don't allow pornography but a pretty face gets lots of clicks every time.

Are there other image sites worth visiting?
I think it's a lot easier now to find cheap resources. There are quite a few sites like morguefile.com namely **sxc.hu**, **ppdigital.com**, **openphoto.net** and **imageafter.com**. The best list of free photo sites can be found at **bluevertigo.com.ar**.

Images

FREE for all!

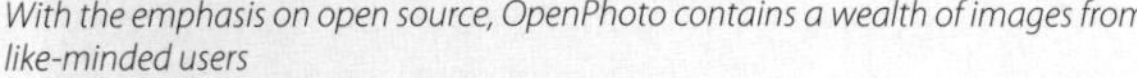

With the emphasis on open source, OpenPhoto contains a wealth of images from like-minded users

SXC looks and feels like a commercial site, but all of the images contained within are completely free

Technology pictures are a speciality at FreePhotosBank (**www.freephotosbank.com**), but there is plenty more

Images on OpenPhoto are protected by a Creative Commons licence. This interesting concept allows you to use the image in any way you wish, including commercially. In return, you must agree to two criteria: firstly, you must credit the author of the original image (this is a common caveat in other resources), and secondly, any image you build using the original can only be distributed under a like Creative Commons licence. This not only protects the original photographer, but also keeps adding more images to the open source network, ultimately benefiting you, the Photoshop user on the lookout for free resources.

Dave Dyer, a frequent image poster at SXC, comments that the "flexibility of various image agreements" makes collaboration possible. You may also be wondering why people like Dave, a mining planner by day, are willing to give up the fruits of their labour to all and sundry. Naturally, he says that he's interested in how people use his images, but he also comments that "sharing is a wonderful way of developing and building on ideas." People often send him a completed project using one of his images. "Most times that will stimulate and inspire other ideas for further images."

> "Photo sites aren't just about grabbing images – there's a continual flow of ideas from those who post the images to those who download"

This community aspect of photo collaboration sites is vital to the people who post their photos online. Frederico Corsini, creator of ImageTemple (**www.imagetemple.com**), has a simple call to arms: "Share your shots. If four designers upload their photos we have some shots to use, but if 100 designers upload, well, the advantage is evident for everyone." This community angle is further reinforced by sites like OpenPhoto, that ask you to register before you download. Not only does this protect the site from attacks, but also helps engender a community via forums and discussions. As Michael Jastremski, creator of OpenPhoto, comments: "People generally do not like to be forced to login to access the site, but it's really for their own benefit."

Photo sites aren't just about grabbing images – there's a continual flow of ideas from the people who post their images to those who download and back again. Not only that, but Dave Dyer believes that learning is an integral part of the experience. "It's a great way to explore and learn about various camera and lighting techniques."

Like many other collaboration sites, OpenPhoto was developed as a location for its creator to store his own photos, before slowly growing into a photo-sharing site. As you ponder utilising the many free images on the site, it's worth remembering the people Michael Jastremski considers to be the most grateful of all users: "I can say that the most appreciative users seem to be non-profit agencies, who simply cannot afford photos."

And finally, we asked Michael for his top tips on obtaining Photoshop resources on the cheap. "I'm an open source person, so I tend to use The GIMP quite exclusively."

Tony Roberts – contributor to MorgueFile

Tony Roberts, a MorgueFile contributor, is developing a new free image site of his own

Why give your images away for free?
I have never actually sold an image yet. It's not intentional – it's just that I haven't actively looked to sell my pictures to anyone. That said, if someone used an image of mine to make profit for themselves, and didn't tell me, I'd have a few issues with them.

What are your thoughts on MorgueFile?
A lot of the pictures are excellent and very professional – SLRs coupled with expensive editing packages etc, that are out of the reach of many people. Similarly the photo sites that focus mainly on places tend to be filled with those beautiful, picture postcard type images, which tell you nothing about the place itself.

I'm currently building a new website, which is based on this kind of community development approach, where people take pictures of their local area and post the images to the site. The site will be at **500yards.com.** As is the case with MorgueFile, all the photographs will be made freely available as long as people use them non-commercially.

What's your advice to people downloading images from free sites?
Check the licence. Some sites say they are free, but you've really got to check out their definition of the word before using any of their pictures. Free could mean copyright-free, but not necessarily cost-free, or else the images may not cost anything but there may be heavy copyright restrictions on their usage.

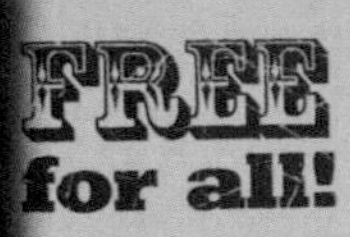

Brushes

Installing brushes

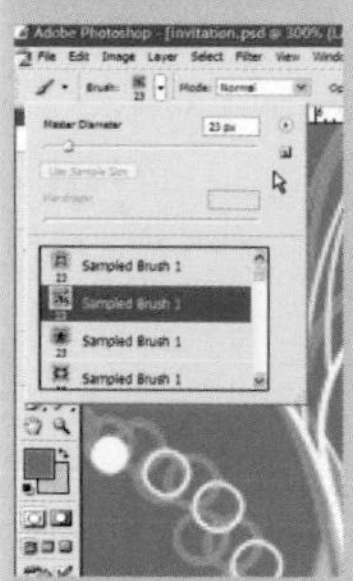

PC and Mac users: Installing a brush set in Photoshop is a doddle. Click on the Brush tool on the main toolbar and click the brush preview in the Option bar. Click on the arrow to bring down the Brushes window, then on the arrow in here for a drop-down menu. If you want your new brushes to be the only ones available, choose Replace Brushes. To add brushes to the existing ones, click Load Brushes. Whichever you choose, browse through your hard drive to the brushes, and you'll be able to use them.

While creating most of the free resources listed here needs a skill that sits outside the Photoshop arena (photography, typography or even some degree of computer programming for a plug-in), anyone who can use Photoshop can create a brush. Indeed, it's the only type of free resource that you can actually use the program itself to make. That said, if you don't have the time or inclination to whip up your own brushes, then once again the internet comes in pretty handy.

Each brush is unique, so if you have a specific purpose you might have to do a fair bit of searching. Make sure you aren't so dazzled by the myriad of brushes on display that you download every one you see. Not only will this clog up Photoshop, but you could also find yourself accidentally taking a 'sheet' download. These are best avoided, because they require you to open up the image file and then create the brush from that, rather than simply installing it. This is fine if it's a one-off special brush, but if you've downloaded a pack of 400 then you can see it's not the easiest way to go! To make things as simple as possible, just make sure that it's .abr files that you're downloading every time.

This shouldn't actually be too tricky, as it's fairly unusual to find massive sets of brushes. Instead you need to find a few sites that really appeal – **www.spy-glass.net** and **www.blinding-light.com** for instance – and then cherry-pick a few sets. Style really is the key here, with things like grunge being particularly popular. Once you find one site you like, you should check if it has any links. The great thing about brushes is that the people supplying them aren't generally thinking about making money. They're usually artists like yourself, who just want to show the world what they've created. Kevin, who is just 17-years-old and is behind **Toastsnatcher.com**, demonstrates this attitude when he says: "to be honest, I never really considered charging for them. All of my favourite sites were free, and I'd offered other free resources on my site before."

> "The great thing about using brushes is that the people supplying them aren't generally thinking about making money"

But while those people are happy as Larry to let you use their brushes in your own work, if you have your own website and want to link to the sites you've found, then you do need to be careful. Some of the sites have some quite specific instructions about how this works.

And once you've exhausted the possibilities, maybe you should think about building a few brushes of your own. If you need a leg-up in the brush-creation business, then head on over to **www.8nero.net** and read the tutorial you'll find there. There's no shame in needing a little help to begin with, as Kevin from Toastsnatcher notes, "It was 8Nero's brush tutorial that got me started with my work, so there you go!"

Blinding-Light.com is a, erm, blinding site to find loads of free brushes that will do you a turn

*The attention to detail in damnedinblack's (**www.damnedinblack.com**) brushes make them very special*

*You'll find a great range of different styles available at **spy-glass.net**, including some neat pixel art helpers*

Steve Upham – Cybia.co.uk

Steve Upham of Cybia.co.uk reveals how he creates his brushes and why he gives so many away for free

How long do you spend making each brush on average?
Each brush can be made within seconds, once you know the procedure. But creating a whole set of, say, 500 brushes in a particular style can take a few days as I usually spend quite a bit of time creating images and experimenting with settings to achieve suitable results.

Why do you give your brushes away for nothing?
I have always been impressed with the online graphics community and how many people share their resources with other users. It really helps to extend programs such as Photoshop when you have extra add-ons like brush packs available. So I decided to contribute in my own small way by making some of my own downloads freely available too. I think it's nice to give something back to the community in appreciation for all the freeware products I've used myself over the years!

What's your favourite Photoshop brushes site, other than your own of course?
Andrew at **www.graphicxtras.com** has the largest collection of brushes available that I currently know of and is well worth checking out. I use a lot of his resources and find them extremely useful in my work.

There are loads of other great Photoshop resource sites online, though, that users should take a look at. Too many to list here but check out the link pages on my website to find more.

Fonts

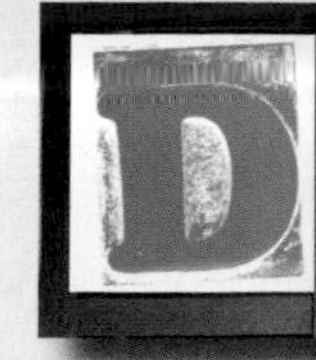

Free font sites are massively popular, mainly thanks to sites like 1001freefonts (www.1001freefonts.com), DaFont (www.dafont.com), Acid Fonts (www.acidfonts.com) and Abstract Fonts (www.abstractfonts.com), where you can download a seemingly endless array of fonts for both Mac and PC. Quickly scan through the various categories on Abstract Fonts, and you'll see the scale we're talking about – at the time of writing, there were nearly 10,000 free fonts.

The main problem with these font collections is that, if you download a font from one of these immensely popular sites, you're liable to end up with something that's being used by millions of people.

If you're after something different, it's worth exploring a different route. Many commercial sites contain a small selection of freebie fonts to tempt you to part with your cash, but often these are more than good enough to use on your projects. The Design Font Maniackers site (www2.wind.ne.jp/maniackers/designfont.html) is a perfect example. As well as a number of shareware fonts, this Japanese site boasts some highly impressive freeware typefaces. BlueVinyl (www.bvfonts.com), Chank (www.chank.com), Fonthead (fonthead.com) and FontMesa (www.fontmesa.com) are all professional fontmakers who kindly allow you to download a smattering for free. Some sites, like Caffeen (www.swank.ca) and Rotodesign (www.rotodesign.com) bear all the hallmarks of professional font companies, but offer up all of their typefaces for free. What's more, you won't find these fonts doing the rounds at other sites.

Another great source of font consternation for many is graphic fonts, or dingbats. You can pick up a world of free dingbats on the web. Jeff Levine is unlikely to win any awards for website design (www.geocities.com/jeffsfonts/index.html), but his free dingbats and alphadings (graphical letter fonts) are not only fantastic, but there are loads of them as well. Renny's Fonts (www.rennysniche.com) proclaims to have the largest collection of graphic alphabets on the internet, and we can fully understand the claim.

Like other free resources, we would implore you to read the small print before you start dashing off creations left, right and centre containing somebody's font. Jeff Levine, for example, will allow you to use his dingbats for non-commercial use, while Jess Latham at BlueVinyl urges you to buy a pay font if you use one of the freeware ones. By far the best example of creative licensing can be found at Robot Johnny (www.robotjohnny.com), though, where the fonts are Toyware. This means they are free for non-commercial use, but if you use them commercially, he asks that you make payment in the form of "a toy or something fun", and helpfully includes his Amazon Wishlist.

1001 Freefonts, as you may have guessed by the name, has oodles of fonts waiting for you

Installing a font

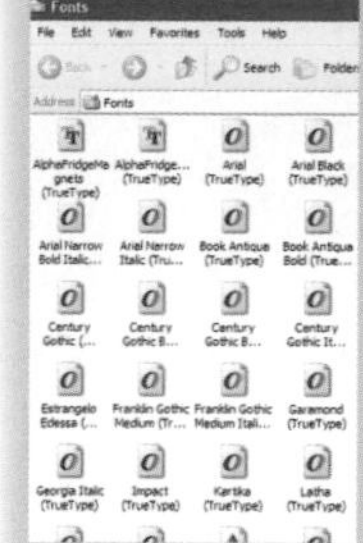

PC users: To install a font, open up the Control Panel in the usual way. Double-click on the Fonts icon, then drop the fonts you want to install into here. Go back to Photoshop, and you should instantly be able to access your new font. Sorted.

Mac users: Double-click on the font to open FontBook. Click Install Font and it should now be installed.

> "Like other free resources, we would implore you to read the small print before dashing off creations left, right and centre"

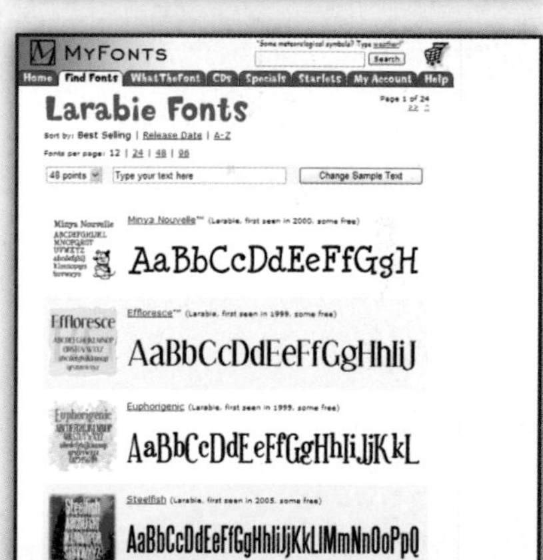

TOP: Use one of Robot Johnny's fonts commercially, and he asks you to send him a toy in return

BOTTOM: Ray Larabie is a true godfather of fonts

Ray Larabie – Larabie Fonts

Ray Larabie explains how he moved from humble font beginnings to providing 384 free typefaces

Tell us about the history of Larabie Fonts. I started Larabie Fonts as a hobby 10 years ago and didn't have plans of making a full-time career of it. The free fonts still bring attention and customers, so I still keep them around and update them occasionally. Now I work full time on my commercial font company, Typodermic. **Isn't font creation an incredibly time-consuming business?**It takes about a week to create a family of four from scratch. Of course, certain kinds of fonts are easier and can be done in a day, and others are more difficult. Then there's an extra day needed to create promotional material and multiple formats.

What's your favourite font?

Th best font I ever made was Tank. It's such an improvement over Machine and similar fonts for certain types of layout. The negative space is completely even, the footprint maximised. Alas, it never caught on as much as I hoped it would. My favourite font when I was a kid is still my all-time favourite: 1963's Compacta. It's due for another comeback (the first was in the early Eighties).

What advice would you give to Photoshop users trying to create amazing images on the cheap?

Buy a scanner that can scan slides and negatives, and offer to scan your relatives' slides for them. Presto! Instant royalty-free photo collection.

Digital photography tricks

Give your digital images the traditional veneer of analogue photography, complete with texture and grain, using these easy-to-follow techniques

When compared to film, digital images can appear a little too polished, which is why many photographers still cling to their old equipment and modus operandi, which haven't changed fundamentally in over 160 years.

Thankfully, with Photoshop, you can duplicate many of the films, processes and techniques of the pre-digital era without having to bump into things in the darkroom or put your hands into dubious, smelly chemicals. Best of all, most of them are easy to achieve in a small number of steps, and in many cases are non-destructive, thanks to the power of Adjustment Layers.

Over these pages, we'll look at eye-catching photographic effects, touch on the important topic of colour spaces, show you how to add convincing film grain to your images and reveal how to convert your colour images into black and white.

Sepia-toning, cross-processing and solarisation are what could be classed as 'darkroom' techniques. Our infrared technique on the other hand shows you how to mimic the appearance of hard-to-find infrared film, which can be difficult to handle in the field. And while nothing can replace the pleasure of using a Lomo Kompakt camera, one of Russia's finest exports, you can still replicate that unique 'Lomographic' style by following our simple steps.

A grainy, gritty image can look amazing, but Photoshop's built-in Grain filter isn't the best solution. Rolling up your sleeves to do a bit of groundwork first, then using small amounts of Noise and Gaussian Blur, will produce better results indistinguishable from the real thing. It's an ideal technique for digital artists who insert new items into a photograph and then have to match the film grain so that the new item doesn't look too crisp.

Thought there was only one way to turn a colour image into black-and-white? Then think again. Here we show you three ways of transforming your RGB images into shades of grey. Usefully, we also explain the pros and cons of each technique, so that you can decide which one's best for you.

You can apply most of the techniques outlined here to any digital image – check out the Photoshop Actions on our CD for one-click access. They're easy to edit, so feel free to fine-tune them to suit your own needs.

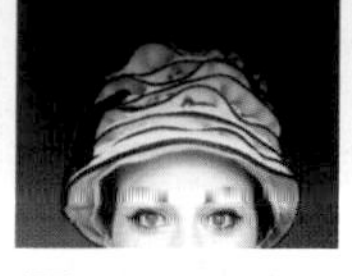

Sepia

Sepia-toning can evoke the stylish look of an aged photograph if used in the right way. In the 19th and early 20th Centuries, the pigment was prepared from the black ink secreted by cuttlefish, but modern photographic processes rely on a chemical dye. You can recreate this look in Photoshop *with a high degree of flexibility*

01 Colorize in Hue/Saturation Open a colour image (or a greyscale one converted to the RGB colour space) and select Hue/Saturation from the Image menu (Image>Adjustments>Hue/Saturation). Click the Colorize checkbox and move the Hue slider until your image is a warm brown colour.

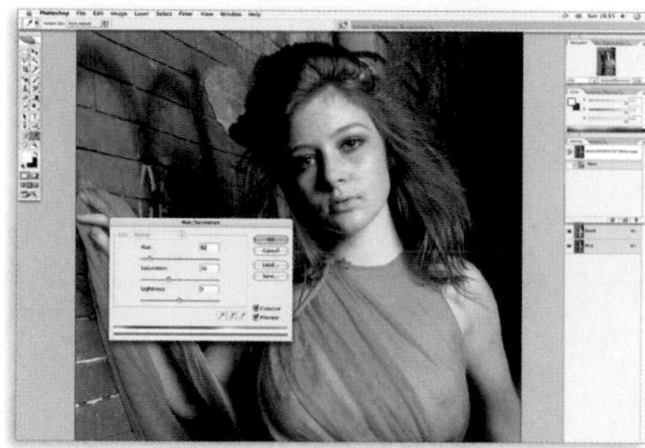

02 Tweak the slider Adjust the Saturation slider to change the amount of colour. Higher numbers will create a richer, more vivid effect while smaller numbers create a subtler, more realistic sepia look. Try adjusting the Hue slider to create the look of blue or green photographic dyes, silver and selenium toning. If you don't want to change the underlying image, use an Adjustment Layer instead

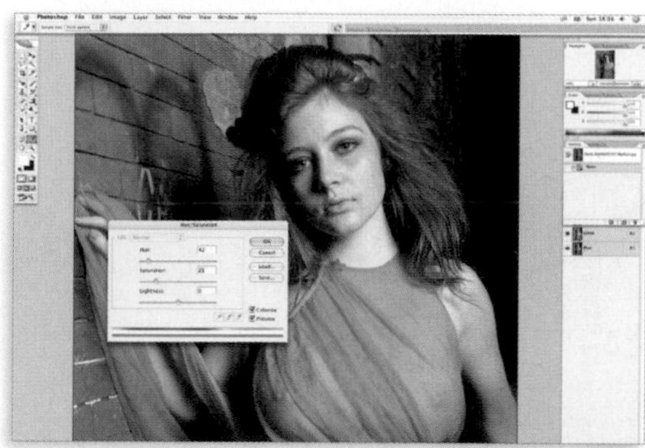

Solarisation

In photographic terms, solarisation is the overexposure of the dark parts of an image and is easily achieved in the darkroom by quickly exposing a developing print to a flash of light. Recreating the effect in Photoshop *is simpler than you might think*

01 Invert image This technique will work with colour and greyscale images. Take an image and make a copy of the layer by dragging it to the New layer icon at the bottom of the Layers palette. Invert the duplicated layer (Image>Adjustments>Invert) to create a negative.

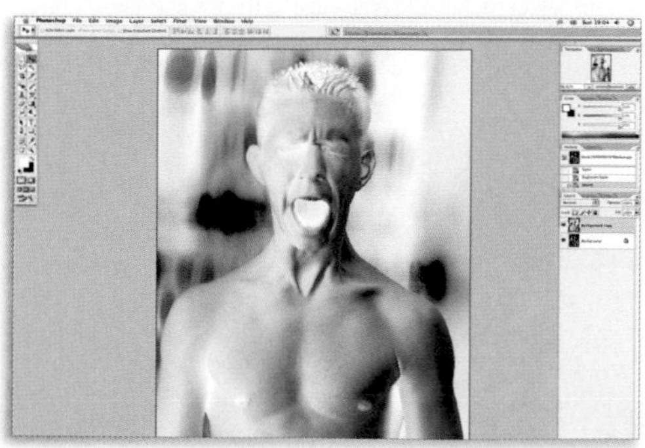

02 Apply Adjustment Layer and tweak Change the duplicate layer's Transparency mode to Exclusion in the drop-down menu at the top of the Layers palette. Create a Levels Adjustment Layer (Layer>New Adjustment Layer>Levels), ensuring that 'Use Previous Layer to Create Clipping Mask' is checked and tweak the Levels to find the correct balance that works for your image. As this process is typically used with black-and-white images, create a new Hue/Saturation Adjustment Layer for the whole image and reduce Saturation to make a greyscale image.

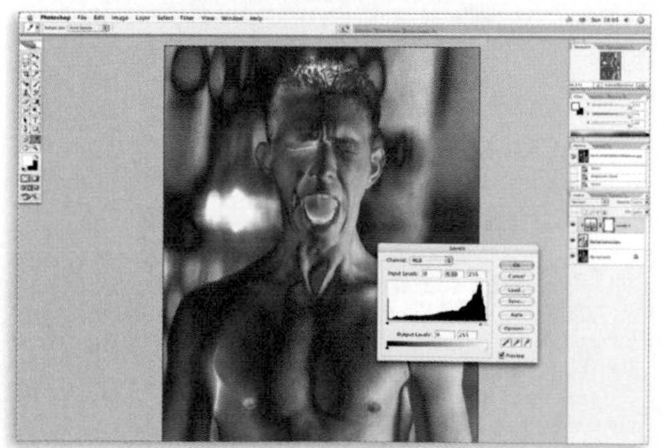

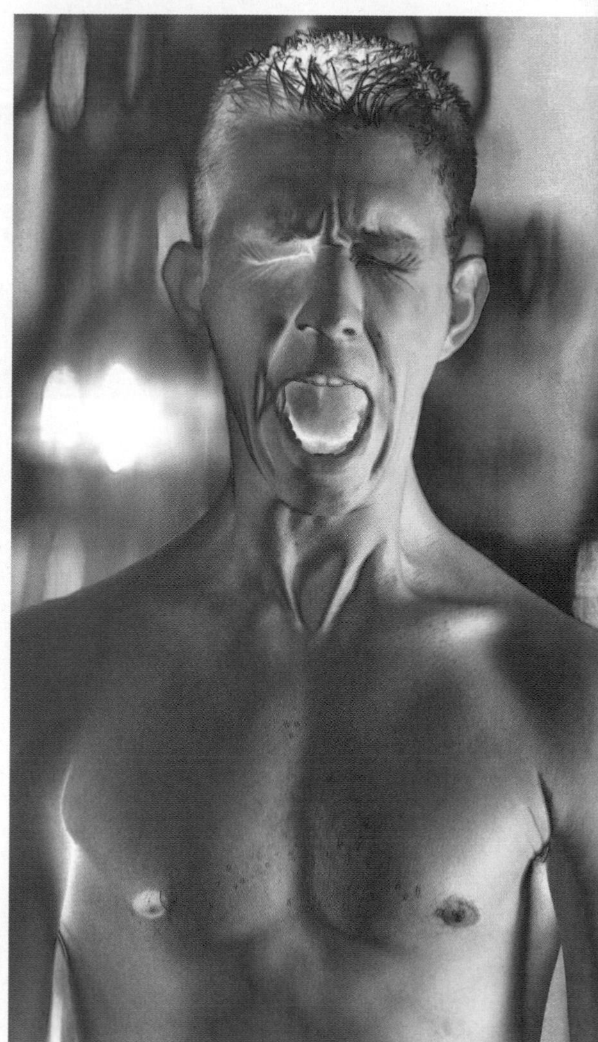

Infrared

Special infrared film can photograph the infrared spectrum, which is invisible to the human eye. Blue skies darken dramatically to black, while foliage develops an unearthly glow. This technique is best used on landscapes, as infrared film can have an unusual effect on human faces, which is beyond the scope of this tutorial

01 Adjust Color Range Open up an image that contains clear blue skies, clouds and some foliage. Using the Color Range tool (Select>Color Range) with a high Fuzziness setting, sample the blue sky and click OK. This will create a selection out of the blue sky. With the help of Levels (Image>Adjustments>Levels), use the grey triangle to darken the sky. Now use the Color Range tool again for the green foliage and boost its saturation using Hue/Saturation (Image>Adjustments>Hue/Saturation).

02 Blur and Grain Go to the Channels palette and click the Green channel. You'll notice that the sky is virtually black and the foliage appears as though the leaves are white. Select all (Select>All), copy the channel and paste it into a new layer in the Layers palette. Use the Color Range tool to select the foliage again (using the original layer), create a new layer, fill with light grey, deselect and then add a touch of Gaussian Blur (Filter>Blur>Gaussian Blur). Finally, flatten the image and add a small amount of Grain from the Filter Gallery (Filter>Filter Gallery).

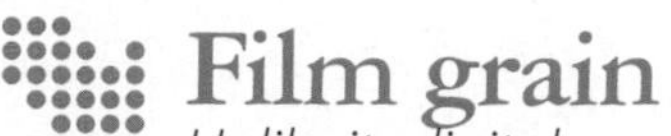

Film grain

Unlike its digital counterpart, film that's pushed several stops and then push-processed often achieves a grainy look which is pleasing to the eye. High ISO ratings on a digital camera, on the other hand, result in digital noise that doesn't look remotely aesthetic. Although Photoshop has a handy Grain filter, it doesn't look realistic because it applies a uniform coating of noise. In film, grain is more noticeable in the midtones and shadow areas and tends to clump. By excluding the highlights and repeating a noise-blur-noise cycle with small values, you can achieve a more lifelike film grain without sacrificing detail

01 Drag background layer to new layer Open an RGB image that's been desaturated or channel-mixed to black and white. Make a duplicate of the image by dragging the background layer to the New Layer icon at the bottom of the Layers palette.

02 Tweaking the channels Click on the Channels palette and duplicate one of the channels by dragging it onto the New Channel icon at the bottom of the palette. For black-and-white images, the channels will all be pretty much the same. On the duplicate channel, invert the image (Image>Invert), boost Contrast using Levels (Image> Adjustments>Levels) and click OK.

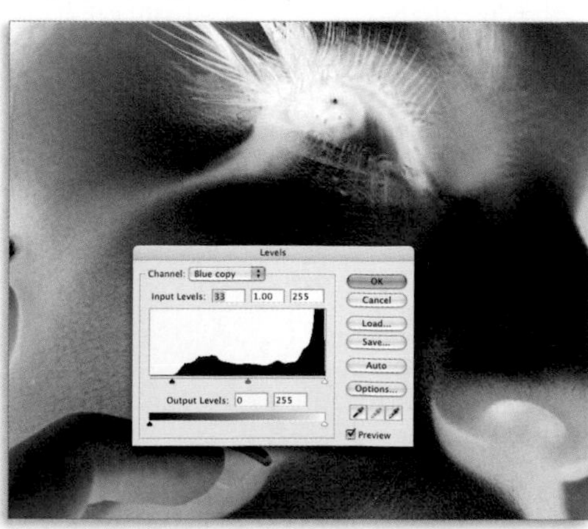

03 Load the selection Making sure that the RGB channels have been selected again, return to the layers and choose Select>Load Selection and load the duplicated channel to create a selection that will exclude the highlights. Apply a small amount of noise (Filter>Noise>Add Noise) – the precise value of which depends on the size of your image, but 10-15 is a good starting point – and ensure that Gaussian and Monochromatic are selected.

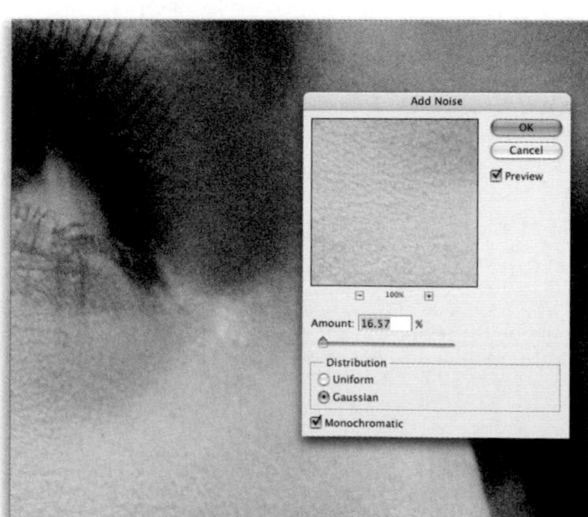

04 Repeat blur-and-noise cycle With the midtones and shadows still selected (you can hide the 'marching ants' selection indicator by turning off View>Show>Selection Edges), apply a Gaussian Blur (Filter>Blur>Gaussian Blur) with a Radius of no more than one pixel. Apply the Noise again and repeat the blurring and adding of noise until a suitable degree of 'grain' is achieved.

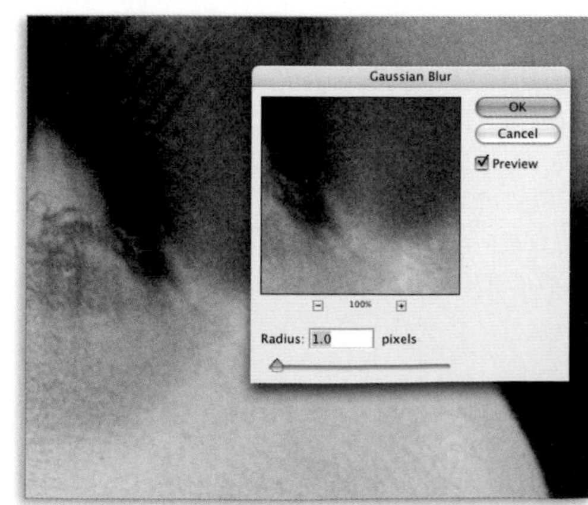

Lomo style

The Lomo Kompact was a Russian-made camera that, thanks to its unique glass lens design and build, somehow managed to produce vivid, saturated images, even of the most mundane subjects. Outgrowing its Communist roots, Lomography has spawned societies and aficionados all over the world dedicated to the Lomo look

01 Retain image details Open up an RGB image and duplicate the layer by dragging it to the New Layer icon at the bottom of the Layers palette. Change the Layer Blending mode to Luminosity, so that details from the image that would be lost implementing the next step are preserved. Now select the bottom layer and create a new Hue/Saturation Adjustment Layer to pump up Saturation to +58.

02 Create new Colour Balance Adjustment Layer To increase the vividness of the image and warm up the tones, create a new Colour Balance Adjustment Layer, and tweak the midtones. Increase the red and yellow values (for example, to +17, 0, -43) and click OK. For absolute authenticity, grab a large soft brush loaded with black and on a new layer add a touch of vignetting to the corners to mimic the camera's optics.

Cross process

Cross processing occurs when you use the wrong chemicals to process colour film – processing negative print film in E6 chemicals and colour reversal or transparency film in C-41 chemicals. This creates unexpected colour shifts and higher-than-usual contrast

01 Remove contrast Take an RGB image and duplicate the layer, turning the top layer's Blending mode to Luminosity to preserve the image detail. With the bottom layer selected, create a new Curves Adjustment Layer and remove some of the contrast with a flattened S-shaped curve (ensure that the light end of the curve is dragged down).

02 Adjust Colour Balance Create a Colour Balance Adjustment Layer. Select Highlights and shift the balance towards the Red and the Yellow (for example +27, 0, -49), then select the Shadows and move parameters towards the Cyan and Blue (for example -70, -15, +32). Finally, create a Levels Adjustment Layer above all the other layers and beef up the contrast by dragging the white triangle to the left.

Converting to black and white

There are many ways to create a black-and-white image from a colour image, and each one has its own advantages and disadvantages

Greyscale

01 RGB to Greyscale The simplest and quickest way is to change Image mode from RGB to Greyscale (Image>Mode>Greyscale). Unless your image is destined for black-and-white output, though, we'd advise against this, since it throws away two-thirds of the image information by condensing three channels into a single Greyscale channel.

02 Duotone, tritone, quadtone An advantage of the Greyscale mode is that it's a stepping stone to exploiting Photoshop's Duotone, Tritone and Quadtone capabilities, which can generate very subtle effects. But this still doesn't change the fact that valuable pixel information is being thrown away. With this in mind, always remember to convert a duplicate image to Greyscale, never the original.

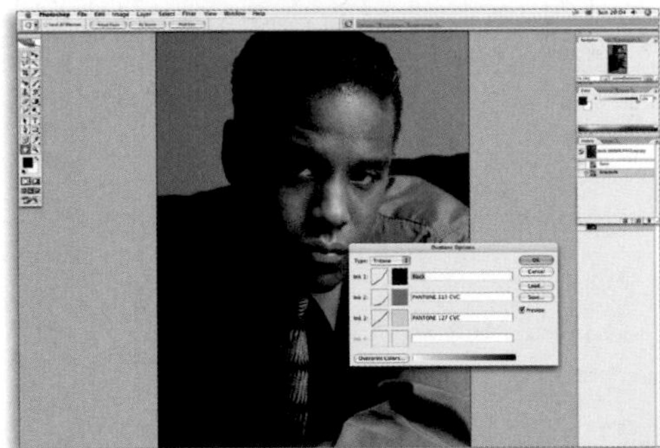

Desaturation

01 Use a Hue/Saturation Adjustment Layer For a non-destructive desaturation approach, open up a colour RGB image and create a Hue/Saturation Adjustment Layer. Take the Saturation slider down to zero and click OK.

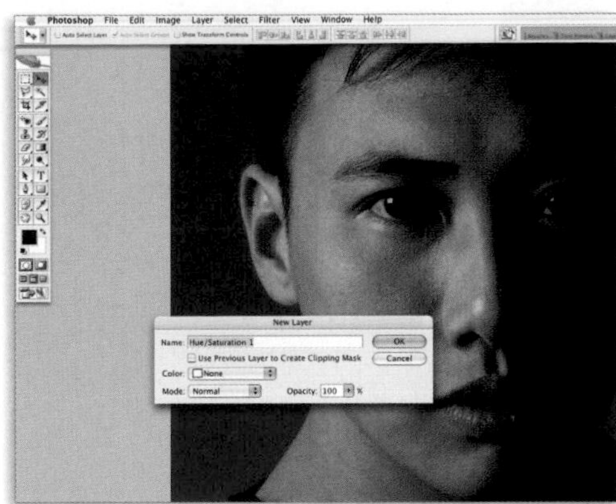

02 Add saturation The advantage of this method is that it maintains all the detail in your original image, resulting in a richer print when it's converted to CMYK and output on a process colour page. By adding a little saturation back into the image, you can create some subtle, aged looks that look almost like hand-tinted photographs.

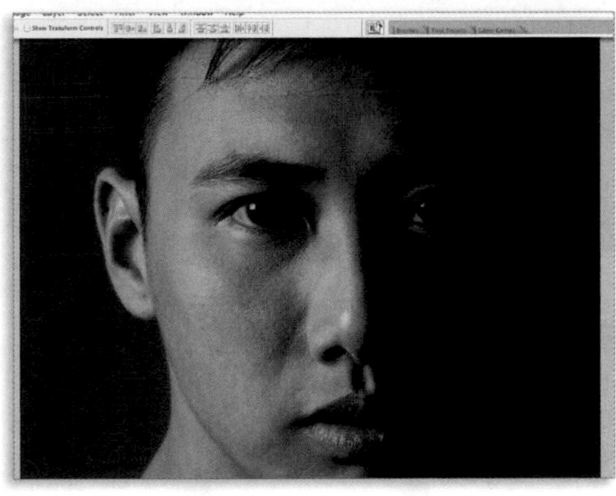

Channel Mixer

01 Use Channel Mixer Adjustment Layer One of the most flexible ways of converting an image to black and white is by using the recently introduced Channel Mixer. Open up a colour RGB image, then create a Channel Mixer Adjustment Layer (Layer>New Adjustment Layer>Channel Mixer).

02 Adjust RGB sliders in Monochrome Tick the Monochrome box and then adjust the Red, Green and Blue sliders so that they're all in roughly the same position, but their values add up to 100 per cent. If the sliders add up to less the 100 per cent, the image may look underexposed, while values above 100 per cent may make the image look overexposed.

03 Experiment! The real fun with the Channel Mixer comes when you experiment with the RGB sliders to achieve 100 per cent values that aren't uniform across the channels. You can make blue eyes paler, darken skin, bring out hidden freckles and completely change the tone of your photograph.

Colour space

Many digital artists, Photoshop users and professional photographers have never really considered colour spaces – or, if they have, decided the subject is far too complex and moved on to the more exciting business of creating images instead. But understanding the topic is vital if you want to get the most out of your work.

To confuse matters, a number of colour 'models', such as CMYK, RGB, HSB and Lab, are mistaken for colour spaces. In fact, the models define how colours can be represented in terms of values, while colour spaces define what the colours should look like. A colour profile is the combination of a colour model and a colour space, which tells external devices such as monitors and printers how colours should be mapped.

Colour spaces essentially tell external devices how to display the material you present them with. This is the crucial part to remember, because a pixel with an RGB value of 39, 210, 26 can look very different on different monitors. For further details, visit **www.microsoft.com/windowsxp/using/digitalphotography/prophoto/colorspaces.mspx**

Tool School

Layer masks

In this tutorial we've used layer masks extensively. Even if you have never used them before, they are really simple and allow you to erase parts of layers in a non-destructive manner. Simply click the Add Layer Mask icon in the bottom of the Layers palette to create the mask. All you then need to do is paint with black as the foreground colour to mask areas of the layer out (press D to adjust the colours). If you want to paint areas of the layer back, simply switch over to white and paint on the layer. Use shades of grey or opacity on the brush to include semi-transparent areas of the layer.

I CAN SEE A RAINBOW

Calm skies ahead

01 Starting the rainbow Download the main image from Stock.xchng (see panel on page 31 for details). Grab the Magic Wand tool and select the tree trunk. From the Select menu choose Similar. Zoom in to the largest tree trunk and hold Shift down while clicking on areas that are not selected. When you have selected enough of the tree, go to Edit>Copy.

02 Paste the trees Pick Edit>Paste to add the trees to a new layer, and rename it 'Trees'. This layer must remain the uppermost layer in this document. From the File menu choose Open, browse to the CD and choose 'nice-clouds.jpg'. We will use these clouds to help create the change in the weather.

03 Add the clouds Drag the clouds over and into your composition. Make sure they are positioned under the Trees layer. From the Edit menu choose Transform and Scale. Resize the clouds to be just over the height of the existing sky and to fit the width of the screen. Now name this layer 'Sky'.

04 Layer mask Click on the Add Layer Mask icon in the Layers palette and paint out the sky over the ground. Now grab the Ellipse tool from the toolbar. Draw a large oval on the screen as shown above. Now double-click the layer in the Layers palette to open the Layer Styles window.

05 Add a layer style Under the Advanced blending options, change the Fill Opacity to 0%. Click on the Stroke category, add a 25-pixel stroke, change the colour to a purple shade and click OK. Copy the layer by dragging it to the New Layer icon. Choose Edit>Transform Path>Scale. Scale up the copied layer to just larger than the original.

06 Change the stroke Double-click the layer and change the stroke colour to blue. Repeat the process until you have each colour of the rainbow. Select each rainbow layer by Shift-clicking the layers in the Layers palette and go to Layer>Merge Layers. Go to Filter>Blur>Gaussian Blur and add a 15-pixel blur to the layer.

07 Fit to the scene Use the Eraser to erase the rainbow over the land section of the image. Change the blending mode to Soft Light and the Opacity to 50%. Copy the layer and change the blending mode to Screen and the opacity of the layer to 90%. The grass doesn't quite fit in with the colour, so select the background layer.

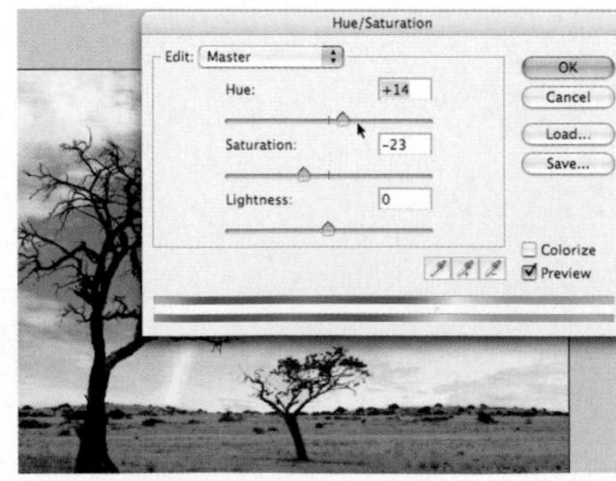

08 Colour correct the grass Go to Image>Adjustments>Hue/Saturation. Change the hue and saturation as shown, then click OK. We've finished the image now, and as you can see we've easily managed to add the rainbow. This was the easiest of the weather effects to produce, so next we'll step up a level to create lightning.

LIGHTNING STRIKES
Darken the sky

01 Start the lightning Open the starting image again and repeat step one and paste the trees to a new layer; name it 'Trees'. Open the image 'darksky2.jpg' from the CD and drag over into the composition, placing it below the Tree layer. Use Edit> Transform>Scale to resize the layer and rename it 'Clouds'.

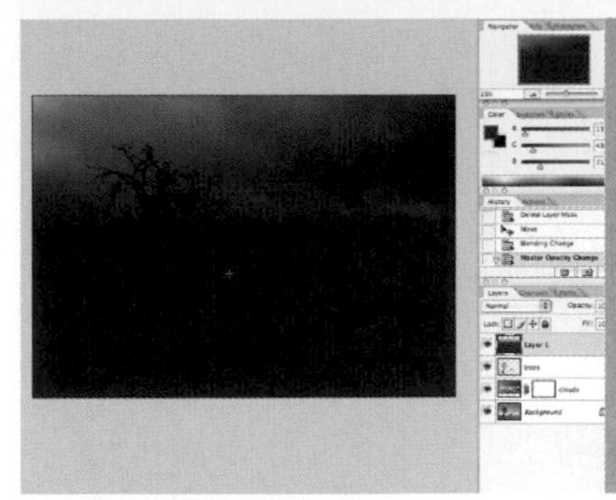

02 Erase the edge Click the Add Layer Mask icon in the Layers palette. Paint out the bottom of the skyline that overlaps the ground. Create a new layer above the trees and name it 'Darkness'. Select a dark blue foreground colour and use the Gradient tool to add a foreground-to-transparent gradient as shown.

03 Blend the darkness Change the blending mode to Multiply and change the Opacity to 80%. This now produces a dark sky that we can add highlights to later on, to reflect the flashing nature of the lightning. Create a new layer again above the others and name this 'Lightning'.

04 Paint in lightning Choose a spot in the sky for your lightning to originate from and then take a soft edged five-pixel brush and draw in some forked lightning. Use the Eraser to thin the edges of your lines. Create another layer of lightning and place that behind the first, reducing the opacity to 60%.

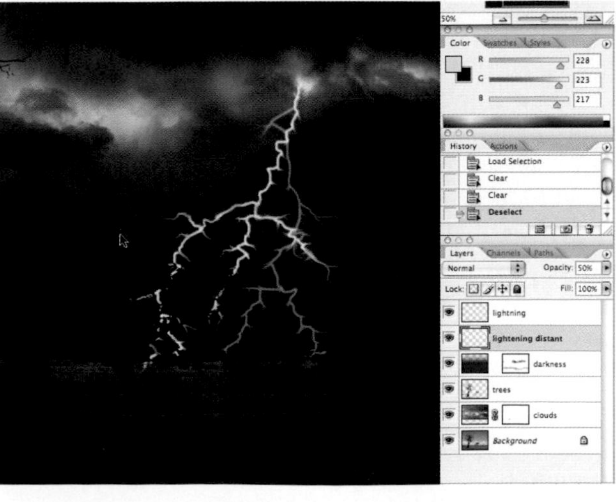

05 Place behind the tree Choose the Trees layer and from the Select menu, choose Load Selection. Click OK in the pop-up window, then select the first layer of lightning and hit Delete. Repeat for the second layer of lightning and deselect. Now select the Darkness layer and add a layer mask, then paint out some of the sky to create highlights.

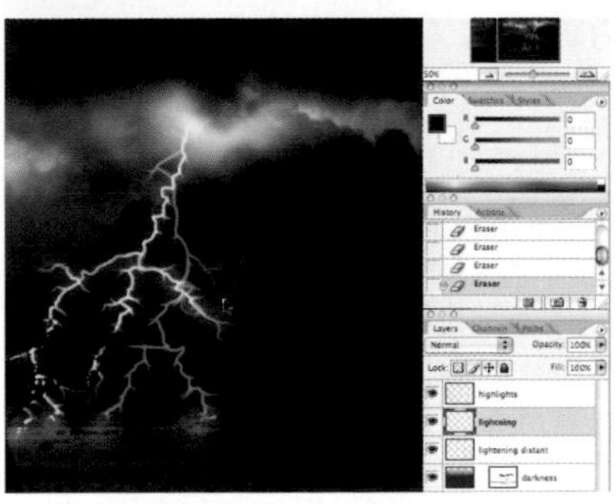

06 Add highlights On the layer mask of the Darkness layer, use a black paintbrush set to 30% opacity to paint in some highlights to the ground below the lightning and to the path of the lightning in the sky. Create a new layer above all other layers and add some white highlights to the clouds and the tips of the lightning.

Expert Tip

Adding shade

If you are adding any content to an already existing image, it's important that the content you add fits in with the existing colours. In order to get the right colours, simply click on the Eyedropper tool and then sample colours from the document. This way you'll be sure that the additions you paint in will fit. We used this technique when adding the twister and then painting in the blend with the clouds. It's a good habit to get into, so why struggle choosing your own colours when this will give you the right hue every time?

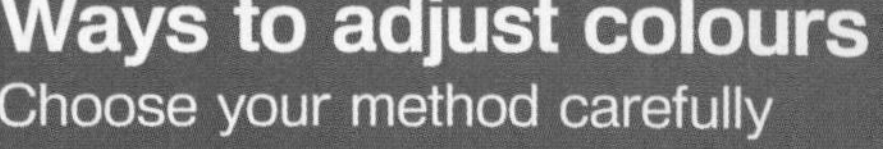

Ways to adjust colours

Choose your method carefully

To create many of the weather conditions in this tutorial, we used colour correction and adjustment tools to get the best effect for the images. Here we explore three ways of adjusting the colour, and discuss the benefits and pitfalls of each. The method used can make or break a project…

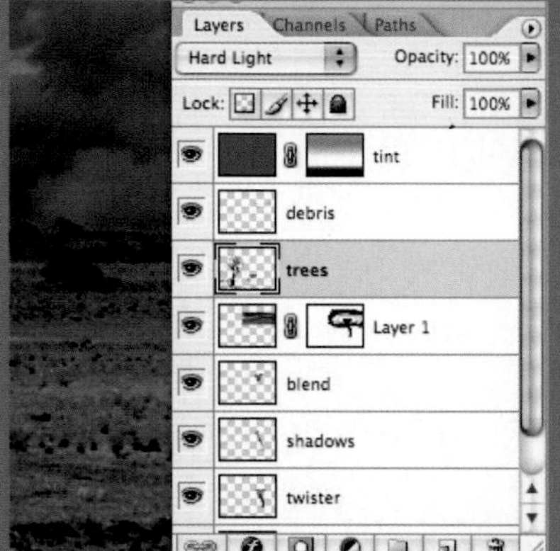

01 Coloured layer

The easiest way to affect the colour of a document is to create a new layer, fill it with a colour then change that layer's blending mode. This will in turn affect all the layers below and accordingly adjust the colour. This technique is good, because you're not changing the colour of layers permanently.

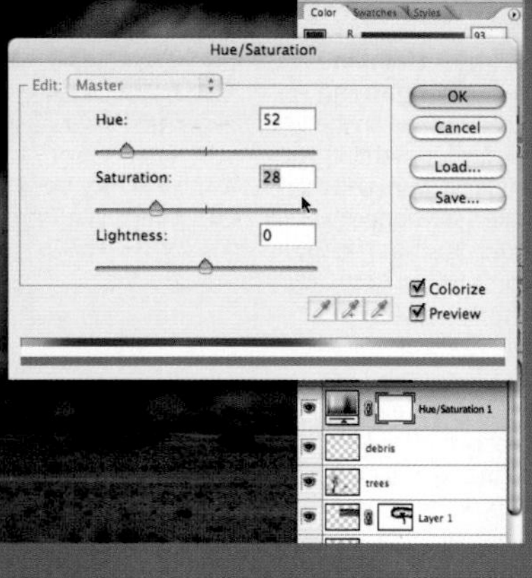

02 Adjustment layer

Very similar to the above technique. It doesn't change the colour of individual layers, but affects layers below the current one. To add, go to Layers>New Adjustment Layer. There are a few, so experiment with them – you can adjust colour, levels, curves and the like.

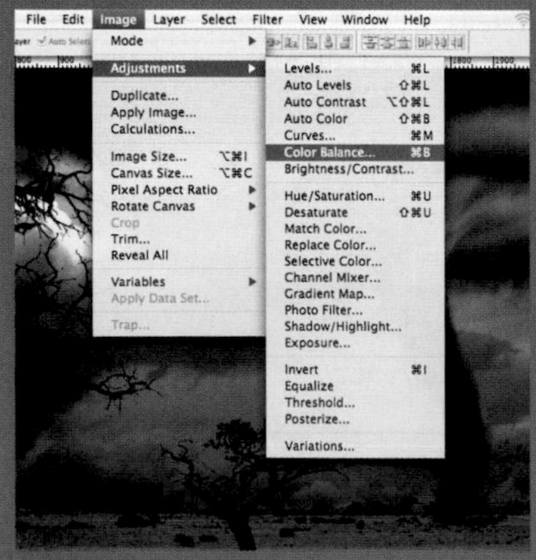

03 Adjusting manually

Each layer can be adjusted manually by selecting it, going to Image>Adjustments and opting to edit a host of settings, including Hue/Saturation, Color Balance, Levels and Curves. The changes will adjust the layer permanently, so be quite sure that you want to make them before applying.

WINDY WEATHER

Add drama to tranquil settings

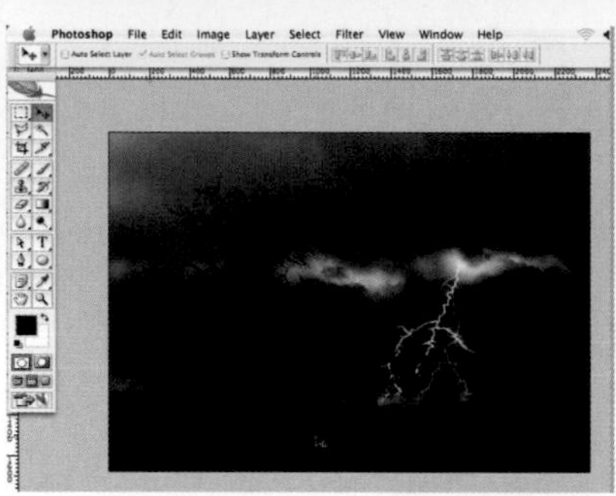

01 Twist and shout Save the image as 'Lightning.psd' and close. Open the starting image again and, as in the previous weather effect, apply the first step. Now paste the trees to a new layer and rename the layer 'Trees'. This is the most complicated of the tutorials and we will re-create a twister.

02 A new sky Open the image 'darksky.jpg' and use the Rectangular Marquee tool to select the sky above the ground. Use the Move tool to drag this across into the composition. Go to the Edit>Transform>Scale menu. Resize the sky to fit in the composition and position as shown above.

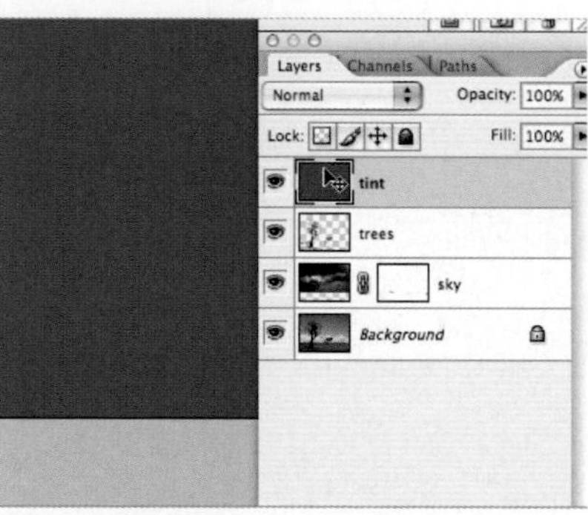

03 Add a mask Call this layer 'Sky' and add a layer mask to it using a black paintbrush to paint out the sky that overlaps the land. Change the blending mode of the Sky layer to Luminosity. Now add a new layer above all the other layers and fill it with a murky brown colour as shown.

04 Change the layer Rename this layer 'Tint', change the blending mode to Color and the Opacity to 50%. Add a layer mask and paint in black around the area of the horizon. Now use the Gradient tool with a mid-grey as the foreground colour and add a foreground-to-transparent gradient to the top of the mask.

05 Merge layers Now the document's the right colour, we need to get our layers in order. Select the background layer and Shift-click the Sky layer. Go to Layer>Merge Layers. Create a new layer above the background layer and name it 'Twister'. Select a dark and light colour from the sky as the foreground and background colours.

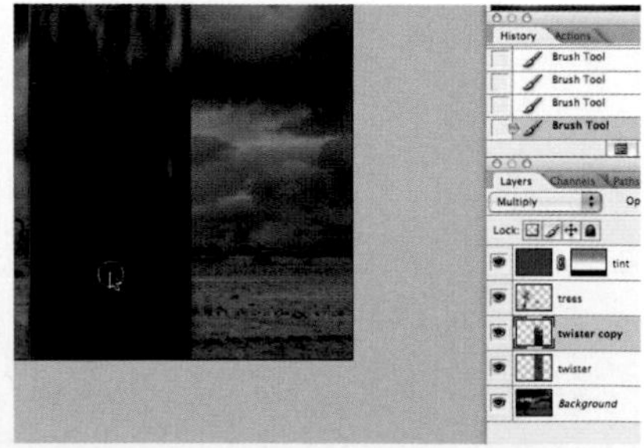

06 Render clouds Choose the Filters>Render>Clouds menu. Select Edit>Transform>Scale and reduce the width of the layer. Duplicate this layer and set the blending mode to Multiply. Now use the Eraser set to 50% transparency to reduce the opacity at the top of the copied layer. Paint in a darker area for shadow at the bottom of that layer.

FUNNEL VISION

Get the twister in the picture

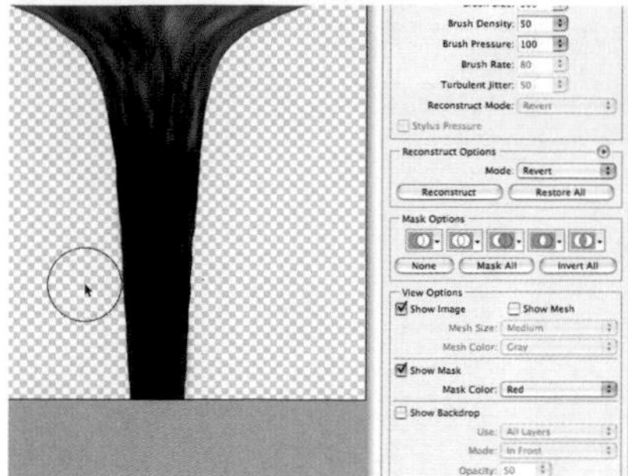

07 Create the funnel Shift-click on the first Twister layer and merge the two layers. Now select Filter>Liquify. Use the Forward Warp tool on the highest setting to push the rectangle into a funnel. You will need to change to a medium-sized brush to fine-tune the edges before clicking OK and returning to your document.

08 Copy the sky Select the background sky; copy/paste to a new layer. Go to Select> Load Selection; hit OK. In Filters>Blur>Radial Blur add a 15-pixel blur; deselect. Place the layer above Twister in the Layers palette.

09 Resize the twister From the Edit> Transform>Scale menu, resize the twister to fit between the new Cloud layer and the floor. Now add a layer mask to the cloud over the twister. Paint out the edges to blend it with the existing cloud. Also paint the mask over the cloud, which is covering the twister.

10 Reshape the twister From the Filter menu choose Distort>Shear. Set up the sheer and add points as shown in the screenshot above to get a slight kink in the way the twister is moving. Once you've done this, add a slight motion blur from the Filter>Blur>Motion Blur menu. This just gives a little movement.

11 Increase the shadows Create another layer just above the twister and use a soft-edged brush with the same dark cloud colour. Set the brush to Multiply and paint in some dark shadows to the left and base of the twister. Add another layer and set the paintbrush back to Normal so that we can blend in the top of the twister.

12 Blend the colour Now just paint at the top of the twister – use the Eyedropper tool to select colours and paint them. The idea is to create a smooth transition at the top of the twister with the clouds. Finally, add a last layer and place this just under the Tint layer. Name the new layer 'Debris'.

13 Finishing touches Use a small dark paintbrush to add an assortment of debris at the base of the twister. From the Filter menu choose Blur>Radial Blur and add a 15-pixel zoom blur to the debris. Ensure that you move the blur centre to the base of the twister. Now save this image as 'Tornado.psd'.

Web resources

Picture credits

The source images for this tutorial came from a variety of people, all found on the excellent **www.sxc.hu** site.

The clouds used in the rainbow piece came from Ryan Smiley (username 'smiley4151'). The sky image used for the lightning was taken by Luc Sesselle (username 'leonbidon') while the clouds used in the tornado image came from Christophe Libert (username 'mordoc'). You can see more of his work at **http://mordoc.deviantart.com.**

But the whole tutorial hung around the fabulous tree shot taken by Carlo Scherer. His Stock.xchng username is 'carlosch'. We used his 'green spot' image, ID number 457002.

Tip

Intense crumpling

If you want an extremely crumpled effect across your image, try increasing the contrast even more. Alternatively, paste your scanned paper onto several layers in order to build up the effect.

FILTER USAGE

Use filters and brushes for a vintage feel

09 Make it noisy Select the layer with your image on it and choose Filter>Noise>Add Noise. Move it to a setting of 12 for a natural effect. Set the Filter to Gaussian and Monochromatic, so no colour is added to the image.

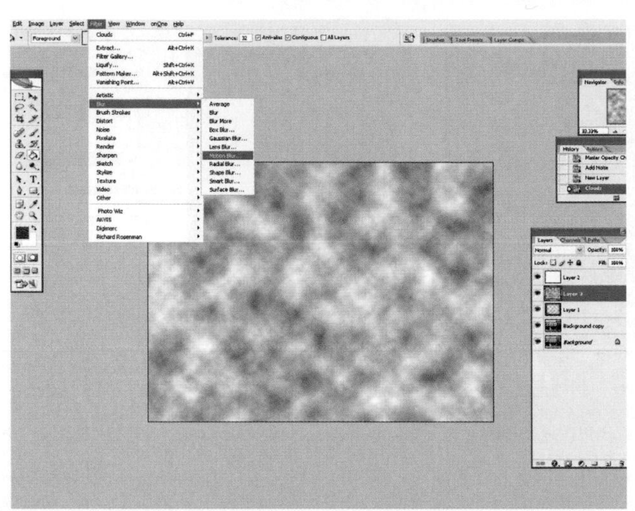

10 Make it cloudy Create a new layer below the white layer. Set the foreground colour to the colour settings Red 153, Green 95 and Blue 56. Set the background colour to white. With the new layer selected, choose Filter>Render>Clouds.

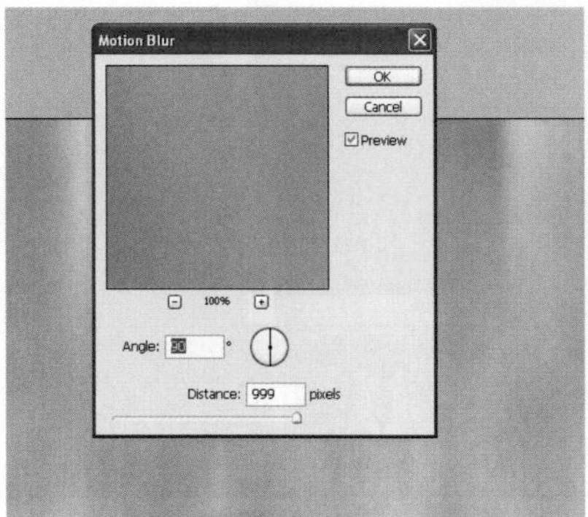

11 Clouds and Blur Choose Filter>Blur>Motion Blur. Enter 90 into the Angle box and move the Distance slider to the maximum. Change the blending mode of this layer to Hard Light. Set the Opacity to 39%.

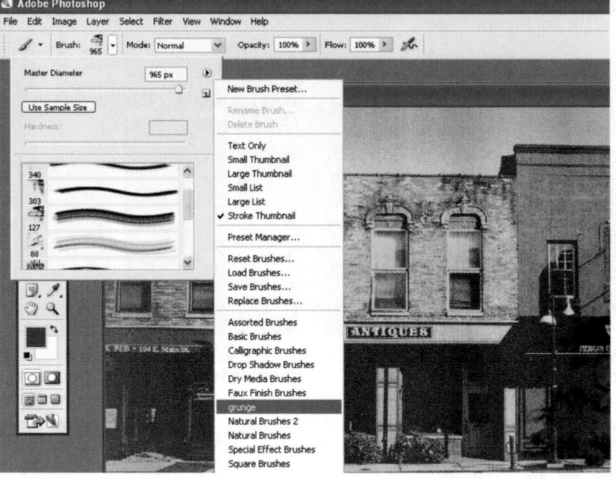

12 Loading brushes We downloaded a grunge brush set from the Photoshopbrushes site (**www.photoshopbrushes.com**). Place your brushes in the Photoshop Application folder under Presets>Brushes. In Photoshop, select the Brush tool and click on the arrow on the right of the Brush listing in the Options bar, and then locate a brush you like.

Tool School

Rip it up some more

If you wanted to create a more severely ripped edge, then instead of enlarging the layer with the scanned paper so it's bigger than the photograph, make it slightly smaller. Now use the same Wet Media brush as before, and follow the edge of the paper you have ripped. Finally, use the Burn tool, as before, to make the edge look more worn.

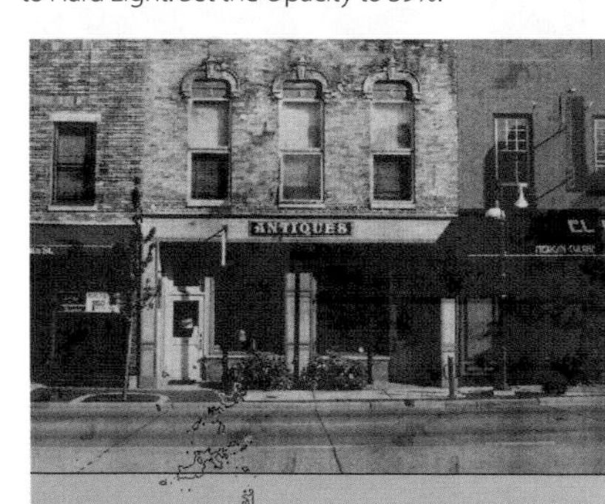

13 Add brush strokes Spread the brush applications over several layers. Lowering the opacity of some layers produces a varied effect. Make sure your foreground colour is a dark brown. Now resize the brush and apply marks sporadically over the image.

14 Scanning paper The best way to create a creased effect on a photo is to take a plain piece of A4 paper and crease it. Scan in your creased paper at 300dpi using your scanning software, or in Photoshop by choosing File>Import. Scan with a piece of dark card behind it so you can remove the edging. If you haven't got a scanner, do as we did and download a texture for free from **www.imageafter.com**. We searched for 'paper'.

15 Incorporate the paper Copy the crumpled paper and paste it on a new layer in your other document, below your photograph. With the paper layer selected, choose Edit>Free Transform and resize your paper so it's larger than your photograph.

FINAL TOUCHES
Create that authentic look

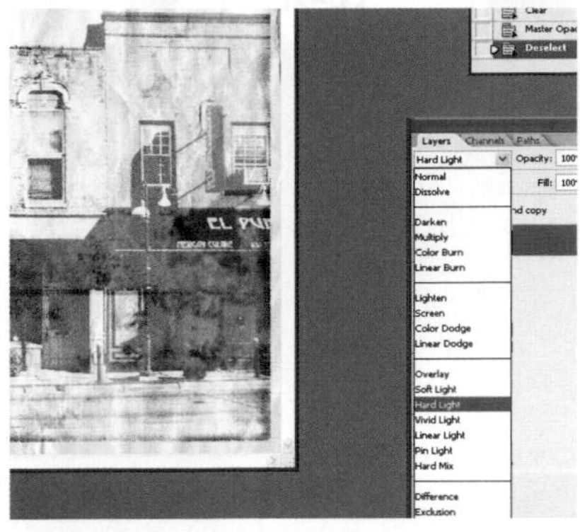

16 Blending mode Move the paper layer below the layer your aged photograph is on. Now set the blending mode of the layer your photograph is on to Hard Light. This will let your texture show through.

17 Show the wrinkles Now, to get the folds and wrinkles from the paper, begin by choosing Image>Adjustments> Desaturate and then select Image>Adjustments> Brightness/Contrast. Move the Brightness down to about -53 and the Contrast up to around +37. Choose Layer>Merge Visible.

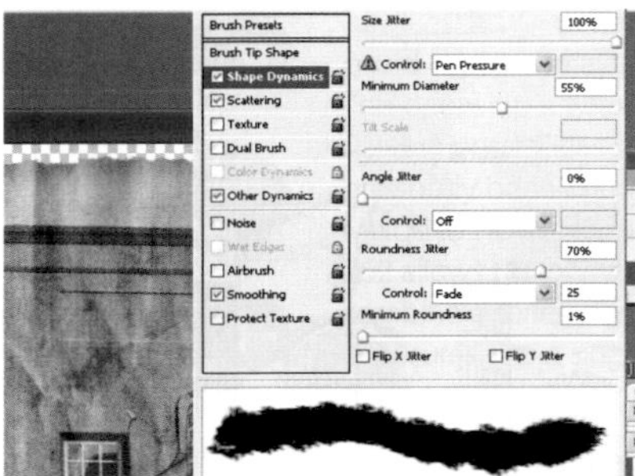

18 Brush settings Choose the Eraser and select Window>Brushes. In the Wet Media brushes, pick the Heavy Flow Scattered brush. In the Brush window, under Shape Dynamics enter Size Jitter 100%, Minimum Diameter 55%, Angle Jitter 0%, Roundness Jitter 70%, Control 25%, Minimum Roundness 1%. Tick Scattering and move the Scatter setting to 71%, Count to 3 and Count Jitter to 7%.

19 Worn edges Rubbing away the edge manually provides you with extra control to alter any parts that may not have ripped the way you want – making them narrower or thicker. Erase the edge of the image.

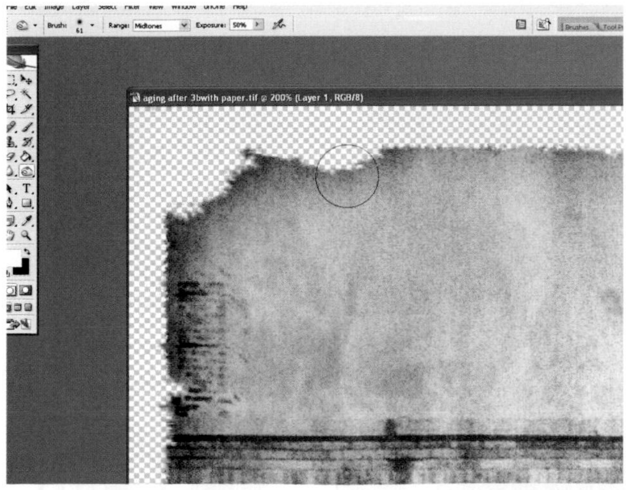

20 Burn it Now select the Burn tool and begin to burn into the edges of your image. This makes them look more worn and creates a slight shadow. Vary your degree of burning so it doesn't look like a solid brown border.

Tip

Using your old photograph

Now you have your authentic-looking aged photograph, there are so many ways you can use it. Why not incorporate it into a postcard or greetings card design? We will be showing you how to integrate it into an old newspaper in a future issue.

The layer structure
Creating your vintage masterpiece

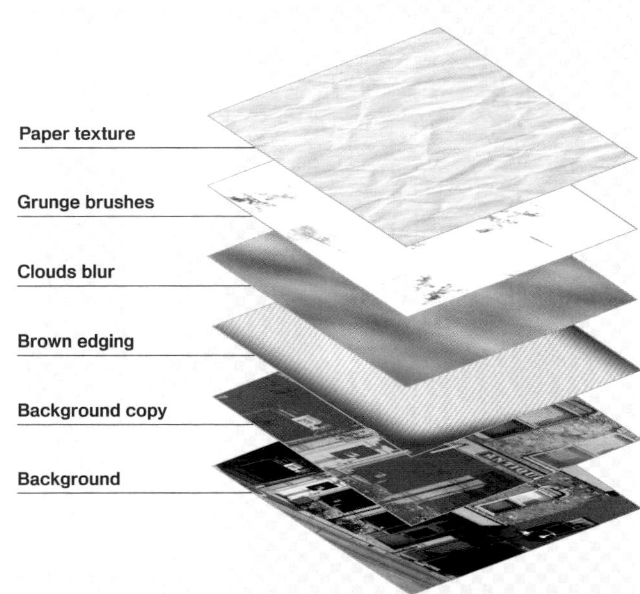

Use Merge to HDR to reduce shadow noise

Even if your scene does not require more dynamic range, your final photo may still advantage from a side benefit: decreased shadow noise. Ever noticed how digital images always have more noise in the shadows than in brighter tones? This is because the signal-to-noise ratio is higher where the image has collected more of a light signal. You can take advantage of this by combining a properly exposed image with one which has been overexposed. Photoshop always uses the most exposed image to represent a given tone – thereby collecting more light in the shadow detail (without overexposing it).

CHANGE THE BIT RATE

Cut your rate in half

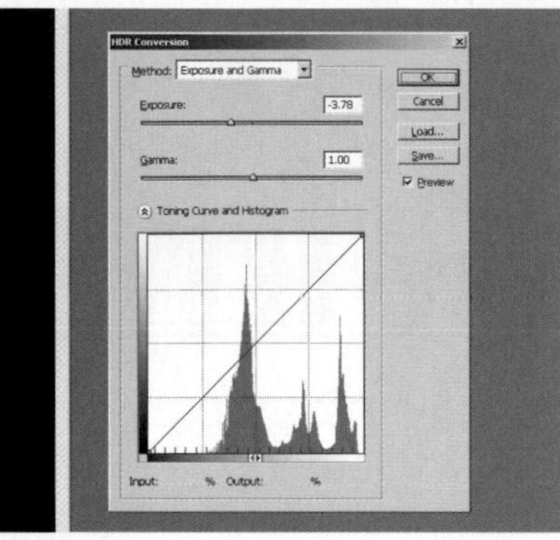

04 Convert 32-bit HDR into 16-bit Convert into a regular 16-bit image (Image>Mode>16 Bits/Channel…) and you will see the HDR Conversion tool. Click on the double arrow next to Toning Curve and Histogram to show these.

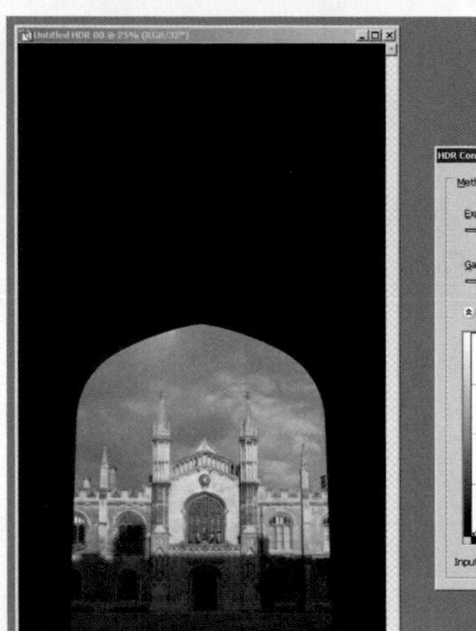

05 Select method Select Local Adaptation because this is the most flexible conversion method. Note how the image preview becomes bright and washed out.

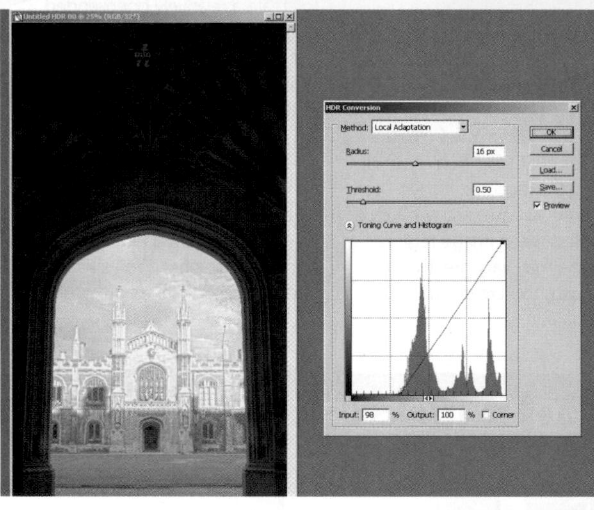

06 Set black and white points Drag the small squares in the bottom left and upper right-hand corners to the edges of the histogram. This sets the black and white points, respectively. Note how the highlight region still appears washed out, but the shadow contrast has greatly improved.

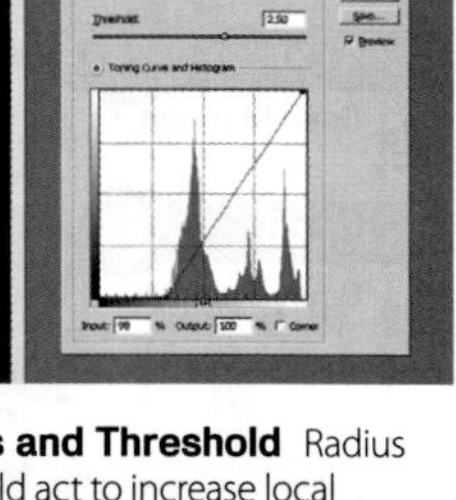

07 Set Radius and Threshold Radius and Threshold act to increase local contrast instead of small-scale sharpness. A high threshold improves local contrast, but also risks inducing halo artefacts, whereas too low of a radius can make the image appear washed out. Adjust each of these to see their effect; for this image, set the Radius value to 250px and then the Threshold to 2.50.

Exposure tip

Capture bracketed photos

Creating an HDR image hinges around the user capturing a series of separate exposures, so a sturdy tripod is essential. Photoshop has a feature that attempts to align the images, however the best results are achieved when this is not relied upon. Make sure to take at least three exposures, although five or more is recommended for optimum accuracy. It is essential that the darkest of these exposures includes no blown highlights in areas where you want to capture detail. Each exposure should be separated by one to two stops and these are ideally set by varying the shutter speed (not aperture or ISO speed). Follow these rules and all should go smoothly!

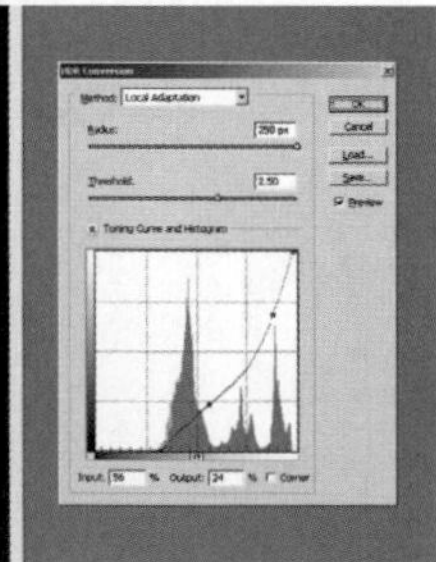

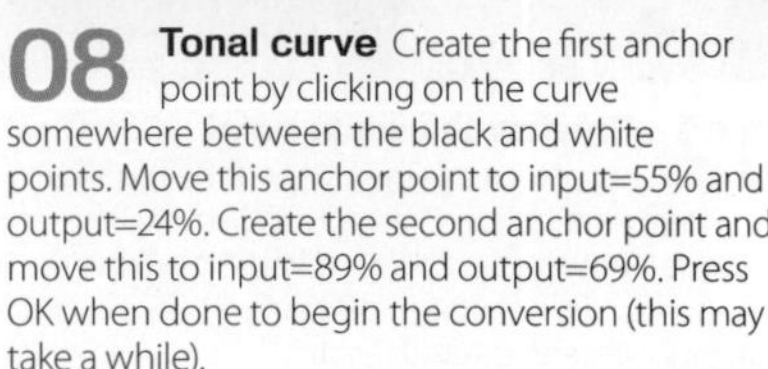

08 Tonal curve Create the first anchor point by clicking on the curve somewhere between the black and white points. Move this anchor point to input=55% and output=24%. Create the second anchor point and move this to input=89% and output=69%. Press OK when done to begin the conversion (this may take a while).

09 Compare with originals HDR images which have been converted into 8 or 16 bit often require touching up. In our image the shadows have become more saturated and the highlights have lost contrast. Load image numbers 1 and 4 from the CD-ROM to see what the shadows and highlights originally looked like.

WEB | A FURTHER DISCUSSION OF 32-BIT FILES AND CAPTURING PHOTOS INTENDED FOR HDR CAN BE FOUND AT **WWW.EARTHBOUNDLIGHT.COM**

CONVERTING TO HDR

Get perfect tonal control by moving to HDR

If you're serious about your digital photography, then getting to grips with HDR images is a massive bonus. They allow you to have unprecedented control over your final photos, and as we see here, let you capture a whole scene without sacrificing detail. Here's a look at what options are open to you in the HDR Conversion window

Exposure and Gamma This method lets you manually adjust the exposure and gamma, which serve as the equivalent to brightness and contrast adjustment, respectively.

Highlight Compression This method has no options and applies a custom tonal curve to the image. This curve greatly reduces highlight contrast in order to brighten and restore contrast in the rest of the image.

Equalize Histogram This method attempts to redistribute the HDR histogram into the contrast range of a normal 16- or 8-bit image. This uses a custom tonal curve which spreads out histogram peaks so that the histogram becomes more homogenous. It works best for image histograms which have several relatively narrow peaks with no pixels in between.

Local Adaptation This is the most flexible method. Unlike the other three methods, this one changes how much it brightens or darkens regions on a per-pixel basis. This has the effect of tricking the viewer's eye into thinking that the image has more contrast, which is often critical in contrast-deprived HDR images.

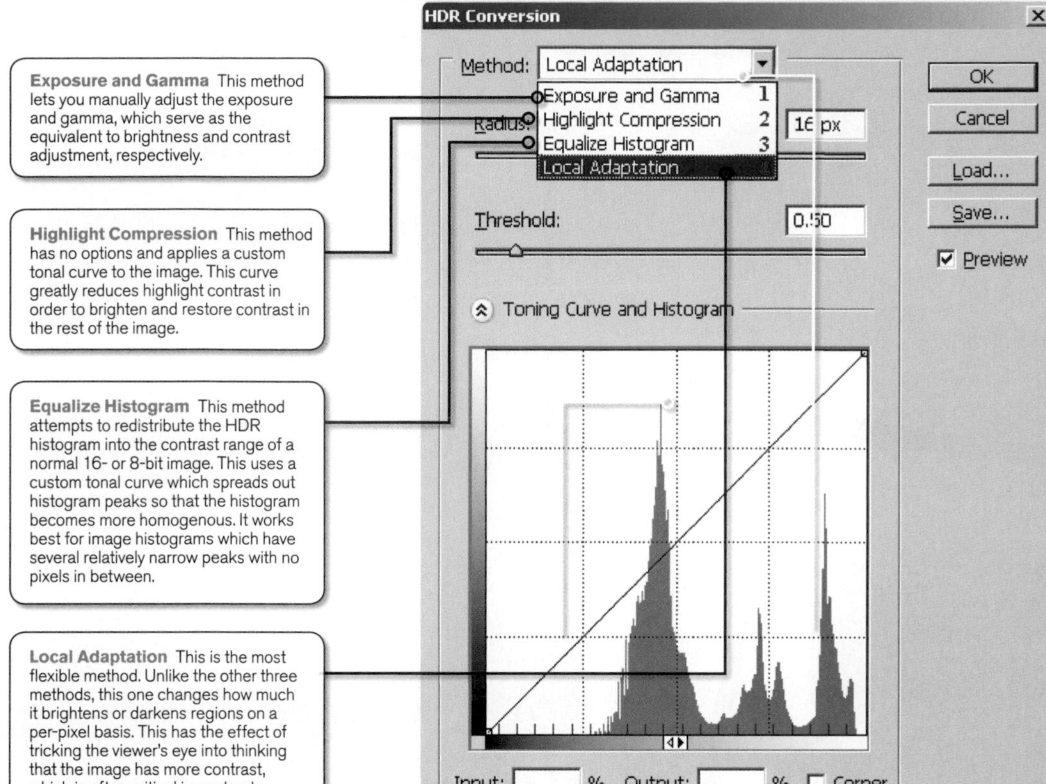

The best use of HDR

When you're working with HDR in mind, be aware that there are certain types of scenes that work much better in the format. There are also other tricks you can deploy to guarantee results. For example, you will achieve outstanding results by using images that are divided into large and clearly defined brightness regions (landscapes) usually producing better results with a graduated neutral density filter.

CONVERSION METHODS

Learn what the different conversion methods mean

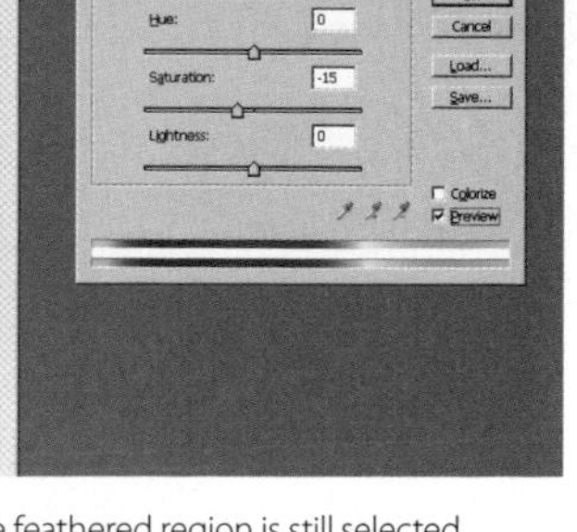

10 Highlight selection Roughly select everything within and below the doorway using the Lasso tool in the image toolbar. You then need to feather this selection by 150 pixels so that any changes will not occur abruptly along the selection border.

11 Highlight touch-up Open the Levels and drag the black point slider inwards until it reaches the edge of the bulk histogram. Then drag the midpoint slider to the right until it has a value of 0.95. These restore contrast within the doorway so that it looks closer to the original underexposed image (#4).

12 Shadow touch-up While the feathered region is still selected, invert this selection (Select>Inverse) so we can now focus on the darker region around the doorway. Decrease the Saturation so that it more closely matches that in the original (Image #1). A setting of -15 was used for this example. Press OK when done and you are left with the final image. Now try using it on your own shots.

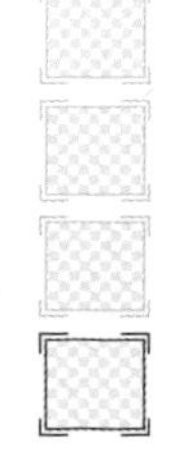

Transform an object's shape

BEFORE

Creating a square apple requires more than a trip to Hogwarts – the Liquify filter beats any magic wand!

essentials

SKILL LEVEL
Beginner
Intermediate
Expert

TIME TAKEN
1 hour

YOUR EXPERT
Matthew Smith

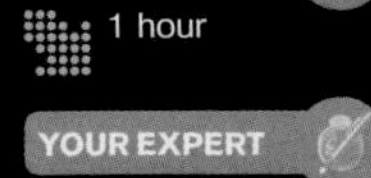

ON THE CD
Apple original

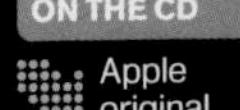

Part of Photoshop's charm for many people is its ability to take a familiar object and turn it completely on its head. This could take many formats – maybe a colour change that goes against nature, or placing items in environments they would never usually occur. This type of image editing can be a lot of fun and produce images that wouldn't look out of place in a clever advertising campaign.

For this tutorial we're going to take the humble apple and give it a new spin by turning it square. Turning a round object square is no easy task, particularly if there's texture that can get warped, stretched and distorted to give away the game. The apple we worked on here contains an incredible amount of lines, swirls and spots in its texture that can easily begin to look unreal if the natural shape is noticeably altered. Much of the hard work then, isn't in the physical reshaping of the object's proportions but in maintaining the detail while this reshaping takes place.

As with any Photoshop task, there are a number of different methods that could be used to achieve this effect, but the Liquify filter certainly produces the most lifelike result in the shortest length of time. It's marvellous at this sort of thing when used with care – there's a real art to selecting which bits to drag at which brush size, to prevent rather unsightly stretch marks. But the great thing about fruit is that it's not a uniform size and contains many imperfections. You're actually better off having slightly wonky edges than having them all perfectly square. Which is a good thing, because perfectly square is not something the Liquify filter does particularly well!

It might possibly seem something of an exercise in futility, but there's more than the fun factor in this application. If you are able to get the hang of preserving detail while changing the fundamental properties of a shape, you will have mastered the Liquify filter and realised just how powerful a tool it really is. It's certainly one of Photoshop's most underrated features!

IT'S HIP TO BE SQUARE

Have fun with nature

01 Set horizontal positioning Open the apple image from the CD. It's more accurate to make a square out of an apple that's properly horizontal, so Select All Ctrl+A (PC) or Apple+A (Mac), then use Edit>Transform>Rotate to square things up a little if needs be. Use Ctrl/Apple+D in order to deselect.

02 Duplicate background layer It's good practice when working on any image to duplicate the background layer. That way, if you mess up you've still got the original to go back to. Either select Layer>Duplicate Layer, or drag the layer to the Create a New Layer symbol at the base of the Layers palette.

03 Fire up the Liquify filter Make sure the Background Copy layer is selected, then select Filter>Liquify. Select the biggest brush size you can, using the slider or the] key. Divide the apple into four sections in your head and drag each upwards and outwards.

04 Work the corners more Next, take the brush size down a third or so and pull outwards and upwards again, this time starting a little closer to the corners – though not at the corner tips. If necessary, move the brush further inwards to another spot and pull to prevent overstretching a specific area.

05 And some more Take the brush size down a third again and tease the corners out a little more. You're aiming to square them off to reduce the rounded effect, but avoid going too far because we still want some corner rounding.

06 Correct edge bow You'll probably find now that the left, right and bottom edges of the apple are beginning to look like they're bowing slightly. Take a large brush and bring them back in line, so the edges look relatively flush.

07 Straighten things up After all this pushing and pulling, you may find the apple appears a little wonky, so take a large brush and pull at the four sections again so the apple looks relatively horizontal and symmetrical.

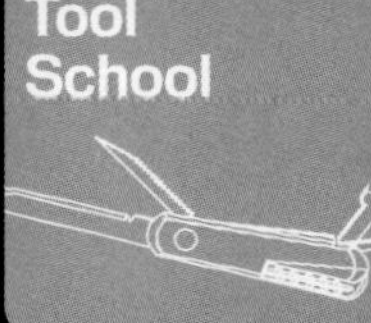

Liquify max brush size

The maximum size brush that the Liquify filter can use is 600 pixels, which is a little underpowered for pushing about objects shots on today's mammoth megapixel cameras. It works best on an image of around 1000 x 1000 pixels, as this allows large drag movements. For bigger images you'll have to make do with a number of smaller movements to achieve the same effect – which requires that little bit extra patience and precision.

Boost colours with the Photo Filter command

Photographers often use coloured filters to enhance a photo's hues – you can do exactly the same in Photoshop

Photoshop is festooned with tools that mirror real-world counterparts and the Photo Filters command is an excellent example of this. The digital equivalent of filters that are put in front of a camera lens, Photo Filters allow you to tweak and improve the colour balance and temperature of an image, either as a whole or by targeting one particular hue. Found in the Adjustments area of the Image menu (or the Adjustments Filters if you're an Elements user), they are a quick and easy way of tweaking colours or applying a totally different effect.

For more traditional edits, the Warming filter (85) and the Cooling filter (80) are painless ways of fixing the white balance of a photo. If you have an image that looks yellowish, a quick blast of the Cooling filter will get things back on track by injecting some blue into the proceedings and evening matters up. The same (but in reverse) is true of the Warming filter. To get rid of colour casts, choose the complementary colour from the ones available.

However, you can also use the filters to bolster an image's colours, as we are doing here. By applying different filters to certain areas, it's possible to turn a lacklustre photo into a gloriously rich colour-fest. By working through this tutorial you'll see how the Photo Filters command is the perfect solution for when you want hassle-free image editing.

essentials

SKILL LEVEL
Beginner
Intermediate
Expert

TIME TAKEN
Approximately 20 minutes

YOUR EXPERT
Jo Cole

ON THE CD
Original photo

COLOUR ME GOOD

Colour correction the easy way

01 Start selecting Open the hay on the CD. Create a copy of the background layer and name it 'Copy'. You need to select all the different areas on the image, so start with the grass. Select the grass area, copy and paste into a new layer. Name this 'Grass'. Now repeat with the trees, hay, sky, trees and field, placing each selection in its own layer. Remember to click on the 'Copy' layer when making your selection!

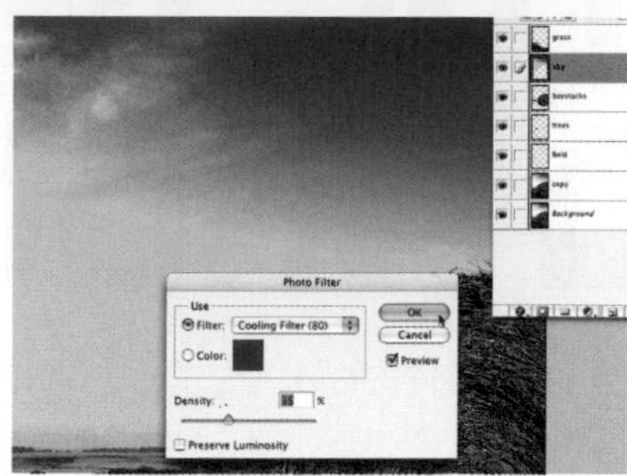

02 Sky captain With all your selections made, click on your Sky layer. Go to Image>Adjustments>Photo Filters (Filter> Adjustments>Photo Filters for PE users) and select the Cooling Filter (80) option. Set the Density to 35% to boost the blues and click the Preserve Luminosity box to uncheck it. This will get rid of the bleached-out area of sky at the bottom. Click OK.

03 Playing the field Click on the Field layer and call up the Photo Filter dialog once more. This time pick the Warming Filter (81) option and set it to 70%. The fields now look a lot more appetising. Click OK.

04 Tree surgeon Select the Trees layer and open the Photo Filters. This time scroll down to the Green option and drag the Density slider to 10%. Also uncheck the Preserve Luminosity box. This darkens the trees, and will make the field and grass more striking. Click OK to continue.

05 Green, green grass of home Click the Grass layer and pick the Green filter once more from the Photo Filter menu. This time, whack the Density slider up to 50% and uncheck the Preserve Luminosity box. This will result in a rich, intense green that matches the overall feel of the photo. Click OK again.

06 Giant haystacks Time for the most important part – the hay. Click their layer and pick Warming Filter (85). Move the Density slider to 72% for a really rich result, but keep the Preserve Luminosity box checked. Click OK to exit the Photo Filter dialog and if happy, click the right arrow in the Layers palette, pick Flatten Image and save. If you think you may want to edit later, save as a layered PSD file.

Tool tip

Pick your own colour

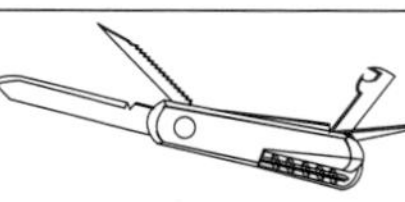

Although there are specific hue options available in the Photo Filter dialog, you can also set your own colours to be used as a filter. With the Photo Filter dialog open, click the colour square to bring up Photoshop's Color Picker. Now select a colour as normal, either by using the palette or entering specific values. When you click OK your colour will be used as a filter.

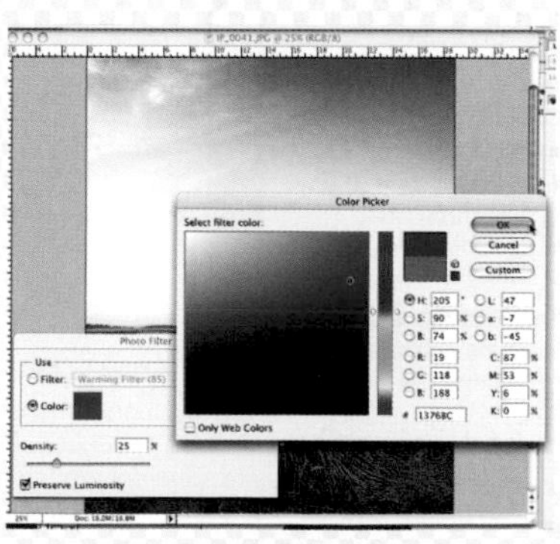

Tool School

To preserve or not to preserve?

The Preserve Luminosity checkbox is worth experimenting with, because it can give you the exact effect you're after. If it's checked, the filters will keep the brightness in the image, so highlights etc will remain as they are. Uncheck this and the filter is applied to all selected areas. Generally, if it's unchecked the result is darker and gives interesting results when applied to skies. So experiment with it!

WORKS WITH | PHOTOSHOP ELEMENTS 3 AND ABOVE, PHOTOSHOP CS AND ABOVE

Merge text with photos

You don't have to take the obvious route with applying text to photos – instead of just writing on top of a photo, why not make the typography part of the image?

One of the very best things about using Photoshop creatively is being able to make gifts for friends and family and there are plenty of things that you can choose to create. You could make a CD of photos from a holiday or maybe a photo montage of family members. At some point you will probably put text on your creation and maybe add a layer style or some other effect. But if you tire of this and are looking for a new way to mix photos and text, we have just the thing. By some cunning use of selections and layer positioning, you copy text into a photo and turn the image into a glorious mixture of the two.

In addition to looking really eye-catching, this opens up a new way of presenting old favourites. Let's say you've just got back from holiday. Instead of getting one of your photos and adding some text like 'Holiday 2005', use this method to add words that sum up your trip. You could apply any sort of text to any sort of image, whether it's a story, poem, song lyric or just a collection of words. According to how you position the text determines how much of the photo you see, and the size you make the text also affects how the photo is viewed.

This kind of effect is best if it has some room to breathe and is seen from a bit of distance away. Dig out your favourite photos and add some text in a simple yet effective way.

ADD YOUR TEXT

Build up the effect

essentials

SKILL LEVEL

Beginner
Intermediate
Expert

TIME TAKEN

30 minutes

YOUR EXPERT

Zoe Mutter

01 Pick a font As text is one of the main components in this exercise it is very important to choose the correct font. Experiment with different types until you find one that is satisfactory. First we tried the Kunstler Script font but found it to be too fussy for this exercise.

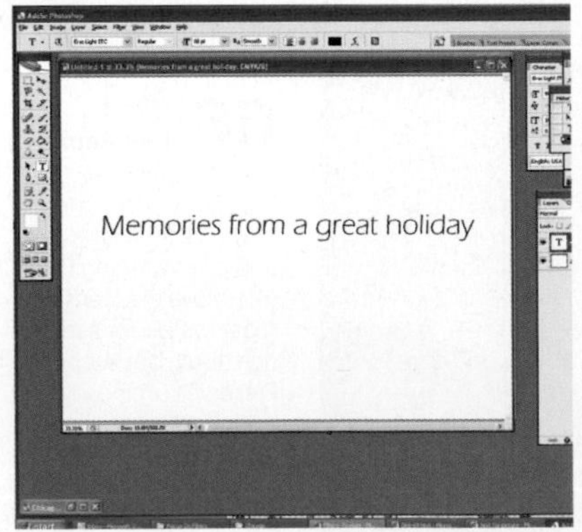

02 Too thin The second font that was tried was Eras Light ITC which was far too thin and did not have enough weight. As the image will be placed on the text this was not suitable.

03 The right choice The perfect kind of font to use for this is thick and bold because it will allow large areas of the underlying image to be revealed. The font we chose was Impact. Set the font to Smooth using the pull-down menu in the top text tool bar (alternatively this can also be found in the Character window).

WORKS WITH | PHOTOSHOP ELEMENTS 3.0 AND ABOVE, PHOTOSHOP 7.0 AND ABOVE

04 No white Create a new document and fill with white. Copy over the image you want to use for the effect. We've decided to make the text relevant to the image, in this case a recent holiday in Chicago. Uncheck the visibility of the white background layer; you will use this later as a background to your merged photo and text.

05 Think about the image Spend a moment thinking about the important areas of the image. In this case it's the skyscrapers and a bit of the sky. Small text will be used in the focal area of the image, because this will still allow the important details of the image to show through. The sea and sky areas do not contain as much detail and is where the larger text will be placed, in a sparser fashion.

06 The first bit of text Type your text over the main focal area of your image. As this is the region that will need to show through most, choose a relatively small font size, such as 30, and closely space the text by adjusting the kerning in the Character palette.

MORE AND MORE

Add some content to the Layers palette

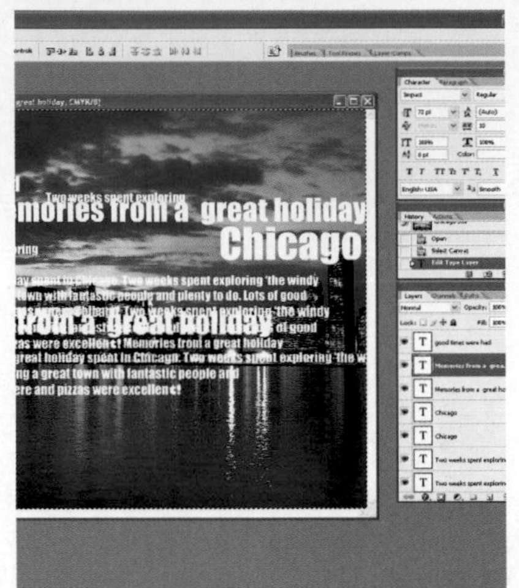

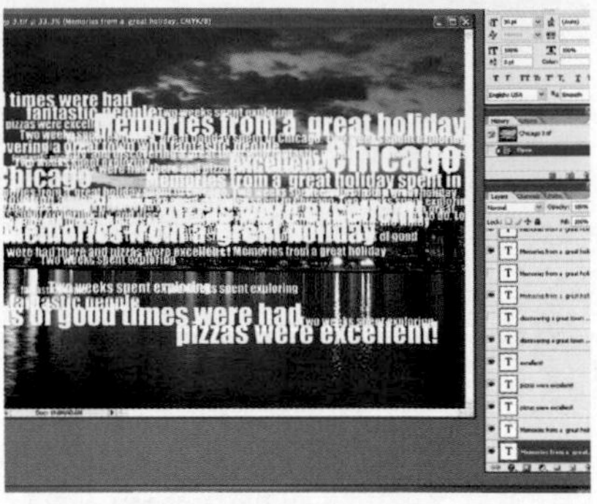

07 Layer it up Duplicate the text by dragging and dropping the layer onto the Duplicate icon at the bottom of the Layers palette. Move the copy of the text to cover another area of the buildings. It doesn't matter if text overlays each other or isn't completely legible as you can select the most important words or sentences later and make sure they're seen.

08 Slightly bigger Now you can start adding larger text in other parts of the image, such as the sea and sky. Don't worry if the text isn't close together as they are just to give a general feeling of the photo underneath.

09 Pick the important parts Gradually build up type of varying sizes and spacing to cover the different parts of the underlying image. Use a large font size for words or sentences that are particularly important or relevant to the image's subject matter.

One size doesn't fit all

You need to think in threes

Because text in Photoshop doesn't take too well to being resized, we'd recommend that you build up your text layers with small, medium and large font sizes

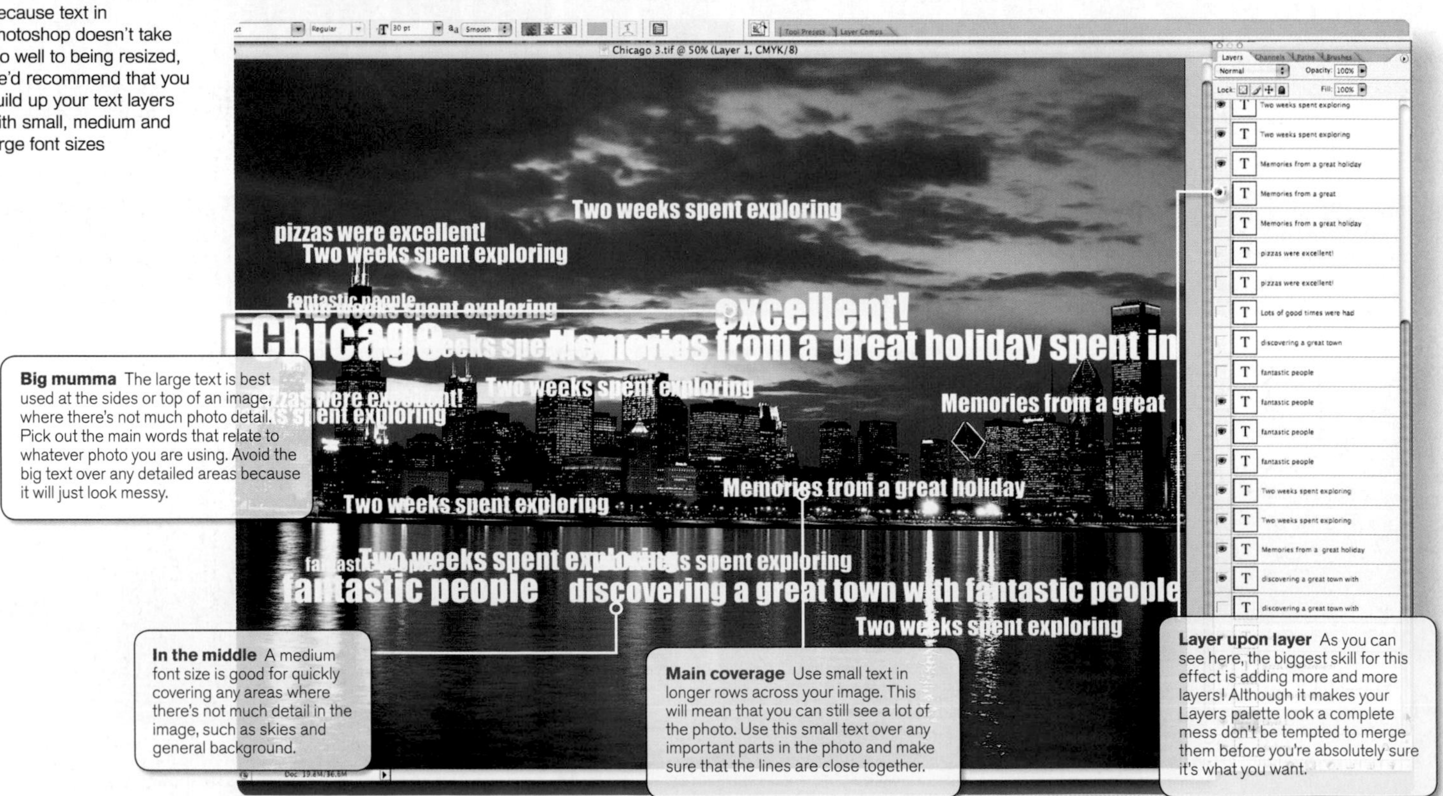

Big mumma The large text is best used at the sides or top of an image, where there's not much photo detail. Pick out the main words that relate to whatever photo you are using. Avoid the big text over any detailed areas because it will just look messy.

In the middle A medium font size is good for quickly covering any areas where there's not much detail in the image, such as skies and general background.

Main coverage Use small text in longer rows across your image. This will mean that you can still see a lot of the photo. Use this small text over any important parts in the photo and make sure that the lines are close together.

Layer upon layer As you can see here, the biggest skill for this effect is adding more and more layers! Although it makes your Layers palette look a complete mess don't be tempted to merge them before you're absolutely sure it's what you want.

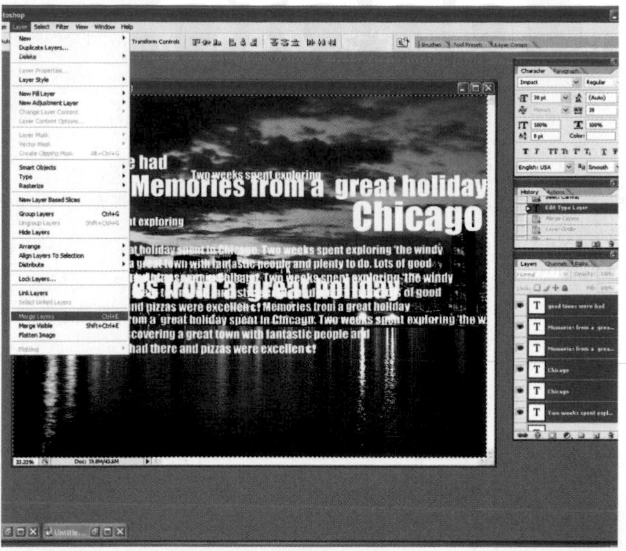

10 See how it goes You can check the effect before adding too much text and see if you are revealing the correct areas of the underlying image. This is done by selecting/linking all your text layers in the Layers palette (Shift-Click) and then choosing Layer>Merge Layers.

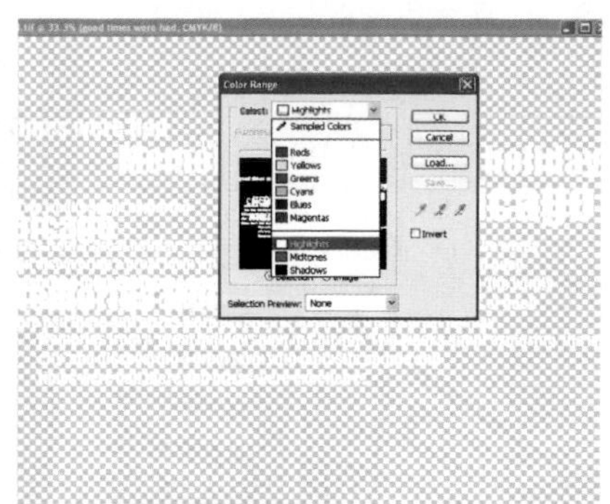

11 Pick it all Turn the visibility icon off on the cityscape layer and make sure the white background layer you created is still invisible. With the layer containing the merged text selected, choose Select>Colour Range (Elements users Magic Wand a letter in Elements and then pick Select>Similar). Now choose Highlights from the Select drop-down menu to select all the white text.

Expert Tip

Try it and see

We're afraid this is one of those really annoying tutorials where we can't give you exact settings and positions. Once you have the basic technique of what you need to do, it really is just a case of building up layers and deleting as you see fit. As long as it's possible to still make out areas of the photo you can't fail!

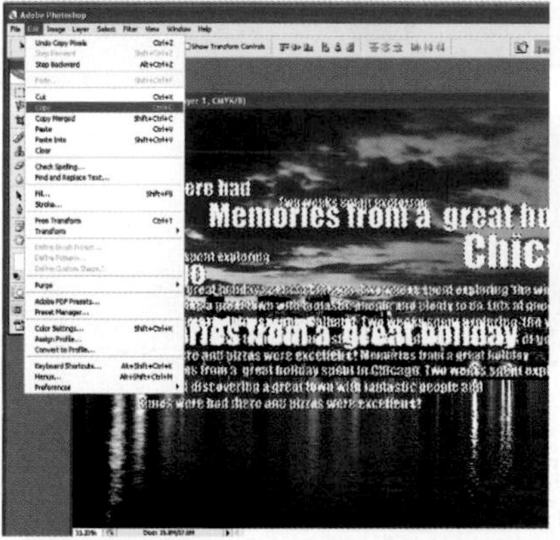

12 Add the text Now choose the cityscape layer in the Layers palette and turn on its visibility. Select Edit>Copy and then Edit>Paste and the merged photograph and text will appear on a new layer.

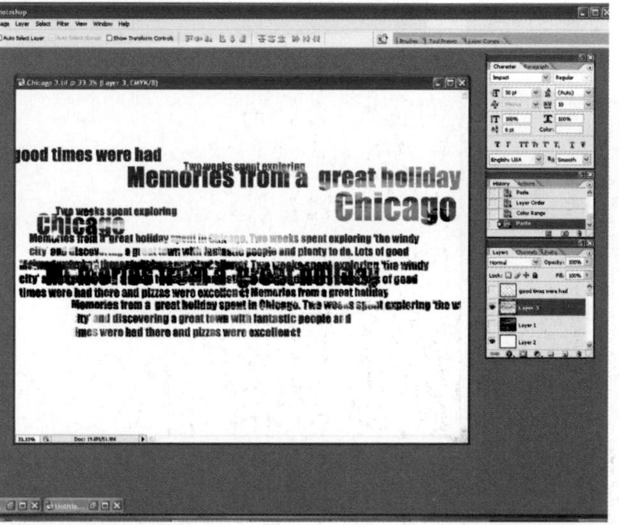

13 Make a decision Now it is possible to judge any areas that may need more text added to them in order for more of the underlying image to show through.

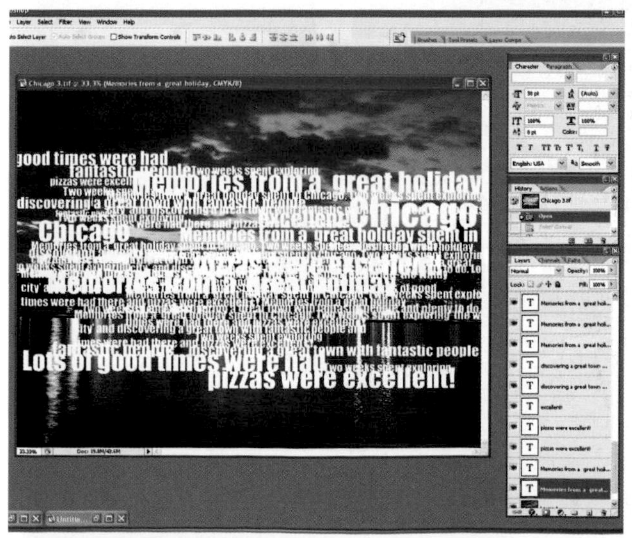

14 Go back in time Select Window>History to bring up the History palette (Window>Undo History for Elements users). Revert back to the stage before you merged the layers to continue adding more text. Now build up the layers of text of varying sizes until you are happy with the overall layout and that all the important areas of cityscape will be revealed.

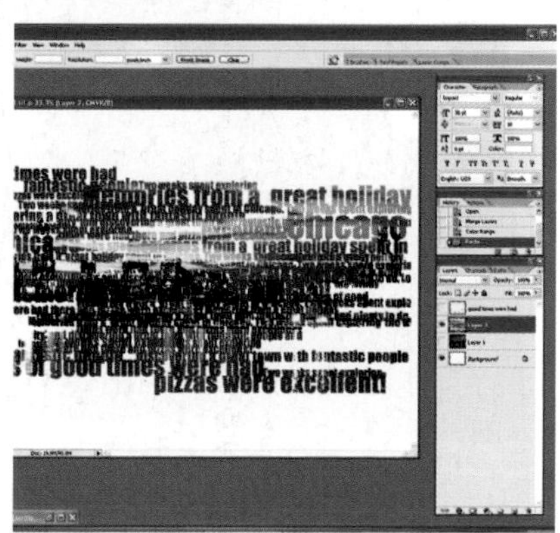

15 All done Finally repeat the steps of merging all the text layers, selecting the Highlights (Select>Colour Range>Highlights) and copying and pasting the cityscape image as before. Turn on the visibility of the white background layer to see the finished merged photograph and text.

Tool School

Creating paths

You may wonder why we had to create a new path in the Paths palette. This is done because if you start to draw on a new layer with the Pen tool, the layer automatically becomes a vector shape layer.

SEEING LIGHTS

Light up the sky

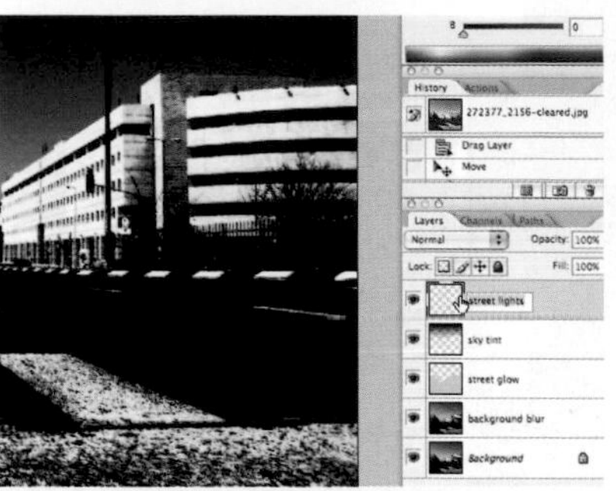

08 Another blend Change the blending mode for the Sky tint layer to Multiply. Press Ctrl+D (PC) or Cmd+D (Mac) to deselect the sky area. Create another new layer call it 'Street lights'. Click on the Gradient tool and then click on the gradient bar in the options to open the Gradient Editor (Elements users click Edit).

09 Edit the gradient In the Gradient Editor select the Blue, Red, Yellow gradient. Click on the blue colour stop and change this to white by double-clicking the Color box at the bottom and selecting white from the Color Picker. Select the red colour stop and drag this towards the white colour stop. Change this to a pale yellow as shown.

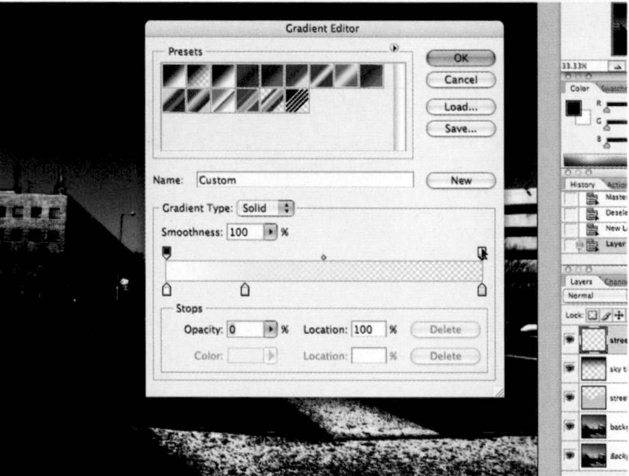

10 Finish the gradient Click on the black opacity stop at the top-right of the gradient bar above the yellow colour stop on the right of the gradient. Reduce the opacity here to 0%. Now click OK to close the Gradient Editor. Choose Radial Gradient from the Options bar.

11 Add lights Click and drag downwards slightly at the top of the lampposts in the scene to add glowing lights to the scene. Make the lights closer to the camera larger and continue making the lights smaller as they are further down the street. When you are done click your gradient to amend.

Expert Tip

Blurred layer

By adding a blurred copy of the background image in step three we have helped to create our night scene by reducing the visibility that occurs at night. The blurry loss of detail found in the image emulates the fuzzy detail of night photography scenes. This helps the overall aesthetics and to make it seem a little more convincing. By blending the layer using Multiply it allows just enough detail from the layer below to peek through.

12 Go light Change the two yellow colours in the gradient to green now; the one nearest the white should be kept pale. Click OK to continue and add two green lights to the traffic signals on the right-hand side of the document. Edit the gradient again and change the green colours to red, then click OK to close the Gradient Editor.

13 Stop light Add a stop light to the left-hand traffic light as shown above. Copy the layer and then go to Filters>Blur>Gaussian Blur. Add an 11-pixel blur and click OK. Now change the blending mode of this copied layer to Color Dodge to make the lights blurrier.

14 Windows layer Create a new layer and name it 'Windows'. Use the Polygonal Lasso tool to select some of the windows in the left-hand side building. Hold down Shift to start selecting another window so that you have multiple selections. Fill this area with white using the Paint Bucket tool.

Turning day into night

Fundamental rules for believable results

Changing an image from day into night is done by altering the overall colour. The image is desaturated and then hues mirroring those of artificial light sources rather than the sun are applied

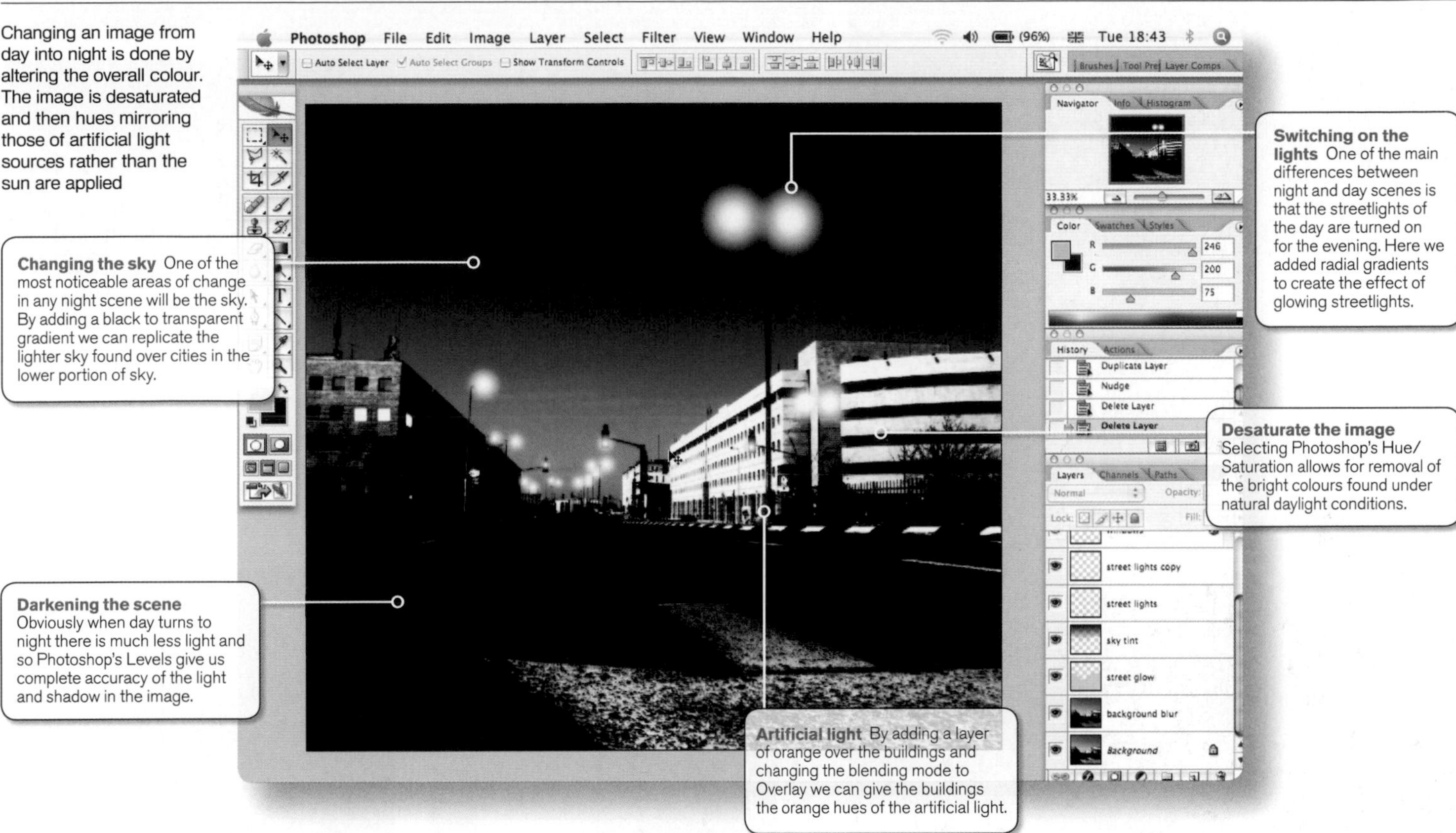

Changing the sky One of the most noticeable areas of change in any night scene will be the sky. By adding a black to transparent gradient we can replicate the lighter sky found over cities in the lower portion of sky.

Darkening the scene Obviously when day turns to night there is much less light and so Photoshop's Levels give us complete accuracy of the light and shadow in the image.

Switching on the lights One of the main differences between night and day scenes is that the streetlights of the day are turned on for the evening. Here we added radial gradients to create the effect of glowing streetlights.

Desaturate the image Selecting Photoshop's Hue/ Saturation allows for removal of the bright colours found under natural daylight conditions.

Artificial light By adding a layer of orange over the buildings and changing the blending mode to Overlay we can give the buildings the orange hues of the artificial light.

THROUGH THE WINDOWS

Who left the lights on?

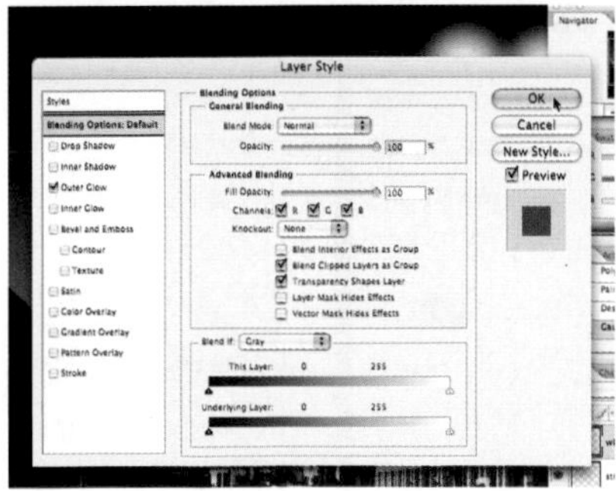

15 Window glow Add a white fill and press Ctrl+D (PC) or Cmd+D (Mac) to deselect. Go to Filters>Blur>Gaussian Blur. Add a three-pixel blur and click OK. Now double-click the Windows layer to open the Layer Styles dialog box. In the Categories click on Outer Glow to apply and then click OK.

16 Darken markings Select the Background blur layer and click around the large road markings in the foreground of the image with the Polygonal Lasso tool. Once you have done this it will be selected. Change the foreground colour to black and select the Gradient tool.

17 Add the gradient Choose the Foreground to Transparent gradient and change the gradient from Radial to Linear. Drag down from the middle of the image to the bottom of the document in order to darken them up slightly. Press Ctrl+D (PC) or Cmd+D (Mac) to deselect.

The power of the Pen
Essential skills

The Pen tool is one of the most difficult tools to get to grips with in Photoshop, yet its power can be used for many common tasks such as cutting out difficult objects. Simply Alt-click (PC) or Option-click (Mac) to change the Pen into the Direct Selection tool and then edit the line. In the tutorial we have used this as a way to draw the lines that will become the light streaks.

01 Straight lines After selecting the Pen tool and creating a new path (Paths palette, right arrow to select New Path) click anywhere on the image. Now click again in another location. A single click produces a straight line between these points. So far so good, but sometimes we need curves, right?

02 Love handles Now click somewhere else to add a new point, but this time continue to hold the mouse down and drag in the direction that your line is going. A handle appears this is not the line but dictates which direction the curve will go next.

03 Sleek curves Add another point lower on the screen than your last point, and still holding the mouse down, drag in the direction towards where you would like your next point to be. Add another point and you will see your curved edge. You can use the Alt key (PC) or Option key (Mac) to edit the curve at any time.

LEAVE A TRAIL
Glowy light effects

18 Create the light trails We are now going to create the light trails to give the impression of cars screaming through the city. To do this create a new layer and name this 'White light'. In the Layers palette click on the Paths tab and then click the New Path icon at the bottom of the palette.

19 Draw paths Click on the edge of the document to start the path and then click towards the centre at the point that the road seems to dip. Hold down Ctrl (PC) or Cmd (Mac) and click off the path to deselect it and do another path above it as shown, keeping in the perspective of the road.

20 Stroke the path Hold down Ctrl (PC) or Cmd (Mac) and click off the path. Select the Brush tool and select a seven-pixel brush with 15% hardness. Make sure that the foreground colour is white. In the bottom of the Paths palette click on the Stroke Path with Brush icon.

21 Another path Create another path in the Paths palette. Select the Pen tool and draw a curve from the end of the first line into the vanishing point. Ctrl-click off the line and do the same for the other light streak, Ctrl-clicking off that one when finished. Mac users need to Cmd-click.

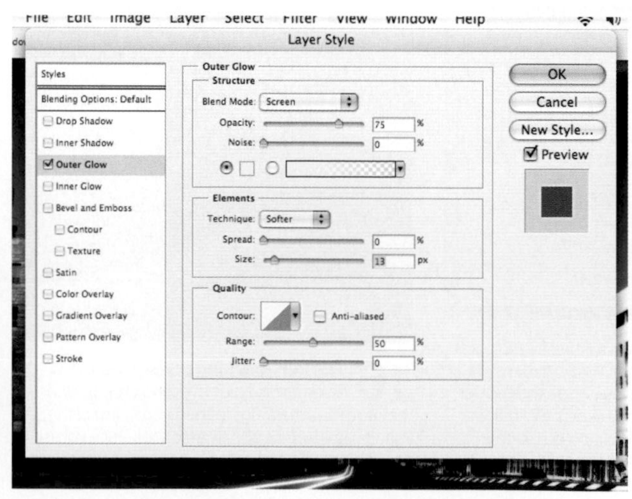

22 Smaller stroke Click on the Brush tool again and change the size of the brush down to four pixels, then click on the Stroke Path with Brush icon again. Change back to the Layers palette and double-click on the layer to access the Layer Styles. Add an Outer Glow and increase the Size to 13 pixels.

Photo credit

We'd like to thank Eli Ratner for letting us use the street scene photo. Eli is a member of Stock. Xchng and you can see more photographs by visiting **www.sxc.hu/browse.phtml?f=gallery&l=ratner**

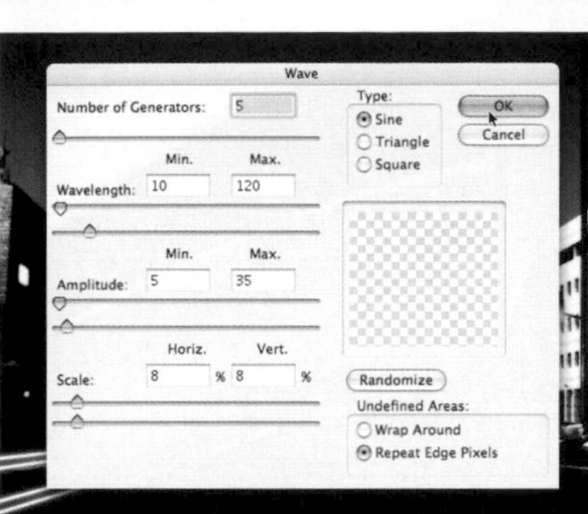

23 Duplicate the layer Drag the light streak layer down to the new layer icon in the Layers palette, in order to duplicate it. With the copied layer selected go to Edit>Transform>Distort. Pull the handles around until you have a slightly different set of light streaks as shown.

24 Waving the lines Go to the Filter menu and choose Distort and Wave. In the Wave dialog window, change the horizontal and vertical scale to 8% then click OK. This gives the impression that the light has moved along bumps in the road. Select the first White light layer and add a 6% wave.

25 More light paths Duplicate the first light streak layer as before. Go to Edit>Transform>Distort. Move the handles around and create another slightly random set of light trails. Double-click to apply. Now Shift-click all of the White light layers. Go to Layer>Merge Layers menu.

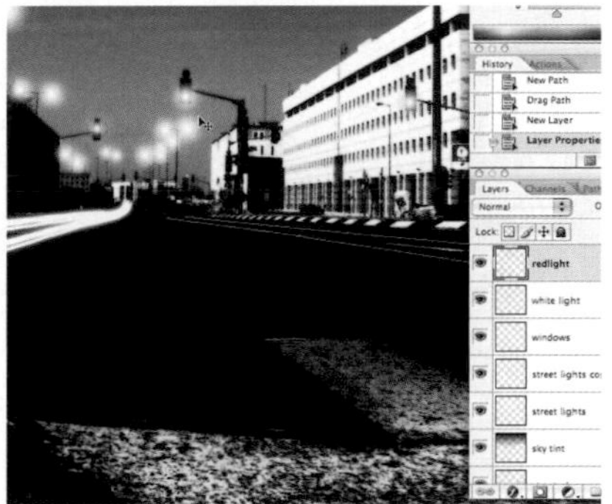

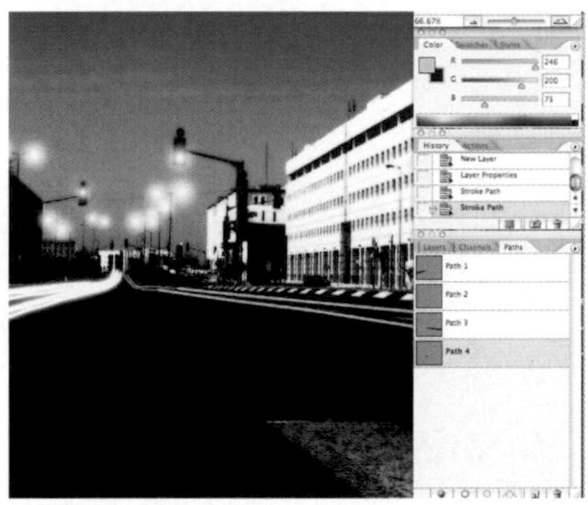

26 Rename the layer Make sure this merged layer has the name 'White light' (you may need to change it from 'white light copy'). Now click back on the Layers palette and follow steps 18 to 26 for the opposite side of the road. This time you will have to name your layer 'Red light'.

27 Change the light colour In order to get the right look for the tail lights you will need to use an orange colour for the brush stroke. Don't forget to use a six-pixel stroke for the foreground light and four pixels for the distant light as shown in the screenshot above.

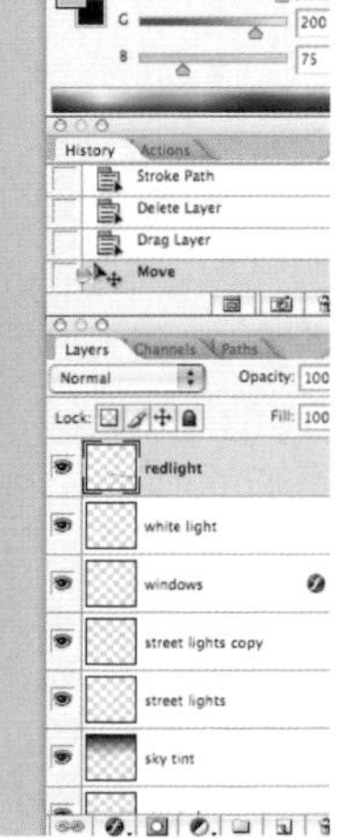

28 Red glowing edges Double-click the layer to edit the layer styles. Add a red outer glow and a white inner glow this time. Then you can duplicate and distort your layers before adding some random waves with the Wave filter. To finish, merge the red light layers together.

How to turn night into day

The layer structure you need

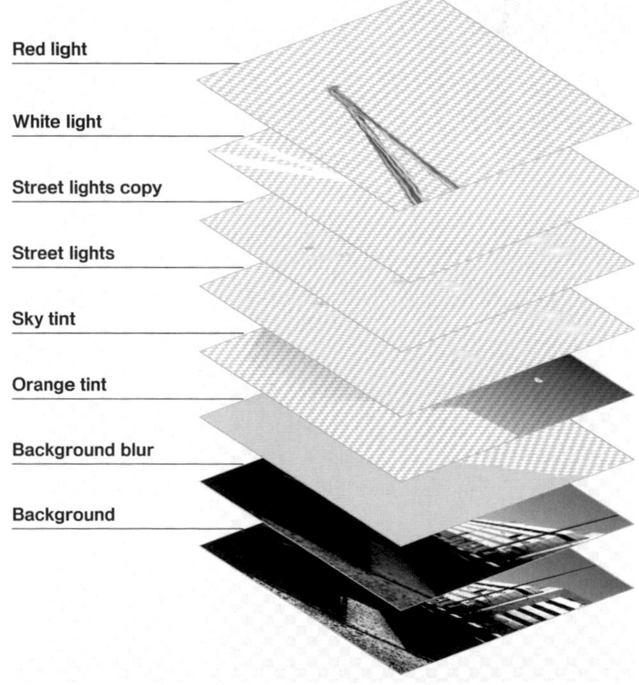

Secrets of successful montages

Although this technique can work on pretty much any photo, there are a couple of things you can do to make sure you get optimum results. If you are working on a portrait photo, try not to cut the face up – use one square for the whole face area. Also be careful to keep the square selections reasonably close together. If they're too far apart you won't be able to see what the original photo was!

MAKING SELECTIONS

Start building up the squares

04 Hip to be square Go to the toolbar and select the Rectangular Marquee tool. Now make a selection of about 6cmx6cm over the face. Copy and Paste onto a new layer and call it 'Square'.

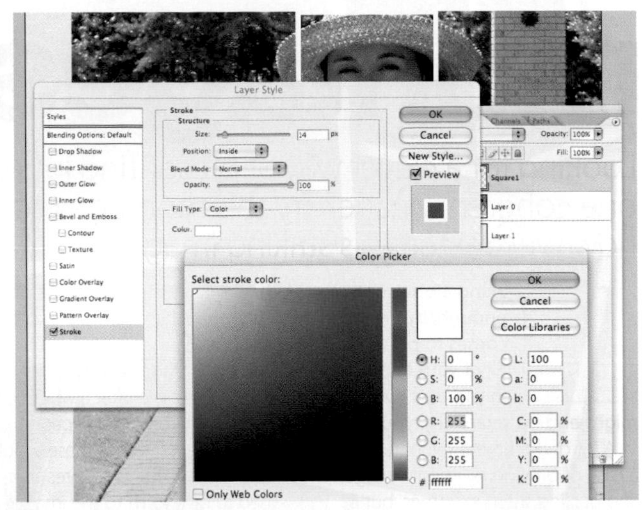

05 Stylish addition Double-click on this newly created layer in the Layers palette to bring up the Layer Style dialog. Click on Stroke at the bottom left-hand side. Change the Size to 14px and set Position to Inside. Click on the colour rectangle at the bottom and choose White.

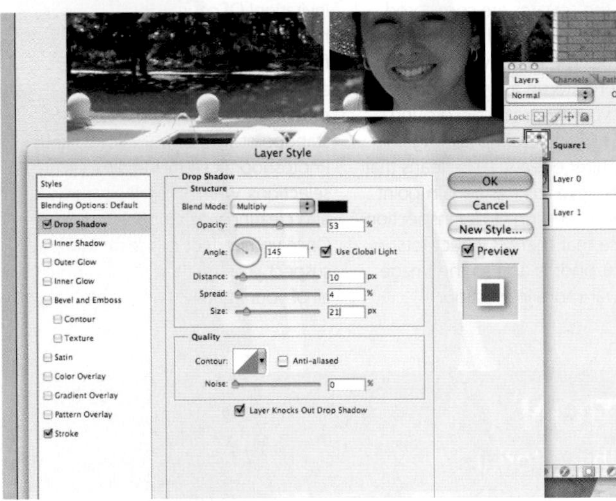

06 Not finished yet Still in the Layer Style palette, choose Drop Shadow. Set the Blend Mode to Multiply and change the Opacity to 53%. Move the Angle to 145 and check Global Light. Change the Distance to 10px, Spread to 4% and Size to 21px. Click OK. This layer is now our template for the layer style and we can copy the style into each square layer once they've all been cut out (see step 10, 11).

07 And again To get identical selections for the rest of the image, go to Select>Reselect. This brings up your last selection. Click back on the 'holiday photo' layer in the Layers palette. Pick the Rectangular Marquee tool once more and move your mouse over the marching ants of your selection. When you see a white arrow, click and hold your mouse button down and move the selection to a new position. Copy and Paste as you did before.

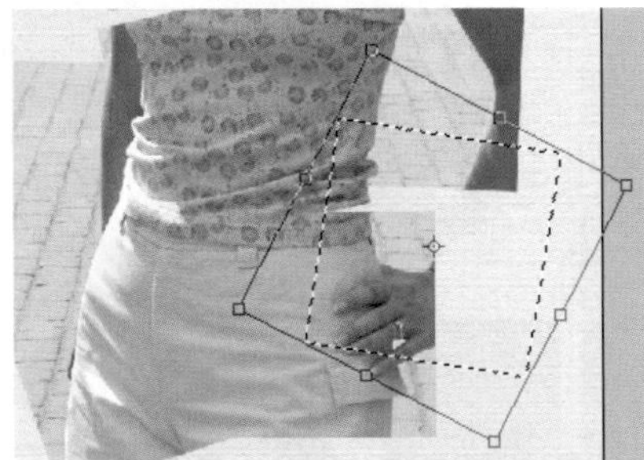

08 Variety is the spice of life To keep the montage interesting, you need to vary the angle of the selections. This gives a nice scattered look. After you have brought the selection back by reselecting, go to the Select menu and pick Transform Selection. You can now click and rotate the selection. When you have your angle, hit Return and then Copy and Paste in the same way.

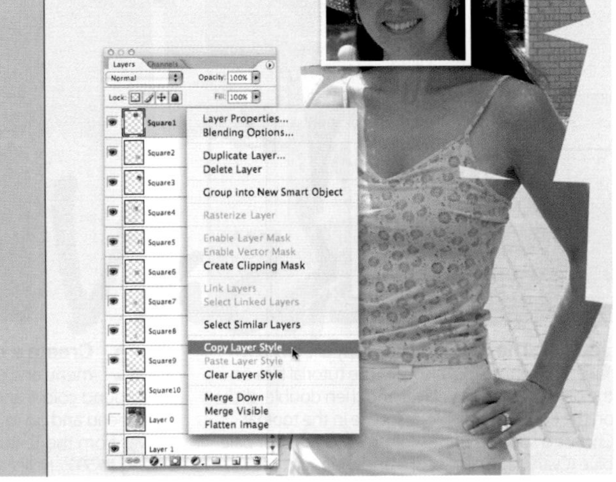

09 The nifty part To apply the Stroke and Shadow effects to all of your selections, Ctrl-click (Mac) or right-click (PC) on the first layer that you have already applied the layer style to and select Copy Layer Style. If you're in Elements, go to Layer>Layer Style>Copy Layer Style.

ADDING VARIATIONS

Mix up finishes for more striking effects

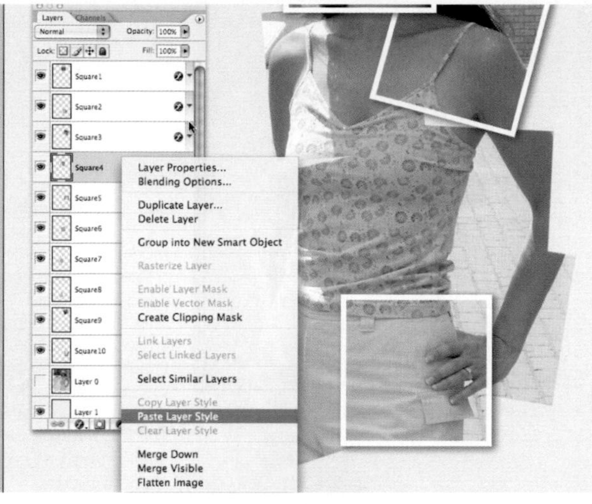

10 Paste layer style Now click on each square layer in turn in the Layers palette and Ctrl/right-click to pick Paste Layer Style. Elements users can go to Layer>Layer Style>Paste Layer Style. Keep doing this on each one until all your squares have white frames and shadows.

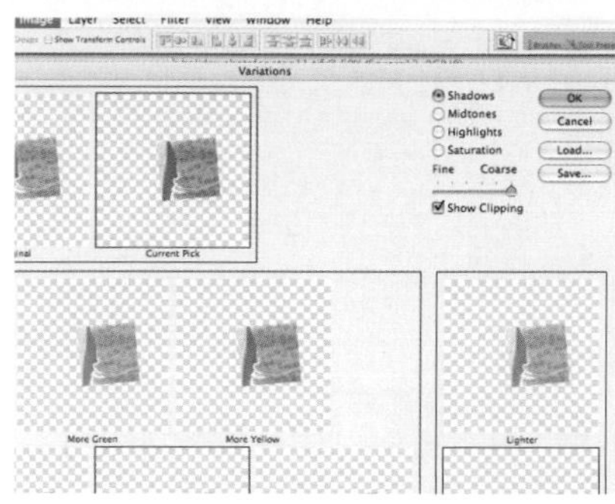

11 Varied finishes You can keep your selections as they are or add some variations in colour. We clicked on random layers and applied some different effects. Go to Image>Adjustments>Variations. Click Shadows and have fun! We chose More Blue and More Yellow for some of our squares.

12 Not just Variations In addition to Variations, you may like to try a quick blast of the Color Balance option (found under Image>Adjustments>Color Balance). You might fancy desaturating some as well. When you've finished adding effects, select all of the square selection layers in the Layers palette and go to Layer>Layer Merge.

13 Photo editing Click on the 'holiday photo' layer and change the blending mode to Luminosity. Reduce the Opacity slider to 44%. With the Rectangular Marquee, draw over the photo, leaving an even border around the outside to neaten things up a bit. Go to Select>Inverse and then delete.

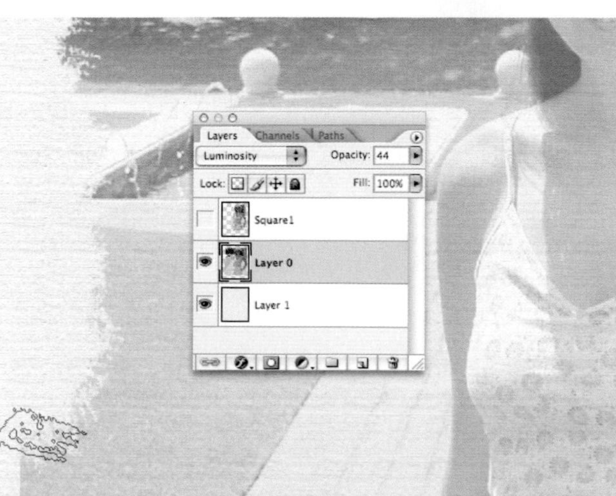

14 Border effect Deselect your selection and then click the Eraser tool. Choose the Large Texture Stroke from the Wet Media brushes set .Make it quite a big brush at around 150 or bigger. Erase around the edges to create a painterly effect. If you're unsure about how to change your brush set, see the side panel on this page.

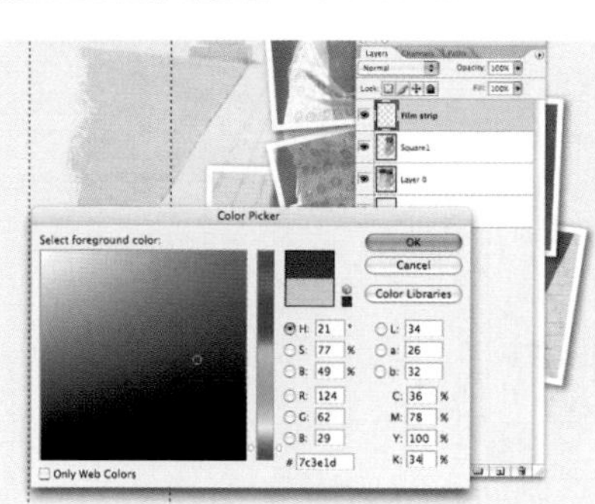

15 The film strip With the main image kind of finished, it's time to create a film strip. Create a new layer and call it 'film strip'. Use the Rectangular Marquee to select a long rectangular section on the left-hand side. Go from the top to the bottom. Choose a reddy brown for the Foreground colour and fill the selection.

Expert Tip

Loading brushes

To alter the current brush set, select the Brush tool and then click the little brush preview square in the options bar. When a window appears with all the brush choices, click the little right-pointing arrow. Select one of the brush sets and then click OK. You'll see the new brushes appear in the window.

Adding extra elements to the montage

In our montage, we decided to add the effect of a film strip, to enhance the photography feel. It works well and is an idea that you might like to experiment with. For example, you might think about introducing a border of flowers, if you're using a floral shot as the main focus of a montage. As ever, the real trick is to have fun with whatever you decide to do!

USING THE FILM STRIP

Go for the traditional feel

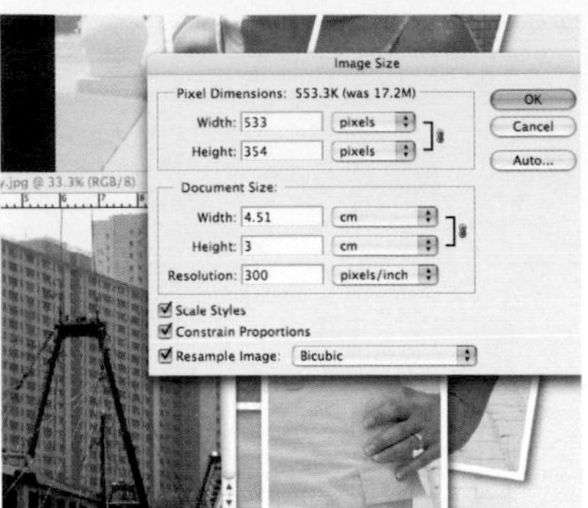

16 On the top Move the film strip layer to the top of the Layers palette. Change the blend mode to Multiply and open the 'jumbo ferry' file from the CD. Go to Image>Image Size and change the Height to 3 and Width to 4.5. Click OK, then select all and copy.

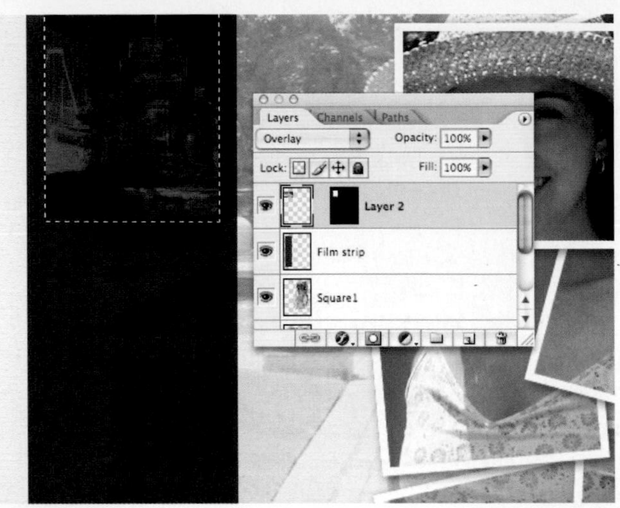

17 Paste it in Go back to the montage document, create a new layer and make a rectangular selection in the shape and position of an image on a negative. Choose Paste Into from the Edit menu. Go to Image>Invert and change the blending mode to Overlay.

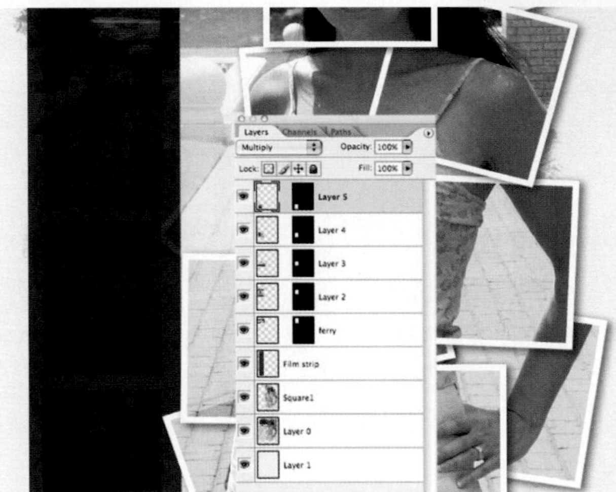

18 Next picture Create another new layer, go to Reselect in the Select menu. Move this selection down where you want the next image to sit on the strip and open 'Sailing again' from the CD. Reduce image size to 4cmx5cm. Select all, copy and paste into the selection on your new layer as before, invert and set the mode to Overlay. Repeat for all the photos on the disc until your negative strip is complete.

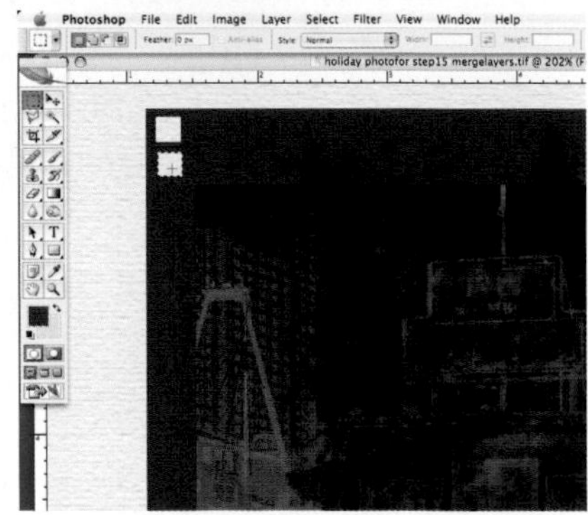

19 Final touches Click on the 'film strip' layer once more, make a small square selection along the side and then press Delete. Repeat the process along both sides of the strip to give it that authentic look.

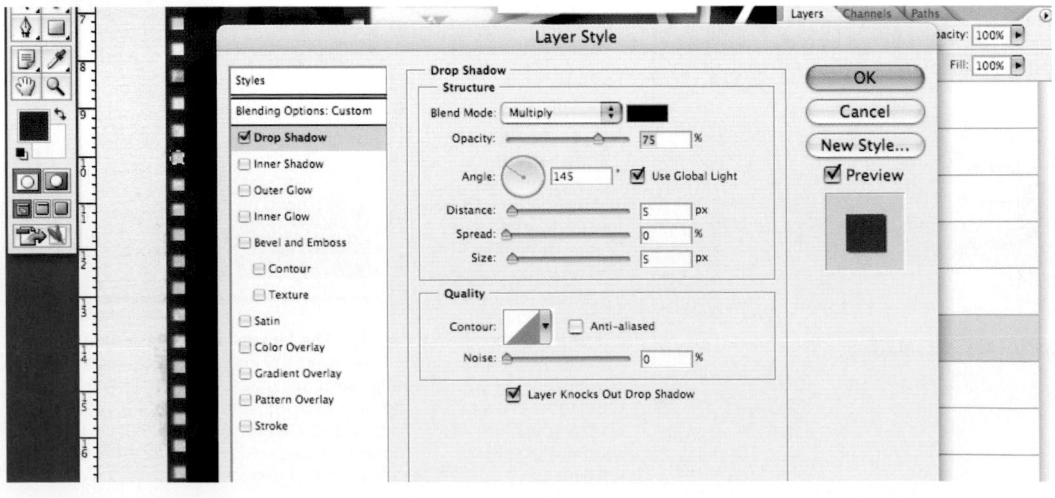

20 Same style You need to apply a drop shadow to the film strip, but the Layer Style command will remember the last values so there's no need to change any settings. They will be the same as the montage shadows which is just what we want, so just click OK. Select all of the film strip layers in the Layers palette and merge.

ADD MORE ELEMENTS
Finishing up the montage

21 In position Go to Edit>Transform>Rotate and move to the angle shown here. Create a new layer and call it 'banner'. With the Rectangular Marquee, make a selection across the bottom of the image and then fill with a cream colour.

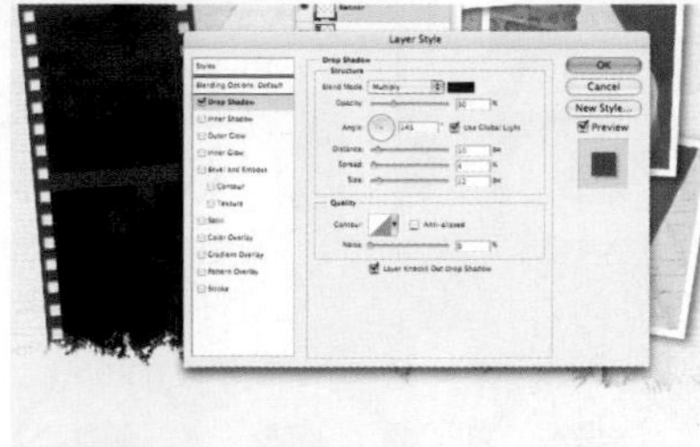

22 More border Use the same Large Texture Stroke brush eraser as before and erase along the sides of the banner. Go to Filter>Texture>Texturizer. Again you don't need to do anything except click OK, as it retains the previous settings you chose for the blue background. Now go to Edit>Transform and rotate to give a slight angle. Go to the Layer Style and select Drop Shadow. Drop the Opacity down to 30% and Size to 12px. Click OK.

23 Type it in Choose a dark blue and select the Type tool. Choose a font you like (we chose Mistral Regular) from the top bar and enter your text. To change the font size or colour, highlight the text and change the value in the top bar.

24 Nice touch Add some decoration to the banner by choosing the butterfly brush from the Special Effect brush set. Open the Brushes palette, click Scattering and move the Scatter slider up to 1000%. Choose two colours for the foreground and background and then click around the banner and text.

Expert Tip

Select brushes

With the current brush set, select the Brush tool and then click the little brush preview square in the options bar. When a window appears with all the brush choices, click the little right-pointing arrow. Select one of the brush sets and then click OK. You'll then see the new brushes appear in the window.

Building up a montage
The layer structure revealed

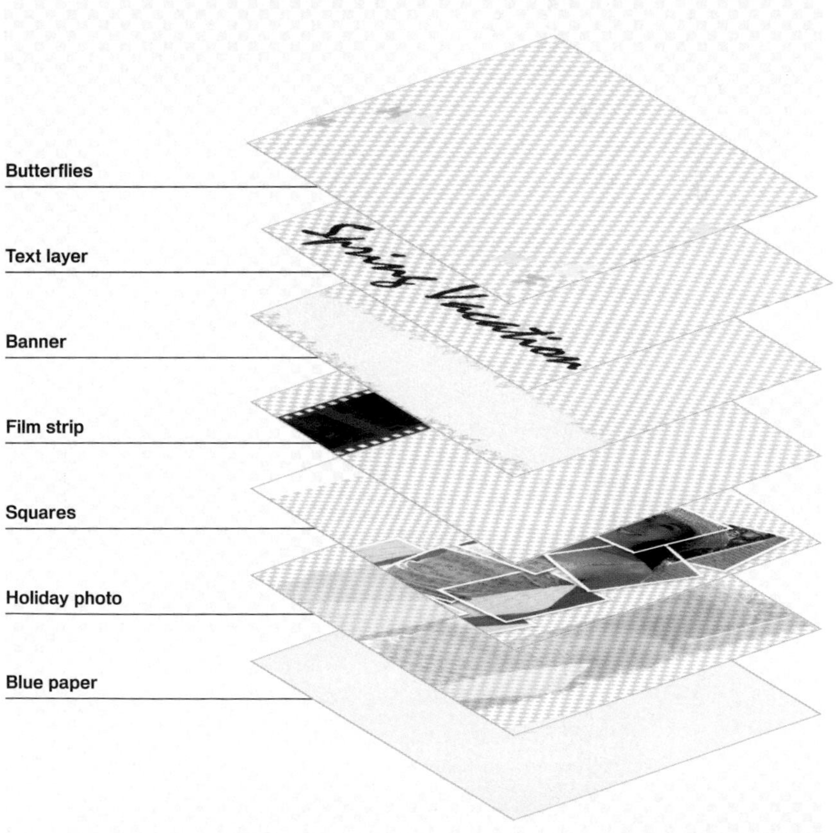

Paint and illustrate with Photoshop

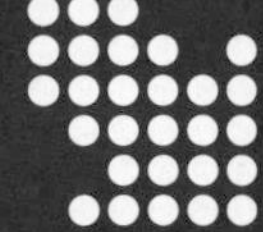

Everybody knows that Photoshop rocks when it comes to editing photos or manipulating them into all sorts of weird and wonderful creations. But there's plenty for those with art in their soul too. Photoshop's Brush and Art History Brush tools turn your computer into a digital canvas, allowing users to produce images that look like they were created in traditional media like watercolours or oil paint. It doesn't even matter if you can't draw or paint – simply use a photo as your guide and let Photoshop do the hard work.

In addition to digital painting, you can also turn Photoshop's hand to illustration, whether it's colouring up line art or re-creating the look of vector. Plus there's the ability to use the inbuilt filters and effects to construct striking images. All will be revealed in this section...

Contents

A typical tablet

Although tablets change slightly, most have similar elements. Here's a look at Wacom's Intuos3 model

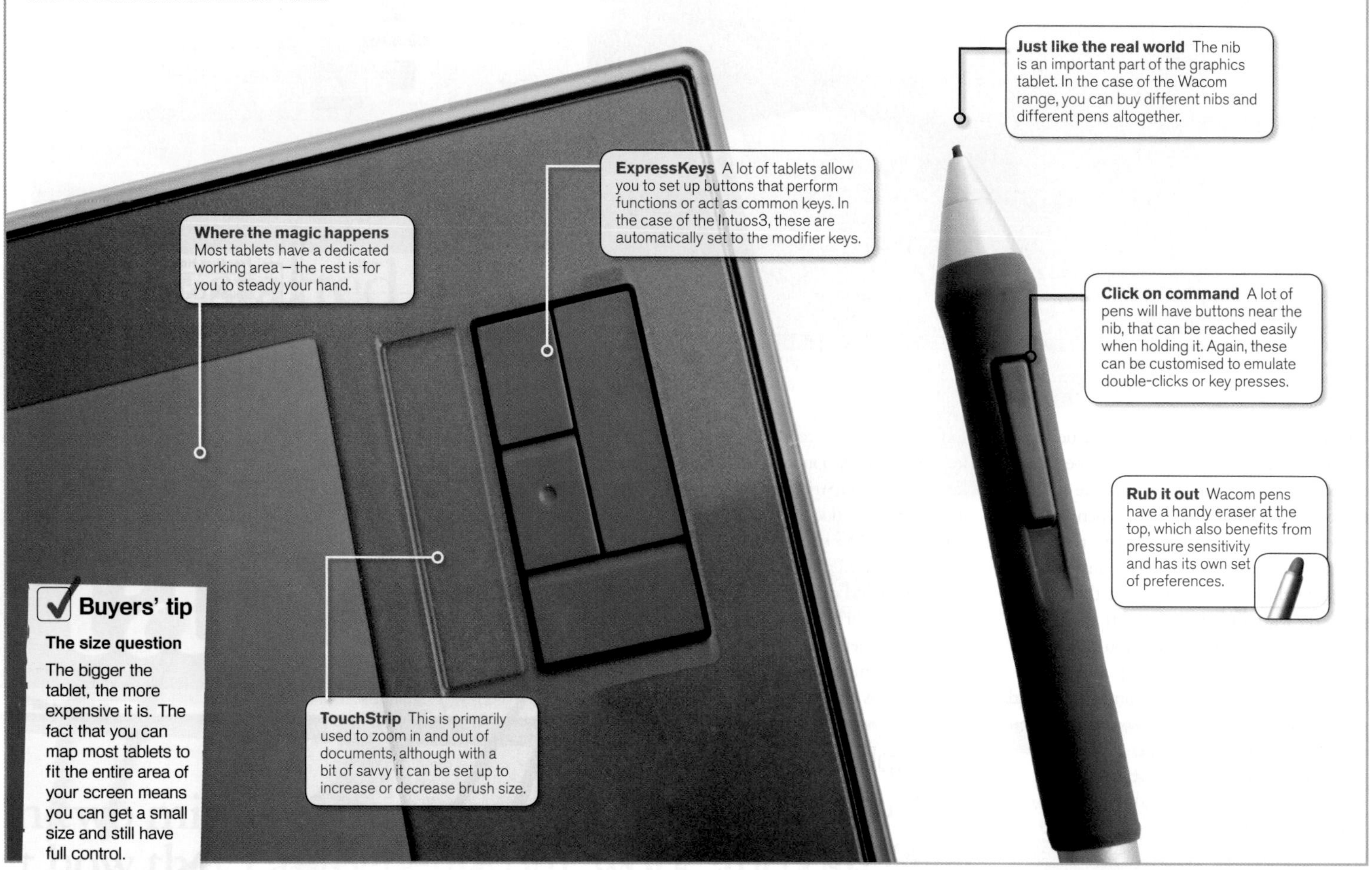

Just like the real world The nib is an important part of the graphics tablet. In the case of the Wacom range, you can buy different nibs and different pens altogether.

ExpressKeys A lot of tablets allow you to set up buttons that perform functions or act as common keys. In the case of the Intuos3, these are automatically set to the modifier keys.

Where the magic happens Most tablets have a dedicated working area – the rest is for you to steady your hand.

Click on command A lot of pens will have buttons near the nib, that can be reached easily when holding it. Again, these can be customised to emulate double-clicks or key presses.

Rub it out Wacom pens have a handy eraser at the top, which also benefits from pressure sensitivity and has its own set of preferences.

TouchStrip This is primarily used to zoom in and out of documents, although with a bit of savvy it can be set up to increase or decrease brush size.

Buyers' tip

The size question

The bigger the tablet, the more expensive it is. The fact that you can map most tablets to fit the entire area of your screen means you can get a small size and still have full control.

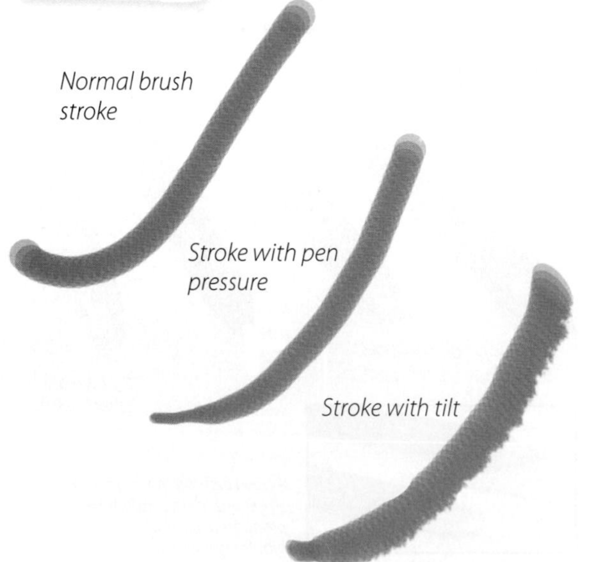

"Tasks you may have once dreaded because they were fiddly aren't such a hassle any more"

levels will be sufficient for most people and give a nice realistic feel, but if you used low pressure on your drawing tools in real life, the Wacom Intuos range is what you would go for. The 1,024 levels of pressure sensitivity will give you the same creative freedom as if you had a sketch pencil in your hand.

Tablets and Photoshop

The real beauty of graphics tablets comes into play as soon as you open up Photoshop. Because of how they work, your everyday tasks become a lot easier. Most of the benefit will take place when you open the Brushes palette. The various brush dynamic settings come with a Control drop-down menu. In here you can determine whether a brush reacts to the sensitivity of the pen (gets bigger/darker the harder you push) or how it reacts to the tilt of a pen (not all tablets support this). Owners of Wacom's ArtMarker pen can also set a brush to react to the rotation of the pen, again providing the same freedom and performance you'd expect from a normal pen.

The fact that you can make the Brush tool in Photoshop act in practically the same way as a brush loaded with paint means that a graphics tablet is perfectly suited to

Controlling Photoshop

Graphics tablets can make certain Photoshop tasks much easier, but you need to set the tablet up to be recognised by the software, otherwise it's no cigar. Here's how to activate Photoshop, using a Wacom Intuos3.

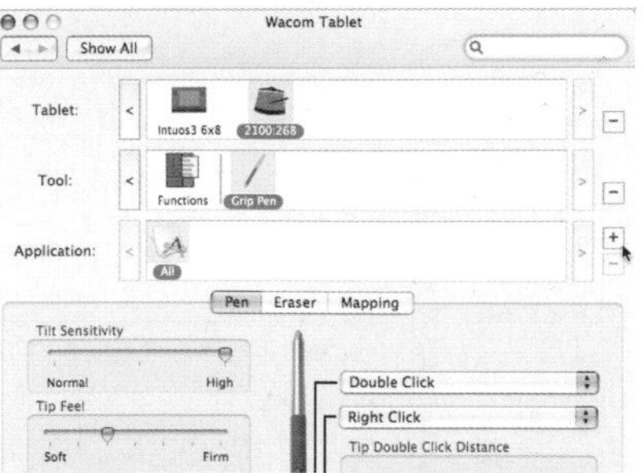

01 What's your preference? Open up your system preferences to access the tablet settings. Go to the Application field and click on the '+' icon. This will allow you to navigate to whatever program you want the tablet to work with (it's not just Photoshop!).

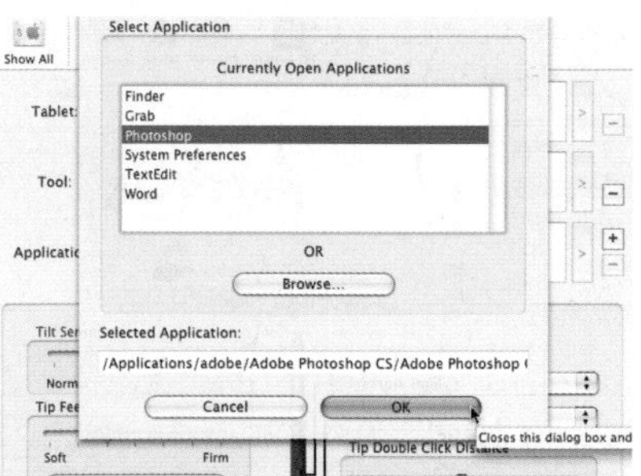

02 That's the ticket As soon as you hit the '+' icon, a window will appear with all the programs that will recognise the tablet. Obviously add whichever ones you fancy, but for this example we are picking good ol' Photoshop. Click to select it and then hit OK.

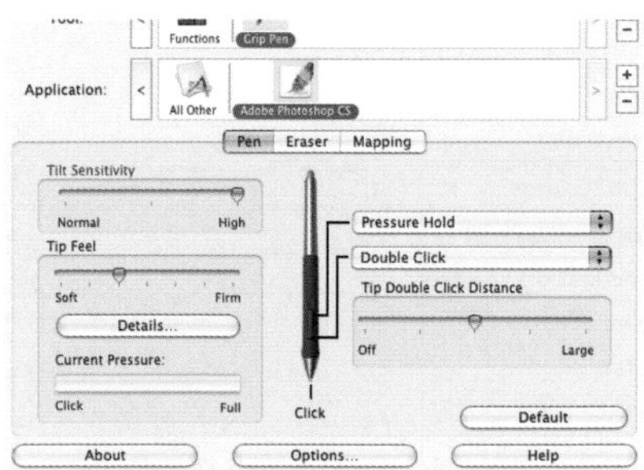

03 All accounted for You'll return to the main tablet preference window, only now there should be a Photoshop icon in the Application section. This means you're ready to take advantage of some serious pen control when using Photoshop's tools.

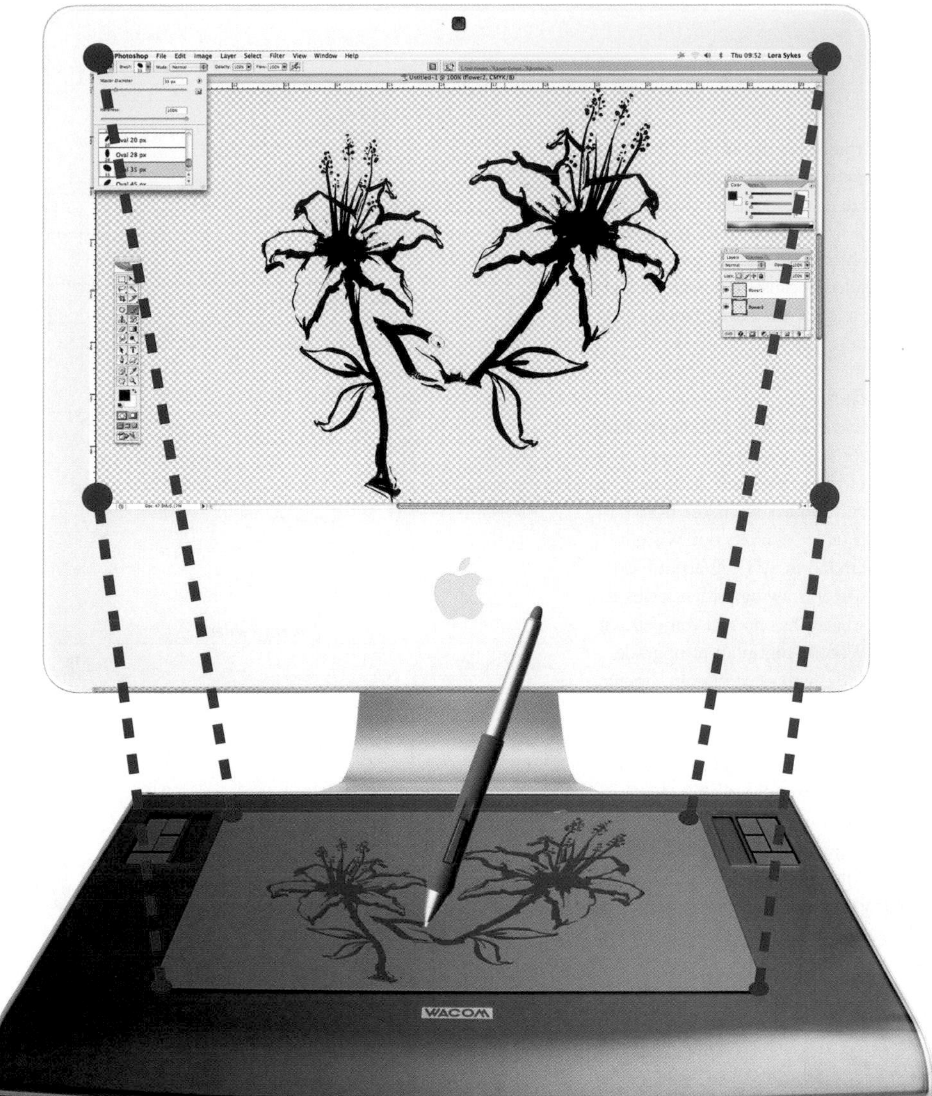

The fact that tablet areas are mapped to your monitor means that wherever you point on a tablet, it will correspond to that area on-screen

the digital painter. By setting up the brush control to react to the pen's movements, you can whirl your way through a painting as if you were painting at a canvas. And even if you didn't have the sensitivity setting activated, the fact you are holding a pen means you can trace, sketch or draw freehand in a far more intuitive way than if you were using a mouse. However well-designed a mouse may be, there's no getting away from the fact that it's a big hunk of plastic that requires a claw-like grip in order to function. An artist wouldn't use a stone to paint a picture, so there's no reason for a digital artist to do the equivalent.

Improved photo editing

The magic of a graphics tablet doesn't just extend to digital painting – day-to-day photo-editing tasks are made much easier. Because the pen is so familiar to hold, your control over tools is dramatically improved. Suddenly the Lasso tools can be just as accurate as the Pen tool for creating paths, meaning Photoshop Elements users don't have to mourn the lack of this powerful tool. Of course, if you have the Pen tool to hand you can make selections far more intuitively by literally tracing around the area on-screen. Wacom users can set the ExpressKeys to the modifier keys, so controlling the tool doesn't interfere with the task in hand.

Creating layer masks is also much easier with a graphics pen. Notoriously tricky selections like hair, clothes and eyelashes are suddenly much easier to make, and controlling tools such as the Clone Stamp is also better. What's more, if

Buyers' tip

Sensitivity

For most people, 512 levels of pressure sensitivity will be enough. There's no point paying out for what you don't really need. More levels won't make you a better artist!

Controlling the brushes

When it comes to graphics tablets and Photoshop, most of the magic happens in the Brush palette. It's here that you can set the brush to respond to the pen. Here's how you set it all up…

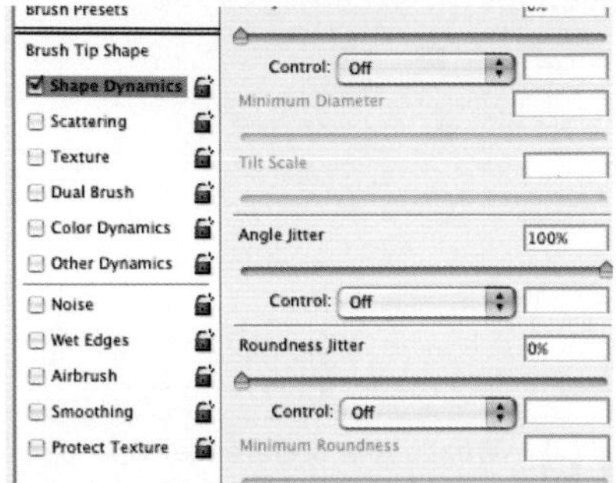

01 Get to the menus Go to Window>Brushes to open the Brushes palette. The right-hand side allows you to decide what part of a brush stroke to control. Some will already have various options ticked, enabling you to control those aspects of the brush's behaviour.

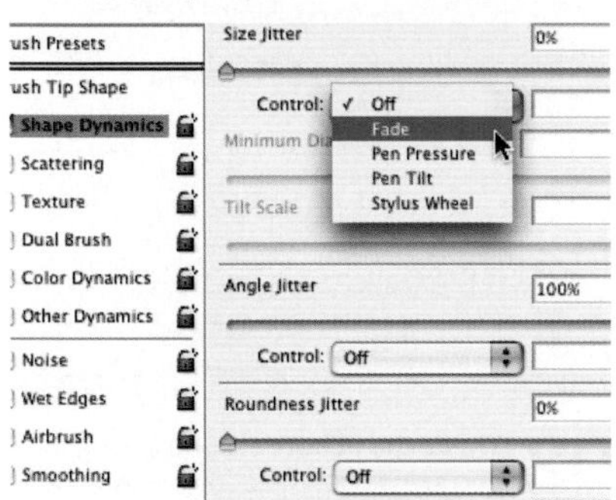

02 The controls The Control drop-down menu lets you decide how the pen's behaviour will affect the brush. The best one to choose is the Pen Pressure option, because this will allow you to control a behaviour according to how hard or soft you use the pen.

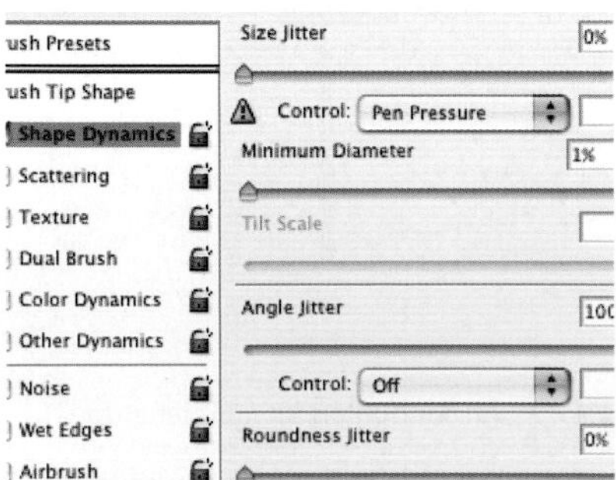

03 The result Here we've picked Pen Pressure, and a preview of the brush appears at the bottom of the palette. It will be different from the original preview, because pointy lines can be achieved by decreasing pen pressure.

you've set the brush dynamics to respond to pen pressure, you can increase or decrease the size of the clone brush without having to lift a finger. And that's the real beauty of graphics tablets; tasks you may have once dreaded because they were really fiddly or took a lot of time aren't such a hassle any more.

What's on offer

So if you have your list of requirements ready and you're eager to buy a tablet, where do you start? Over the years, there have been many makes and models to choose from in the graphics tablet market, but Wacom dominates. Founded in 1983, Wacom has perfected the art of drawing with a stylus to such a degree that it has no real competition. Despite this, Wacom continues to upgrade its range regularly with sleeker looks, lighter, more ergonomically designed pens and improved sensitivity.

The Graphire4 Classic is the smallest and cheapest Wacom currently on offer (12x9cm and roughly £68), aimed essentially at photographers wanting to do a little modest work on their digital snaps. It is, however, a pretty versatile tablet and pen capable of pro level results from Photoshop. Setting up the tablet is a breeze, and the 512 levels of pressure sensitivity means you can get good response from Photoshop's tools. The actual tablet is encased in a slightly see-through plastic case that can be unclipped so you can insert a photo or drawing to trace around.

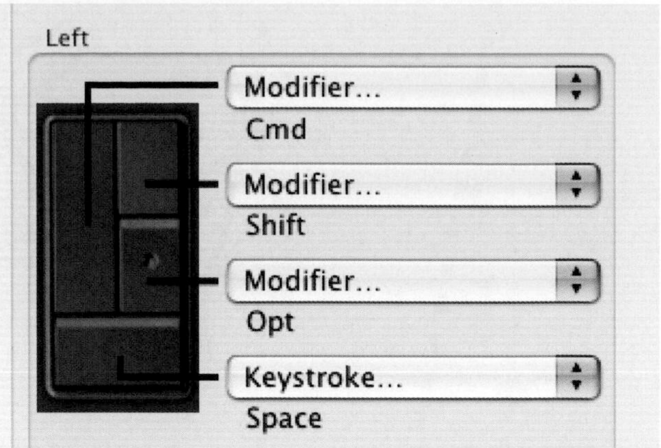

Control common keys using dedicated buttons

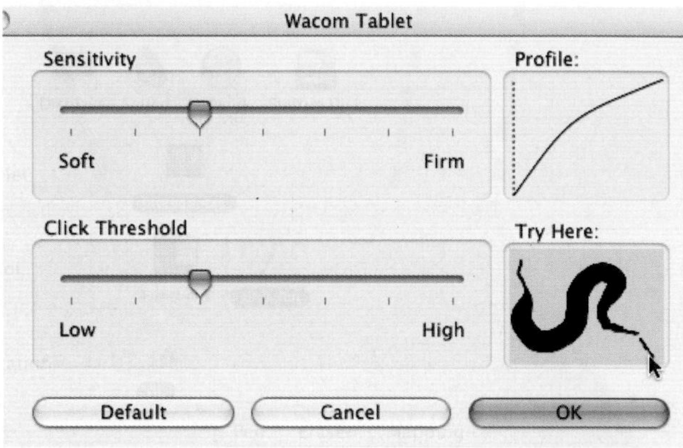

It's important to spend time setting up the pen so it responds to the way you work

> "There are a few choices out there, and you really don't have to pay a fortune for a tablet"

The pen has front and back pen keys, allowing you to perform single and double-click movements with ease. ExpressKeys allow you to assign your preferred creative software shortcuts. Located between these keys is a scroll wheel that functions like that of a traditional mouse. It can be used for zooming in and out of applications, or used for browsing. These additions alone give the Wacom Graphire4 value for money.

More tablet for your money

Wacom's Intuos range recently benefited from a slick redesign and oozes quality, with sleek designer good looks. Aimed at the more serious (or fussy) creative, those extra pounds get you a less 'plasticky' feel and some additional pro level functions. Out of the box it certainly looks the part, with new sloping wrist rest and a tasteful anthracite acrylic overlay.

The Intuos3 Grip Pen benefits from a sleeker, easy-on-the-hand design that feels luxurious and performs exceptionally well. An extended rubberised grip now runs up the barrel for added support, and a rocker switch can be used to access shortcuts. Drawing is intuitive and precise, with wonderful control over what marks you make thanks to 1,024 levels of pressure sensitivity. It now makes drawing with a mouse feel like you're wearing boxing gloves (although there's no ability to lift the top layer and put a photo underneath to trace from). Tilt sensitivity means you can tilt your pen in either direction to create natural-looking pen, brush and eraser strokes.

New ExpressKeys directly on the tablet eliminate the need to switch between tablet and computer keyboard. The newly designed

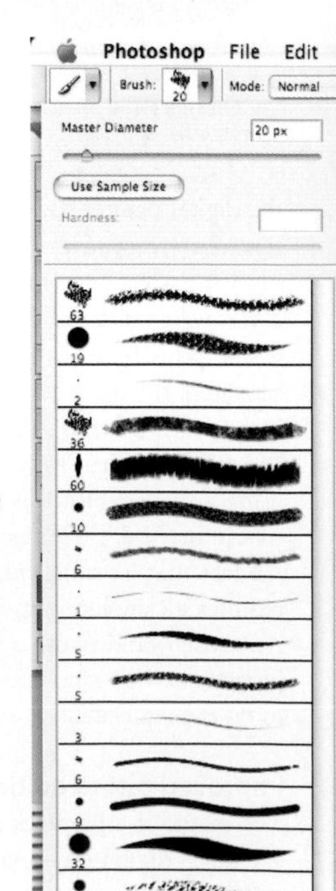

Touch Strip lets you use your finger directly on the tablet, scrolling through applications and zooming in and out.

Other options

Because of Wacom's dominance of the market, it's easy to forget that there are other manufacturers producing decent products which won't take such a mighty chunk from your wallet. Trust is a name that can be found in many PC shops, and it has various tablet options, with prices starting from around £20. The Wireless Tablet TB-3100 is probably the best all-rounder and can be yours for £40. This A5 tablet is big enough for most tasks, and its wireless status will be welcomed by those drowning in cables. The pen does take batteries so there is extra weight, but it's not really any heavier than a posh ballpoint.

In addition to customisable buttons on the pen, there are 12 further function keys on the tablet area itself, which you can use to access common functions and commands. There's a lift-up transparent overlay so you can trace over photos, and the mouse is there if you need it. Talking of sensitivity, the pen has 512 levels so you get plenty of control over your Photoshop brushes. Unfortunately, Mac OS X users are out of luck – drivers are only available for Windows and Mac OS 9 and 9.2.

Another alternative is the range of tablets from Genius. Again, these can be picked up for next to nothing, although we'd suggest the Wireless 8x6 mouse. The pen boasts 1,024 levels of sensitivity and will improve your Photoshop use no end. As with the TB-3100, there's a transparent overlay that you can lift up in order to place a photo or sketch underneath it, which is very handy if you're not too hot on drawing. Again, as with the TB-3100, there's no support for the latest Mac OS so it's not an option for some users, but it can be picked up for £50.

An essential tool?

We've hopefully given you a better idea of what a graphics tablet actually does, and how it can help make your Photoshop work much easier. This is by no means an exhaustive run through, but you should have a better understanding of how a tablet can fit into your normal workflow pattern.They may take a bit of getting used to, but once you get there we promise you'll never look back!

Buyers' tip

Heavyweight

Pens that need batteries, even AAA, will be quite heavy in the hand. If you have a very light way of holding a pen, it's best to go for one that works without the aid of a battery.

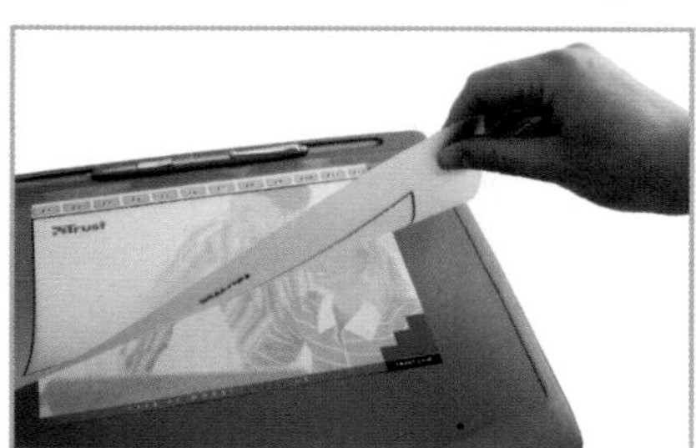

Some tablets have special sheets that you can place a photo under to trace

When combined with Photoshop's brushes, a graphics pen gives remarkable control over paint effects

Graphics tablet sampler

So which tablet should you go for? Here are four products that should appeal to most people…

Product	Wireless Tablet TB-3100	MousePen 8x6	Graphire4 Classic	Wacom Intuos3 A5
Company	Trust	Genius	Wacom	Wacom
Web address	www.trust.com	www.geniusnet.co.uk	www.wacom.com	www.wacom.com
Price	£40	£50	£74.99	£230
PC requirements	USB port, Windows 98/ME/2000 or XP	USB port, Windows 98/2000/ME/2003/XP	Windows 98 SE, Me, 2000, XP	Windows 98 SE, Me, 2000, XP
Mac requirements	N/A	N/A	Mac OS X 10.2.8	Mac OS X 10.2.8
Pen sensitivity	512 levels	1,024 levels	512 levels	1,024 levels
Size	6x8 inches	8x6 inches	4x5 inches	8x6 inches
Customisable buttons	Yes	Yes	Yes	Yes
Included software	Manual, programming software	Corel Painter 8 (trial) PenSuite	Corel Painter Essentials 2	Corel Painter Essentials 2, Elements 3
Included accessories	Wireless 3-button mouse and wireless 3-button pen	Cordless pen and cordless mouse	Cordless pen and cordless mouse	Grip pen, 5-button mouse
Suitable for	Novice photo editors/digital artists	Advanced beginners	Beginner/ intermediate photo editors and artists	Ambitious image editors and artists

Expert Tip

Layer sets and naming

Use folders to organise your layers; it can greatly improve your workflow when you know where everything is. Save certain parts of the image for different layer sets – these can be collapsed or expanded to show which layers are in that set. It saves space in your Layers palette and helps organise and keep everything clean. In this image we used folders for the various additions to the image, such as the circle effects, shapes and brushes. Name your layers too. It helps when trying to find certain parts you added and if you're trying to find a specific layer in a complicated Photoshop file with loads of layers.

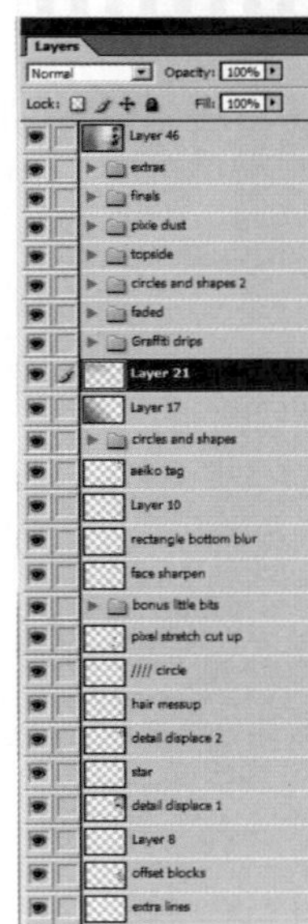

CREATE THE DOCUMENT

Get the photo ready for its filter treatment

01 Set up your canvas Create a new canvas about double the width of the image, making sure it's set to RGB mode and 300dpi. Copy the 'original_image.jpg' file from the CD, open it in Photoshop and then copy and paste it into the new canvas, placing it onto the far right-hand side.

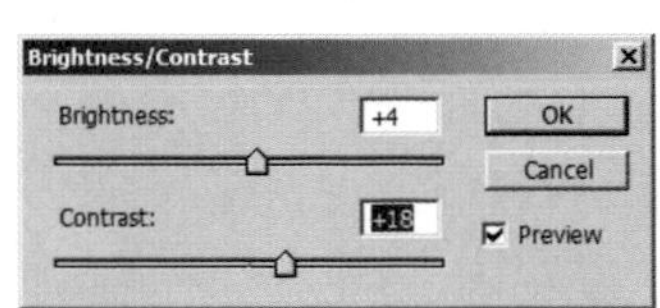

02 Brightness and contrast Go to the Layers palette and click the Add New Adjustment Layer button at the bottom (the circle that's half black and half white). From the options that appear, pick Brightness/Contrast. Lower the brightness just a tad and up the contrast. This will bring out the black more on her clothes and boost some of the subtle areas of her skin.

03 Colour balance Add another adjustment layer but this time for Color Balance. The skin looks a bit pale and bland, so you want to give it more colour and make it look healthier. Under Tone Balance, click Shadows and add more red and magenta. Adjust the midtones and highlights accordingly.

04 Mask the colour balance The colour balance layer you've just created came with a linked layer mask – click on this and use a soft round black brush to mask off some of the areas that you don't want the colour balance layer to affect. Adjust the brush size for more detailed areas and keep the flow of the brush quite low at around 10–20%.

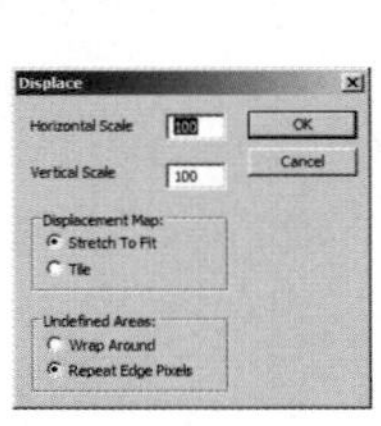

05 Use the Displace filter Hit Apple+A (Mac) or Ctrl+A (PC) to select the whole canvas. Now go to Edit>Copy Merge and then Edit>Paste. This places the whole canvas on a new layer. Go to Filter>Distort>Displace. Set the Horizontal and Vertical scale to 100 and make sure it's on Stretch to Fit. Click OK. Navigate to the 'displace_01.psd' file from the disc and click OK.

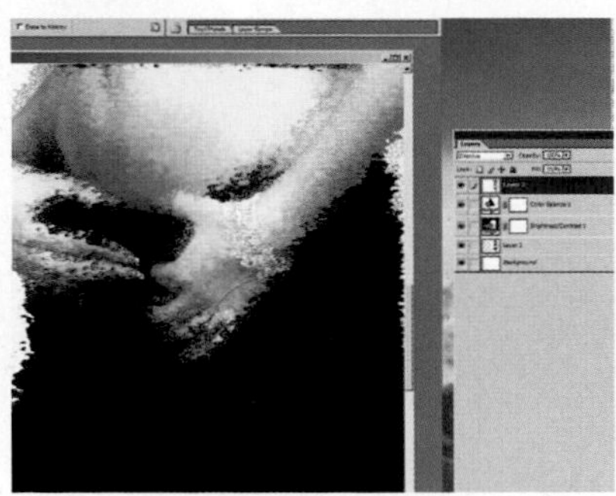

06 Dissolving Use the Magic Wand tool to select all the white on the layer then press Delete. Change the blending mode to Dissolve. Use a soft eraser to erase parts of the image around the woman. The effect you're looking for is one that's pixellated and lo-fi. Move this displaced layer over the top of the original picture.

07 More colour change Create a new layer and add a linear gradient using yellow and pink, although you can change this to whatever you fancy. Set the blending mode to Screen and go to Layer>Layer Mask>Reveal All and then start adding black areas to where you don't want the gradient layer to affect.

08 Add more colour Create a new layer and select the Gradient tool with a colour going to transparent. We picked a light blue and dragged it from the bottom right to the centre. Layer mask areas of the image you want to save from the gradient – we masked the face, hair and arm. Repeat a couple of times, but use pink.

HIGH CONTRAST OFFSET

It's time to up the colour stakes

09 More glitching

Copy merge the whole canvas as before and go to Image>Adjustments >Brightness/Contrast. Turn the Contrast up to maximum, set Brightness a little lower and click OK. Use the Magic Wand tool to delete large areas on the left-hand side, leaving more detail near the woman, set the blending mode to Overlay and offset slightly to the right.

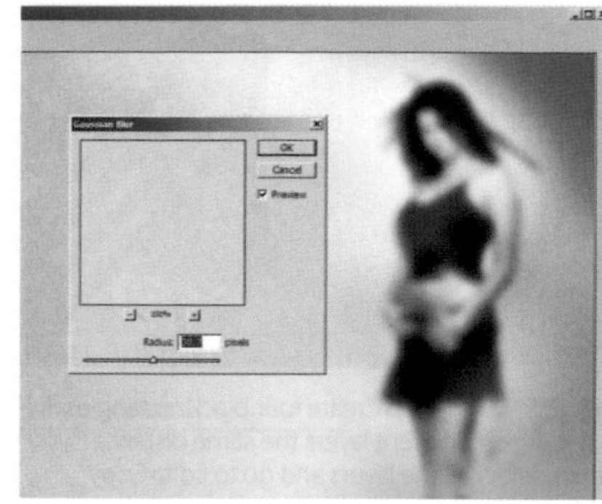

10 Blurring

Copy merge the canvas again and paste into a new layer, then go to Filter>Blur>Gaussian blur. Set the Radius to 30 pixels and hit OK. Scale the layer, set it to Linear Burn turn the Opacity down to about 20%, and place this on the canvas to the left-hand side.

11 CMYK lines

Use the Rectangular Marquee to make a long rectangle, copy three times and place next to each other. Add colour overlays of cyan, magenta, yellow and black and merge all the layers together. Rotate the layer by 45 degrees and place by the woman, erasing parts so it looks like it's behind her. Set the blending mode to Hard Light, 10% Opacity.

12 Using strokes

Copy the canvas and place into a new layer, up the contrast to 100%. Select and delete most of the layer, just keeping the head, top and some skirt. Apply a Stroke to the whole layer (Edit>Stroke). Make sure the colour is white with a Width of 1px. Set the Fill Opacity of the layer to 0% so you are just left with the stroke. Copy the layer, delete some parts and rearrange on the canvas.

13 Organic displace

Select the whole canvas again and go to Filter>Distort>Displace. Set the Horizontal and Vertical scales to 100 with Stretch to Fit and Wrap Around selected. For the displacement map, choose displace_2.psd from the CD and click OK. Erase some of the displacement from the woman, especially the face.

14 Another displace!

Add a few random shapes to the background. These can be created with the Pen tool with a Stroke and Fill Opacity of 0%, or use the custom shapes in Photoshop. Repeat the last step but use the 'displace_03.psd' file from the CD. Delete as required so it gives a nice choppy effect around the woman's legs and also to the shapes you added.

Expert Tip

Stay in control

Although Photoshop has a vast range of filters and effects that can be applied to modify your image, it is important not to over-use them. It's a good idea to get to know each filter individually and know what you want to do to an image before you apply filters. Having said that, sometimes its fun to experiment and mess around with filters. Just don't expect the Photoshop software to create the images for you; remember it's only a tool for visualising your artwork. Nothing can take the place of imagination and experimentation!

SAVE TIME WITH THE BRUSH TOOL BY COPYING THE LAYER AND SCALING IT, FLIPPING IT AND ADDING DIFFERENT BLENDING EFFECTS | **TIP**

Quick mask

After you make a mask, you will get two thumbnails in one layer. If you click the space between these two thumbnails, you link them together. Then you are allowed to move and adjust them together.

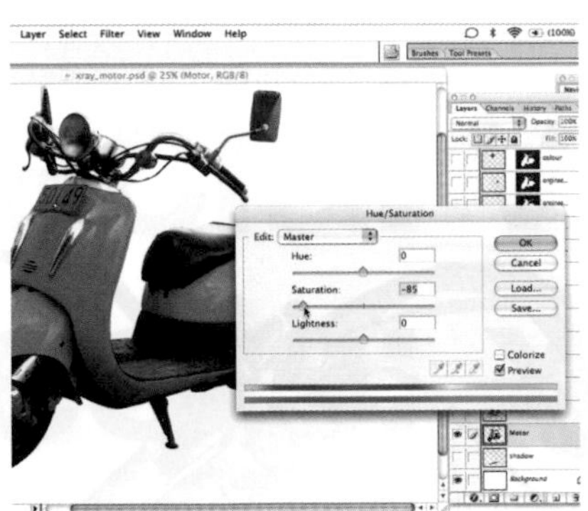

04 Hue adjustments Use Image>Adjustment>Hue/Saturation (Apple+U (Mac) or Ctrl+U (PC)) to adjust the saturation of the image. Make this image incline to grayscale by taking Saturation to the left.

05 Add a filter Now that we have a greyer hue, it's time to start on the x-ray effect. Choose Filter>Stylize>Solarize to make the image look overexposed.

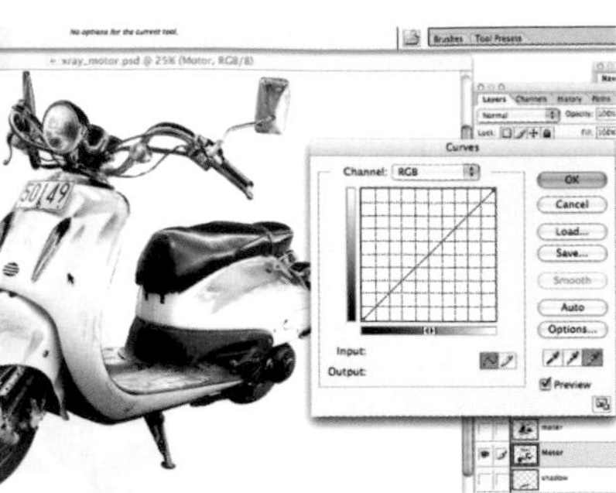

06 Using Curves Go to Image>Adjustment>Curves. Choose the third dropper on the right, underneath the Options button. Use this dropper to click the yellow parts on the image. This sets the yellow as the white point and instantly changes the look of the image to a pinky/purpley bike.

07 Changing colour Use Image> Adjustments>Replace Color. Your cursor will become a picker. Choose the blue point of the image and adjust the Replacement slider on the panel to turn the blue to purple.

08 More variations Use Image> Adjustments>Variations. Click once on More Yellow, and then click once on More Red. This order can make the whole image incline to yellow. Use Image>Adjustments>Curves to adjust the contrast of the image.

09 Opposites attract Use Image>Adjustments>Invert or you can press Apple+I (Mac) or Ctrl+I (PC) on your keyboard. The colours will become blue and green, and the black areas have become ghostly pale.

START YOUR ENGINES

What's inside the bike?

10 Pick the engine Open the 'engine02.tif' file from the CD-ROM. Use the Pen tool to trace the shape and make a selection. Then copy this shape in another layer.

11 Back to grey Use Image> Adjustments>Desaturate to turn the image grayscale. You can achieve the same effect if you go to Image>Mode>Grayscale, but it will change the colour mode of the image. However, the Desaturate command can just turn the single layer to grayscale but keep the file as RGB or CMYK.

12 Adjust contrast Use Image>Adjustments>Curves to boost the contrast of the image. Then use Image> Adjustments>Variation to adjust the colour of the image. Go for a browny look as above.

ALERT | IF YOU USE PHOTOSHOP ELEMENTS, SELECT THE OBJECTS WITH THE MAGNETIC LASSO

Replace colour and variations

Here's a look at two of our favoured options for working with colour

There are many ways to adjust colour of an image in Photoshop. In this tutorial, we used two orders: Replace Color and Variation. Both commands can be found in Image>Adjustments. Replace Color allows you to change the hues in your images while variations allow you to see multiple editing options in one window

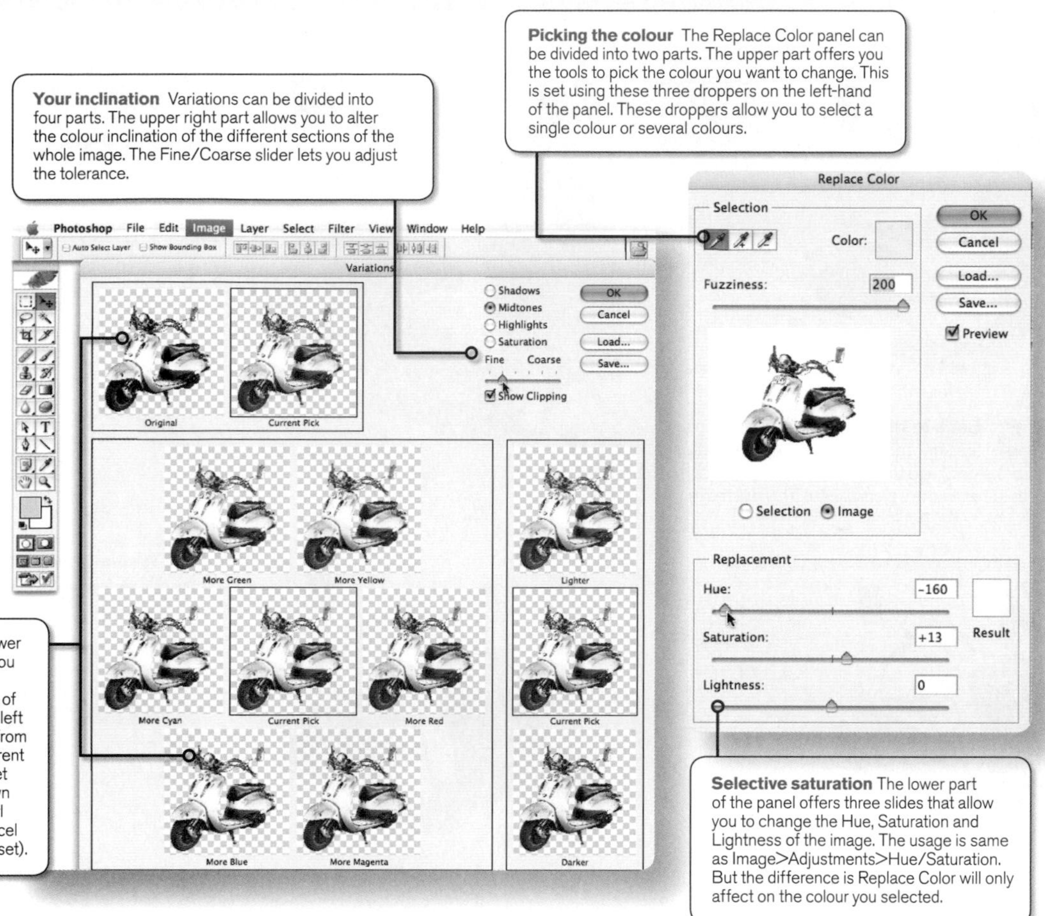

Your inclination Variations can be divided into four parts. The upper right part allows you to alter the colour inclination of the different sections of the whole image. The Fine/Coarse slider lets you adjust the tolerance.

Picking the colour The Replace Color panel can be divided into two parts. The upper part offers you the tools to pick the colour you want to change. This is set using these three droppers on the left-hand of the panel. These droppers allow you to select a single colour or several colours.

Changing colour The lower parts of the panel allows you to adjust the colour. Every small image is the preview of the final effect. The upper left part can allow you switch from the original image and current pick. But you can also reset your image by holding down the Apple key (Mac) or Ctrl key (PC) and clicking Cancel (which has changed to Reset).

Selective saturation The lower part of the panel offers three slides that allow you to change the Hue, Saturation and Lightness of the image. The usage is same as Image>Adjustments>Hue/Saturation. But the difference is Replace Color will only affect on the colour you selected.

Expert Tip

You can select a image, then press Apple+C and Apple+V (Mac) or Ctrl+C and Ctrl+V (PC) to copy and paste. But you also can hold the Option key (Mac) or Alt key (PC) and drag the layer to achieve the copy and paste.

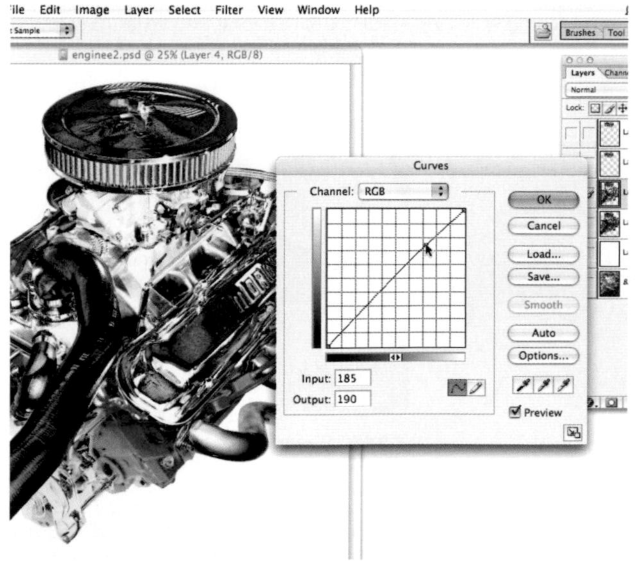

13 Once more with the inverted Choose Image>Adjustments>Invert and then press Apple+M (Mac) or Ctrl+M (PC) to adjust the contrast of the image. Again, boost the contrast for a more dramatic effect.

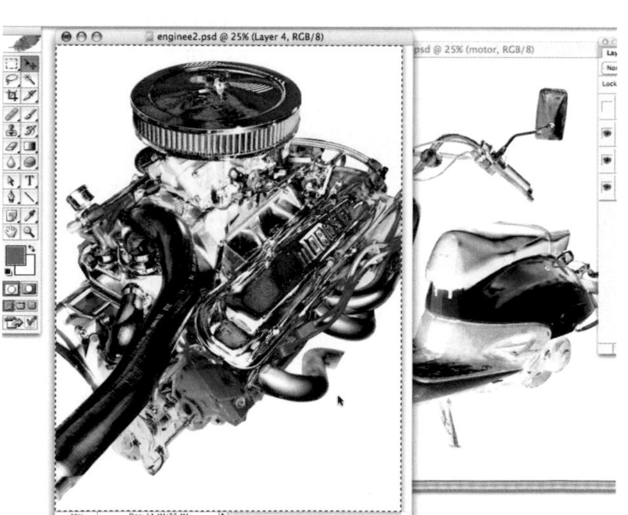

14 Select and copy Now everything is looking more x-rayesque, use Select>All to select the image. Now copy it.

Redo

The colour mode of the final image for print should be CMYK. However if you're not working for print, use the RGB mode. Not only will this keep your file size down, but the RGB mode works with all types of filters, but CMYK only plays with some of them. You can always switch the file after you've finished the image.

BACK TO THE VEHICLE

Adding the inside elements

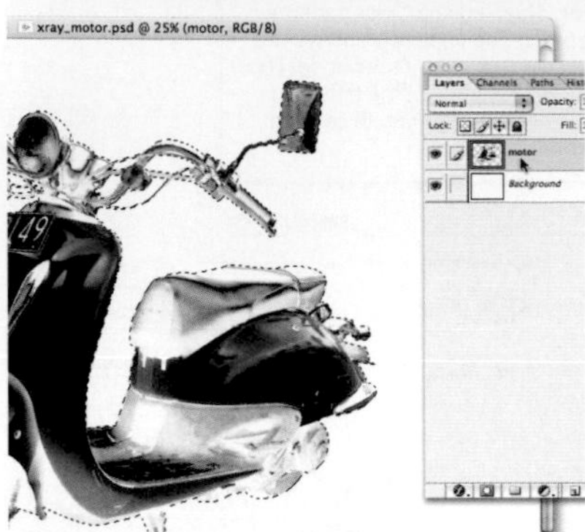

15 Back to the vehicle Come back to the file 'xray_motor'. Hold the Apple key (Mac) or Ctrl key (PC) and then use the mouse to click on this layer in the Layers palette. This will make a selection of the outline.

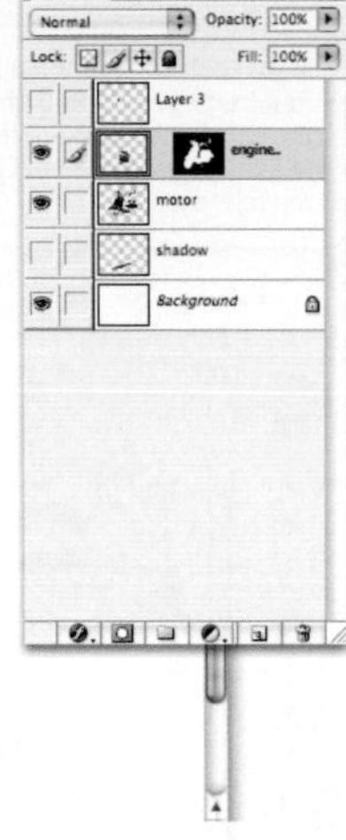

16 Make a mask Use Edit>Paste Into to create a quick mask. The engine image that you copied from the other file will be constrained in the shape of the bike.

17 A new angle Use Apple+T (Mac) or Ctrl+T (PC) to select the Free Transform option. Use this to adjust the angle of the engine so it fits snugly. Once everything fits as it should, change the blending mode from the Layers palette to Soft Light.

18 Copy the layer Select the layer of the x-ray engine, hold down Option (Mac) or Alt (PC) and drag this layer above the motor layer. This key command means that you can move not only the layer but also the layer mask.

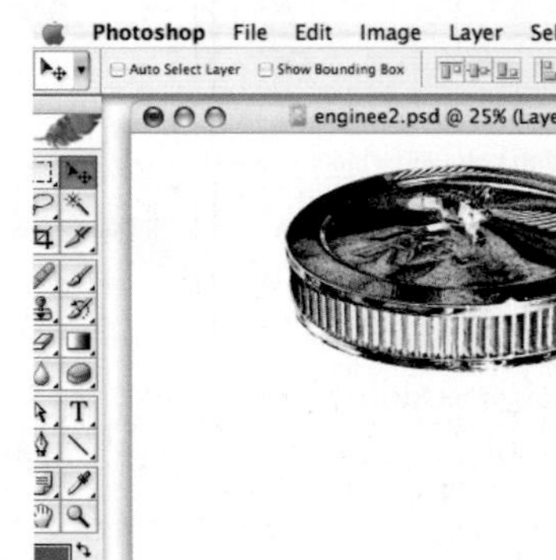

19 X-ray the engine Return to the 'engine02.tif', and use the Pen tool to select the top round disc of the image. Follow exactly the same steps as we used for the engine to create the same effect.

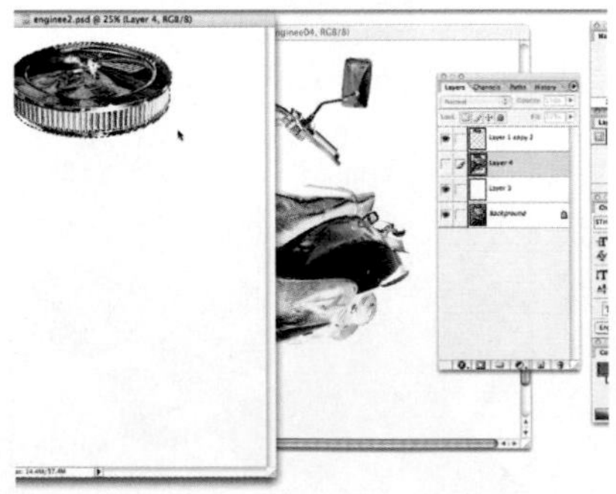

20 Back to the motor Select the cut out image that you've just applied the x-ray effect to, and then Paste Into the xray_motor document as before. As in step 17, select the Free Transform tool to make the elements fit. .

21 Make it fit Use Apple+T (Mac), Ctrl+T (PC) to adjust the angel of the engine disc. Place this one underneath the seat, near the front. You won't need the side grille areas, so use the Eraser tool to get rid of it.

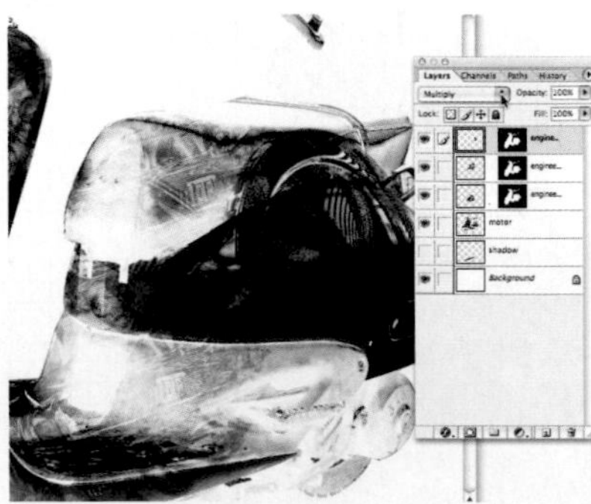

22 See to the blending mode Once the engine section is snugly in position and you've got rid of extraneous detail, change the blending mode of this layer to Multiply. This helps make the engine part sink into the image and really look like it's part of the bike.

NOTES | FIND OUT MORE ABOUT HOW X-RAYS WERE DISCOVERED FROM **WWW.XRAY.HMC.PSU.EDU/RCI/SS1/SS1_2.HTML**

23 More engine fun Open the file 'engine01.tif' from the CD-ROM. Use the Pen tool to make a selection of the gears. Then follow the same procedure as was applied to the engine to achieve the same effect.

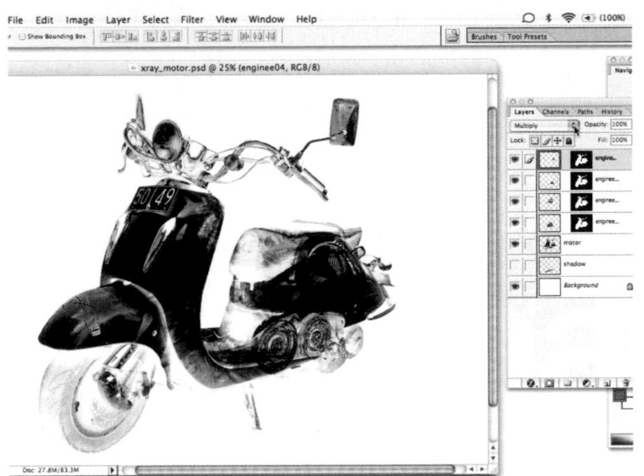

24 Add the engine Follow steps 15 and 16. Copy this layer and use Paste Into to make the selection fit the shape of the bike in the 'xray_motor' file. Then change the blend mode of the layer to Multiply.

Expert Tip

After you use the Pen tool to trace a shape, you can go to the Paths palette and press the small arrow on the right corner and choose Make Selection to turn the shape into a selection.

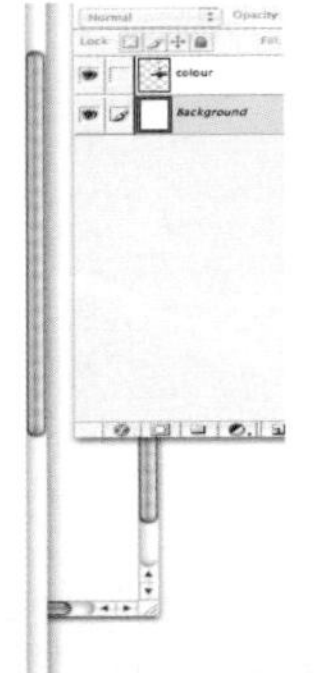

25 Adjust the colour of the handlebars Open the file 'flower01.tif' from the CD-ROM. Use the Pen tool to select the shape of the flower and then copy it to another layer. Use the same procedure as for the engine to achieve the x-ray effect.

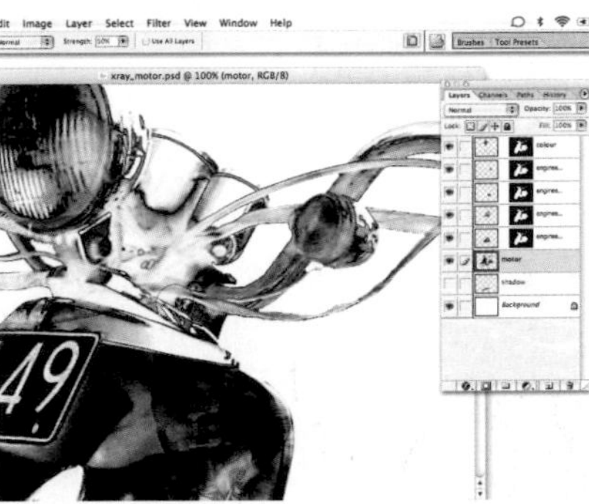

26 Back to 15 and 16 once more Follow the steps 15 and 16, copy the layer and paste it into the shape of the bike in 'xray_motor'. Change the blend mode to Soft Light. Select the motor layer and press Apple+R (Mac) or Ctrl+R (PC) to blur any details that may be too sharp.

SHADOW MAKER

Add a bit of presence

27 Back to the shadow Return to the 'moto_photo' file. Use the Pen tool to select the shadow on the photo. Copy and paste it to the file 'xray_motor'. Follow the same steps as applied to the engine to make this x-ray shadow.

28 All done Now that everything is x-rayed and looking lovely, have a final check to make sure everything fits with everything else. Check that the engine parts are in the right place and once you're happy, save. You've now created a work of visual wonder!

The layer structure

How our bike stacked up

Keep your layers nice and structured with this guide to how they should be presented

Handlebars

Engine 4

Engine 3

Engine 2

Engine 1

Motorbike

Shadow

Tool School

Threshold advice

When you use this technique on your own photos, be warned that it takes a bit of time getting the Threshold and High Pass settings correct. Threshold tends to look thinner in the Preview box than it actually comes out, so keep this in mind.

WORK WITH THE EFFECT

Use different filters for realistic results

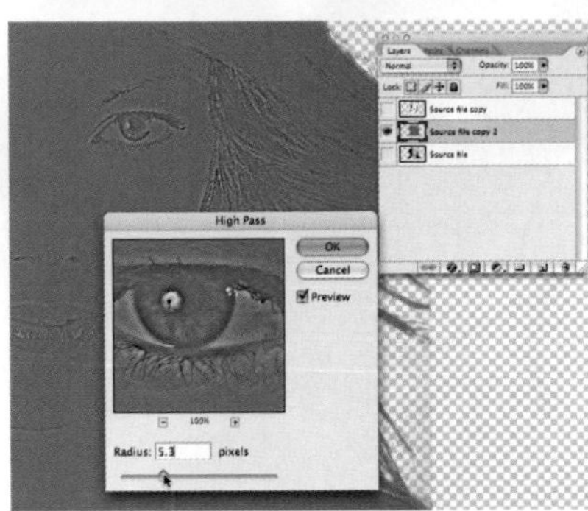

04 Duplicate again Click on the original layer again and duplicate it once more. It's always worth keeping an original image in case you want to go back. This new layer is for a thinner pencil effect (call it Thin Pencil), so use the High Pass filter to 7.2 pixels and the Threshold option to 120.

05 Get the highlights Go to Select>Color Range once more and then Select: Highlights. Click OK and press Delete. You should just be left with the pencil marks (Elements users go for Magic Wand). Repeat this on the other drawing layer. Now create a new layer and go to Edit>Fill. Pick White as the fill colour and place at the bottom of the layer stack. Call it Paper.

06 Old King Coal Click on the thin pencil layer. Make sure that the Foreground and Background colours are set to black and white in the toolbar. Now go to Filter>Sketch>Charcoal. Set Charcoal Thickness to 4, Detail to 5 and Light/Dark Balance to 13.

07 More sketch Go to Filter>Sketch> Graphic Pen. Set Stroke Length to 12, Light/Dark Balance to 6 and Stroke Direction to Right Diagonal. Make sure that the thin layer is on top of the thick layer. Change the blending mode to Multiply and change the Opacity to 90%. Go to the thick layer and set Opacity to 43%.

08 Hair extensions The hair on the left is looking a bit wispy. Duplicate the thick pencil layer and go to Filter>Blur>Gaussian Blur. Set to 8.1. Make the opacity of the layer 62% and then move to under the original thick layer. Select the original thick layer and pick the Lasso tool. Set the Feather to 4 and select some hair. Copy and paste the selection and move to the left-hand side. Repeat until the hair looks nice and full.

Tip

What does it all mean?

At the heart of this tutorial is the Threshold and High Pass filters. If you've never met these filters before, here's an outline of what they do. Threshold basically makes an image high contrast and black and white. You decide on a Threshold level and pixels lighter than this become white and pixels darker than this level become black. The High Pass filter picks out the edges of an image. The higher the Radius you set, the more pixels are picked up.

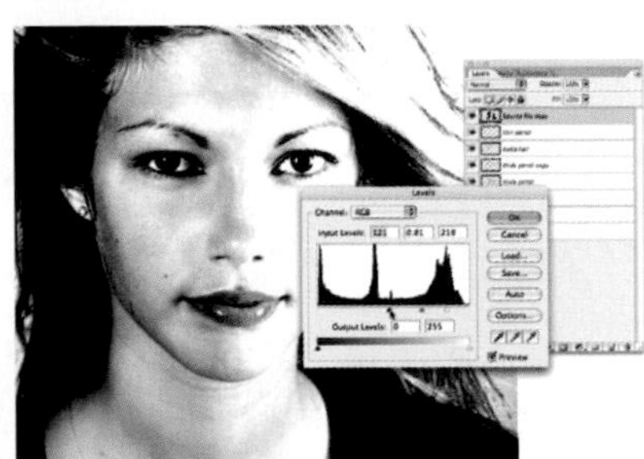

09 Merge together Merge all of the extra hair layers into one. Click on the original thick pencil layer and duplicate it. Position above the original thick pencil layer to bring back some of the markings. Move the duplicate of the original photo to the top of the Layers palette. Go to Image> Adjustments>Desaturate and then bring up Levels. The aim here is to exaggerate the shadows, which can be done by moving the black slider to the right.

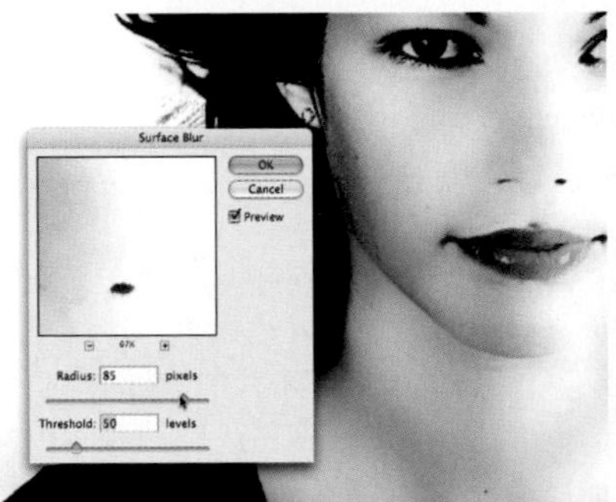

10 Add some blur Hopefully you can see things beginning to develop, but there's still some work to do. Go to Filter>Surface Blur and in Radius put 85 and in Threshold enter 50. If you haven't got CS2, you can do a light Gaussian Blur. The aim is to soften things a bit.

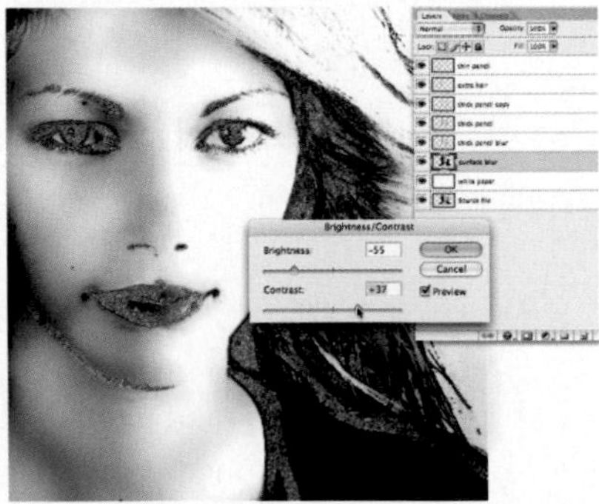

11 Brighten up Put the blurred layer underneath all of the pencil layers and go to Image>Adjustments>Brightness/Contrast (PE users need to go for Enhance>Adjust Lighting>Brightness/Contrast). Enter a setting of -55 for the Brightness and 37 for the Contrast.

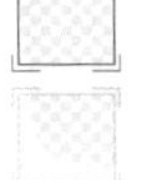

TIP | SET THE THRESHOLD AND HIGH PASS UP TO PRODUCE THICK LINES AND CREATE YOUR OWN COLOURING BOOKS

BRING OUT THE DETAILS

The small things make all the difference

12 Underpainting Still on the blur layer, go to Filter>Artistic>Underpainting and enter 6 for the Brush Size, 5 for the Texture Coverage, Sandstone from the Texture menu, 109% in the Scaling field, set Relief to 27 and pick Top from the Light menu. Click OK and set the layer to 83% Opacity. Change the thick pencil layer and the thick pencil copy layer to Linear Burn.

13 Take away Back on the blur layer, choose a big soft brush and reduce its Opacity to 56%. Start erasing over the eyes and mouth.

14 Dodge and burn Create a new layer and choose a light grey colour. Pick a medium-sized brush and paint over the face and neck. Click on the Burn tool. Run the brush over the areas that need darkening (where the shadows are) and then switch to the Dodge tool and brush over the highlight areas. Reduce the opacity to taste and move this layer above the blur layer.

15 Hatch job Choose a hard brush and set it to three pixels. Reduce the Opacity to 15% and drag it in a left to right diagonal motion on her face and neck. The idea is to create the feeling of rough pencil sketches.

16 Move about Move each of the thick pencil layers underneath the blur layer. Duplicate the thin pencil layer (which is still above all the other layers). Change the Opacity of the duplicate to 44%. Go back to the original thin pencil layer and go to Filter>Blur>Motion Blur. Set 41% as the Angle and 31 as the Distance.

17 Rough it up Create a new layer and move it above the Blur layer. Fill with white and reduce the Opacity to 22%. With the default brushes loaded, pick the Chalk brush. Select the Eraser tool and start erasing away some areas to bring back the shadows. A good place to start is on the hair next to her face.

18 More marks Go back to the grey shading layer and choose a soft brush at 3px size. Set to an Opacity of 17%. Set the Flow to 62% and start making lots of soft, thin eraser marks around the edge of the noise and around the eyes. This will give more definition to the areas and help give the impression of more pencil marks.

19 The grand finale Of course, you don't have to rely on Photoshop to get your pencil marks. We scanned in some pencil marks and smudges and then imported them to place over the image. By changing the blending mode to Multiply, they merged in beautifully with the digital sketch.

Expert Tip

Build up a theme

You can really have fun with the sketch effect. As you can see from our cover and intro image, we've placed it on a sketchbook to really enhance the impression of a hand drawing. If you'd like to do the same, flatten the image and then place over a layer containing your sketchbook image or texture. Change the blending mode to Multiply and marvel at your creation. You can either take a picture of a sketchbook or maybe scan in some textured paper. Alternatively, make use of Photoshop's own Texturizer filter, found under Filter>Texture>Texturizer.

Tool School

Selecting stuff

The Lasso tool isn't the only way to make selections in Photoshop. You can also use the Polygonal or Magnetic lassos, or the Pen tool to make paths that can be turned into selections. Quick Mask (Q) offers yet another alternative, as does the Color Range command (Select>Color Range).

COLOURING IN

Get the base colours sorted

01 In the beginning… Most digital illustrations begin life as a sketch on paper, and this piece is no exception. Our lovely lass was drawn on A4 paper and scanned as a 400dpi Grayscale image. The background was drawn separately and scanned, and the two pictures were joined and resized to 300dpi, which is the normal resolution for printing magazines and books. You will find the lady on the CD.

02 Primary colours Set the sketch layer to Multiply, and create a new layer below it. This is the layer where you'll be putting in patches of flat colour. You'll want to do 'flats' for two reasons – to quickly establish a rough colour palette, and to save yourself the trouble of re-doing selections later.

03 Lasso selection You can fill in large swabs of colour in a number of ways, but for the purposes of this tutorial, select the Lasso tool (L) and start selecting the face and body of the ninja. Make sure that Feather is set to 0. Click the Add To Selection button to make it easier for you to keep on making selections. Alternatively, you can hold down the Shift key.

04 Fill 'er up Once you've made your selections, use the Paint Bucket Tool (G) or Fill (Edit>Fill) to infuse them with colour. Choose a light shade of pink – this will serve as the base skin tone for the ninja. Repeat the process for the ninja's face, hair, clothes, and sai.

05 Background and moon Use the Lasso tool to select the mountains and sky. If you find the Lasso difficult to control, try using the Polygonal Lasso or Pen tools to make selections. When you're done with the mountains, use the Elliptical Marquee tool (M) to create a large circle on another layer and fill that with a light silvery blue.

Tip

We love tablets

The digital tablet is the digital painter's best friend. These lovelies are pressure sensitive, have more precision than a mouse, and just look spiffy on a desk. There are several different brands available, but if you can afford if, a tablet with better sensitivity like the Wacom Intuos series is better suited to graphic work.

06 First stage painting Now that the base colours have been sorted, it's time to start painting. Select the Brush tool, choose a soft-edged brush of about 97px and set the Hardness to 0%. Leave the mode as Normal, with Opacity and Flow at 100%. If you have a graphics tablet, check that the Pen Pressure option is checked in your Brush controls.

07 Spraying shadow Select the layer with the ninja's 'flats'. Using the Magic Wand (Tolerance 1), click on the skin colour. Voila! Unless you checked off the Contiguous box at the top, all areas with the skin tone should have been selected. With the selection still active, create a new layer and start spraying shadows with the Brush tool.

BURN, BABY BURN

Introducing the Burn tool

08 Spray away Keep your selection active. Once you're happy with the shadows, spray on some other colours to give the skin more life. Try adding some pinks to the face and back, and greens and browns to the legs. You can lower the Opacity settings on your brush so that the underlying shadow colour is still somewhat visible through the new colours.

09 Mmm… toasty Right, now for the fun part – burning stuff! The Burn tool (O) is part of a sub-toolset that includes the Burn, Dodge and Sponge tools, and is represented by an icon of a pinching hand.

10 Burning desire Select the layer where you painted the shadows. Set up your Burn tool as follows: Diameter 100, Hardness 30%, Range: Midtones, Expose 25%, airbrush. Now start gently brushing the inner areas where the shadow should be deepest. Notice any difference? The Burn tool should make the dark colours even darker and more intense.

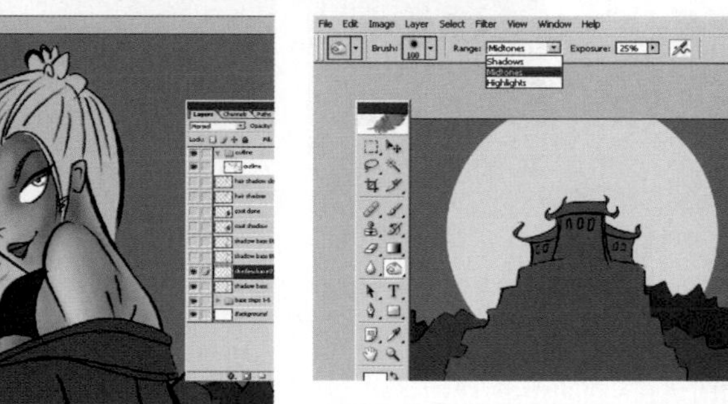

11 Sizzling results Continue burning to achieve dramatic shadows. If you are using a tablet, try not to apply full pressure. Lightly brush the areas you want to darken. The result of the burn can be dramatic but not obvious at first – try using the History palette to go back a few steps to compare the difference.

12 Burn ranges By now, you might have noticed that the Burn tool has a drop-down menu for Range. This affects how the Burn reacts with the colours on a layer. Shadows focus on dark colours, while highlights focus on lighter areas. Midtones is the default and gives a nice overall effect. Try changing the Range while brushing to see the different results.

13 Completed burn When you're done burning in the colours, your ninja should look something like this. She might look a little baked, but part of the reason is because nothing else in the picture has been touched up yet. In any event, you can soften up the offending areas by spraying a lighter colour over with the airbrush later.

14 Dodging Well now that you've gotten the hang of using the Burn tool, it's time we moved on to its fairer sister – the Dodge tool. The Dodge tool is in the same sub-palette (click and hold the Burn tool to see all three tools) and is represented by a black pushpin.

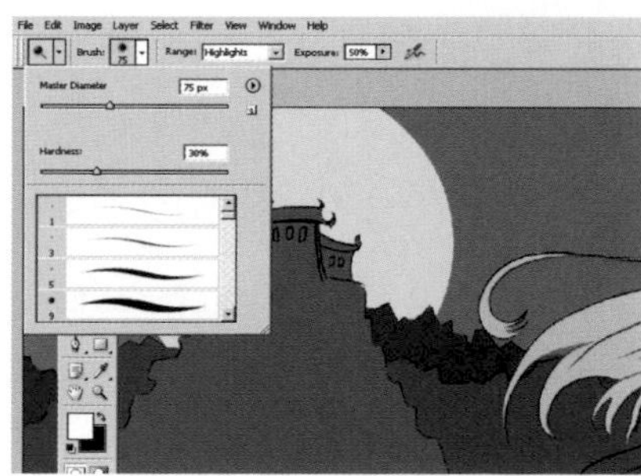

15 Dodging basics The Dodge tool in Photoshop puts a new spin on a traditional technique (see side tip, top-right). It lightens colours, all the way to white if you keep at it, but used correctly it can help achieve effects unlike those produced by other tools. For now, select Dodge, and set the Range to Highlights, Exposure 50%. Reduce the Diameter to 75.

Old faces

The Burn and Dodge tools in Photoshop have their counterparts in traditional photography. Before Photoshop came along, photographers would resort to darkroom tricks in order to get the perfect shot. The burn technique literally meant burning more light onto a print by allowing an area to be exposed for longer. Overexposure would result in a big black blob, so burning had to be done carefully. Dodging, on the other hand, was to prevent parts of an image from being developed. This was a handy little trick for removing ex-partners from pictures, leaving a space for the skilled photographer to later burn in the image of a

Know your own strength
Pick the right settings first time

Part of the success of using the Dodge, Burn and Sponge tools is the strength you use them at. By altering the Exposure slider, you can change how strong the effect of the brush is, and thereby control the look of what you're trying to do.

Dodge tool

The higher up the Exposure slider, the more intense the result and the greater the contrast. High percentile Exposure settings are good for getting dramatic effects.

25%

50%

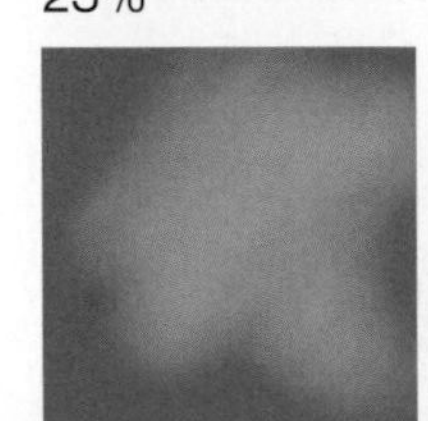
75%

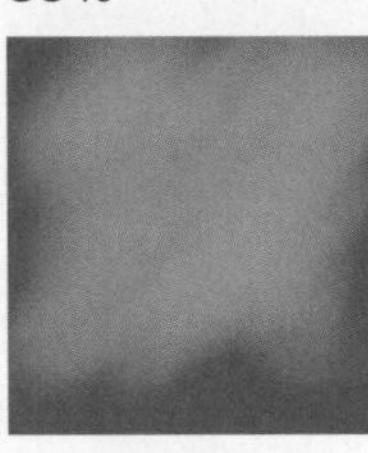
100%

Burn tool

The greater the Exposure setting, the more intense the burn. The result of this tool is also affected by whether you choose to burn the highlights, midtones or shadows.

25%

50%

75%

100%

Sponge tool

The Sponge tool is used to saturate and desaturate colours, and because it isn't very strong in terms of effect, it is helpful in making fine adjustments after burning and dodging.

25%

50%

75%

100%

LIGHTEN UP
Introduce some highlights to the girl

16 The artful dodger Now use the Dodge tool on the lighter areas of the shadow layer. Since the moon is on the left, we can assume that it's illuminating the girl, and hence the highlights should be on her left. Brush gently with the Dodge tool to give the skin tone an overall sheen.

17 Dodge complete The final result of burning and dodging on the ninja. With practice, dodging and burning makes short work of shadows and highlights, saving you time and giving you the freedom to try out different intensities of colour relatively quickly. This is especially helpful if you're timid about creating high-contrast or oversaturated pictures.

18 Sponge Speaking of over-saturation – the last tool of the Dodge/Burn sub-palette is the Sponge. Sponge lets you make adjustments to saturation – if there's an area where you feel the brown is a bit too intense, you can bring it down a notch or two with Sponge. Likewise, Sponge can be used to saturate areas where the colour seems too weak.

AND THE REST
Carry on with the painting

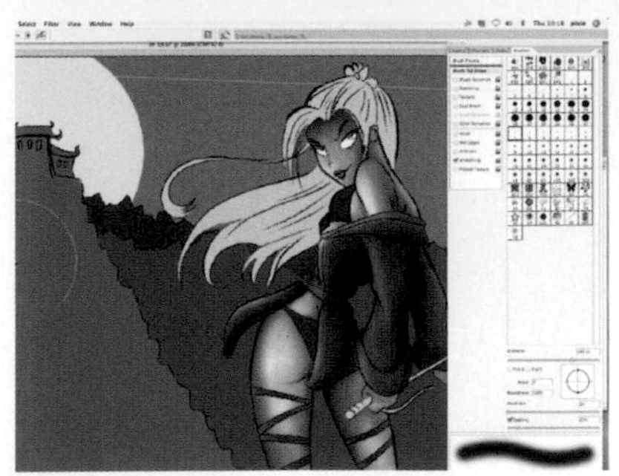

19 Robing the ninja Complete the ninja's robe using the same techniques. Along the way you might want to readjust the size of your brush to suit the needs of your particular painting. The Burn, Dodge and Sponge tools can be adjusted like any other brush in Photoshop from the Brush palette. Elements users have less options.

20 Heavy-duty Dodge and Burn When doing the hair, try turning up the settings for the Dodge and Burn tools. Turn the Hardness way up, and increase the Exposure. Usually these settings generate results that are too harsh, but in some instances they can be used to create neat effects. Use the extreme Dodge and Burn tools to add some interesting effects to the hair.

21 Make the moon You can also create interesting textures using Dodge and Burn tools. The rocky textures on the moon and mountains were created with just fills, gradients, lighting effects and a blatant disregard for brushstroke disciple. To make your own moody moon, start by selecting the silver circle you did right at the beginning.

22 Paint rough! With the elliptical selection active, create a new layer. Fill it with a Foreground to Transparent gradient with light grey as your foreground (your fill should be transparent in the middle). Still using the extreme Dodge and Burn tools, vigorously and randomly paint the new layer.

23 Multiply and enjoy Your extreme exertions should have created a rough, uneven texture – perfect for the surface of a moon! Change the layer's lighting mode to Multiply. Go back to the original moon layer and apply a slight Gaussian Blur (Filter>Blur>Gaussian Blur) to it, and enjoy your new moon!

24 Making mountains You can apply the same trick to create the rugged texture of the mountains. To create an even more dramatic effect, select the mountain shapes and on a new layer, fill them in with a Foreground to Transparent gradient, with Black as your foreground colour. Do the same for the sky behind the moon for maximum effect.

25 Finishing touches Put the finishing touches on your picture; zoom in close to see if there are little gaps in colour (which sometimes happens if you're not careful in making selections). Paint in the eyes and lips, and polish up the bikini. As a final touch, spray on a little blue around the edges to complete the look of a quiet moonlit scene.

Web Resources

The art of Dodge and Burn

Even though the Dodge and Burn tools are easy to use now, it's worth remembering that not long ago they were skills that set apart great photographers from amateurs. While the darkroom arts are not quite as widespread as they once were, there's still a lot to be learnt from them. Here are some sites you can check out if you'd like some more information:

The New York Institute of Photography

It has been educating photographers since 1910. 'Nuff said.

www.nyip.com

Student Curriculum in Photography

Nice easy-to-read article explaining what burning and dodging is all about.

www.scphoto.com/html/dodge_burn.html

Ansel Adams

Online showcase of black-and-white work from the legend himself.
www.anseladams.com

Create space!

Begun these Clone tool wars have. Discover how to make stars, worlds and more without ever having to leave Photoshop

essentials

SKILL LEVEL
Beginner
Intermediate
Expert

TIME TAKEN
You're looking 5 hours

YOUR EXPERT
Ross Andrews

This was possibly the most fun we've had in Photoshop for years. Not because we've been getting bored of Adobe's master app, but just because creating cosmic artwork is something the *Photoshop Creative Collection* team have been dying to get their teeth into for ages.

Inspired by the work of Greg Martin (**www.artofgregmartin.com**) we spent a great deal of time researching the best ways to bring stellar beauty straight to your screen without having to resort to 3D applications. The plan was to make use of Photoshop's filters, shortcuts and tricks wherever possible.

For the most part the techniques in this tutorial are not only deceptively simple; they are also flexible. Once you've followed the individual parts through and understand how they work we urge you to revisit steps and experiment with settings – after all, you're trying to create, not re-create worlds, and with these techniques anyone can play god.

Creating worlds takes a long time, and many of the results shown here get better the more you play with them – this is especially true in the case of the starfield cloning and planet texturing. With that in mind we've split the tutorial up into two sections – creating the planets and then a nebula.

PHOTOSHOP 7.0 AND ABOVE | **WORKS WITH**

Tip top twirling

If your twirl in step 24 doesn't seem quite erm... 'twirly' enough, just repeat the filter until you get the result you are looking for. Many filters can benefit from repeat runnings, such as the Spherize filter you used earlier and the Difference Clouds filter you'll be using to make the nebula.

MAKING PLANETS

Spatter them about

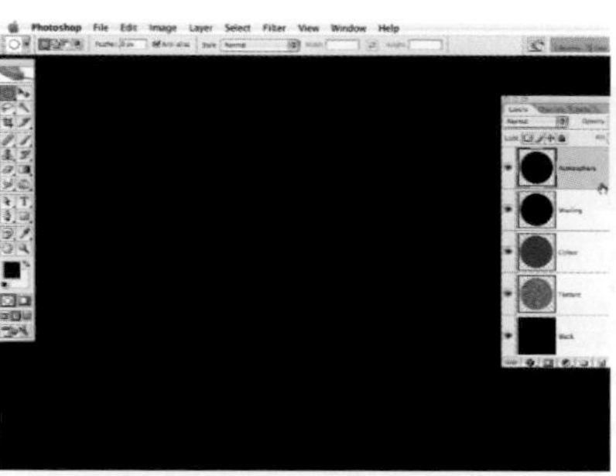

14 Stratus Quo Fill the background layer with black, and then create three layers above your texture. Command-click (Mac users) or Ctrl-click (PC users) the texture layer in the Layer palette to load it as a selection and then use that selection to create a dark blue disc on the first blank layer with two black discs above it. Name them 'Colour', 'Shading' and the top one 'Atmosphere'.

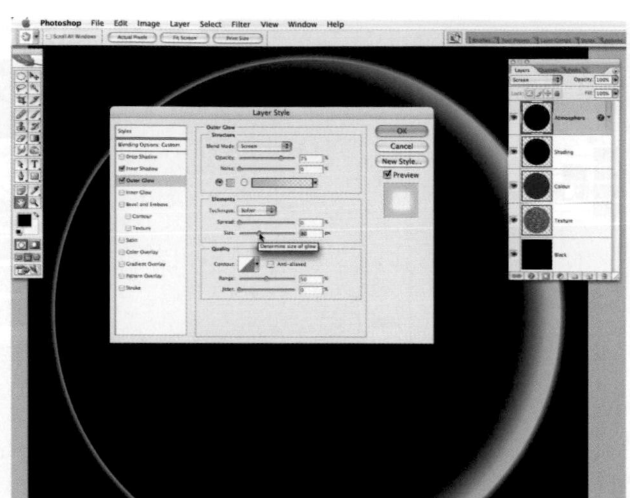

15 Let there be light Now you're ready to bring your planet to life. Select the Atmosphere layer and choose Layer>Layer Style>Inner Shadow. Set the mode to Screen, the colour to a light cyan and the Global Light angle to -10. Drag the Distance and Size sliders right up – depending on the size of your image, but don't hit OK just yet...

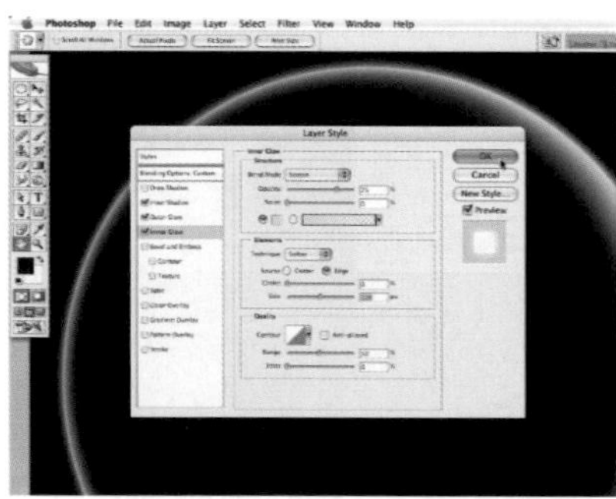

16 World a'glow Add an Outer Glow using the same cyan and a Screen blending mode. Drag the Size slider up to create a halo, then add an Inner Glow; again to a cyan screen. Increase the size of the glow. Hit OK and create a new layer below the Atmosphere. Switch back to the Atmosphere layer and use Layer>Merge Down.

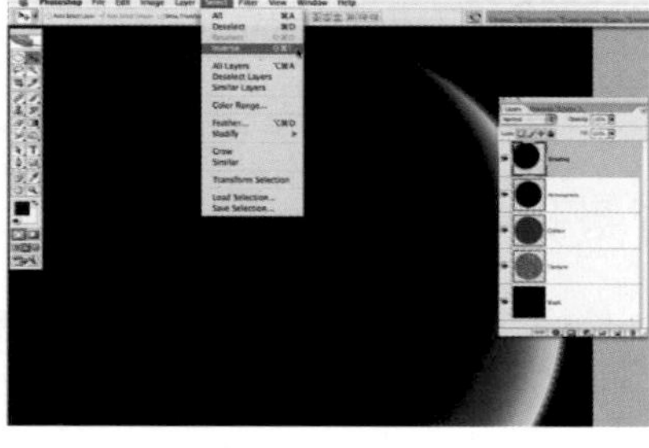

17 Eclipse Switch to the Shading layer and move it above the Atmosphere layer. Drag the disc up and to the right so that it masks the top-right third of the atmosphere glow. Go to Filter>Blur>Gaussian Blur and apply a 95 pixel blur to the circle. With the shading layer still active, load the texture shape selection again (same technique as in step 14), choose Select>Inverse and then hit Delete to remove the surplus parts of the shading shape.

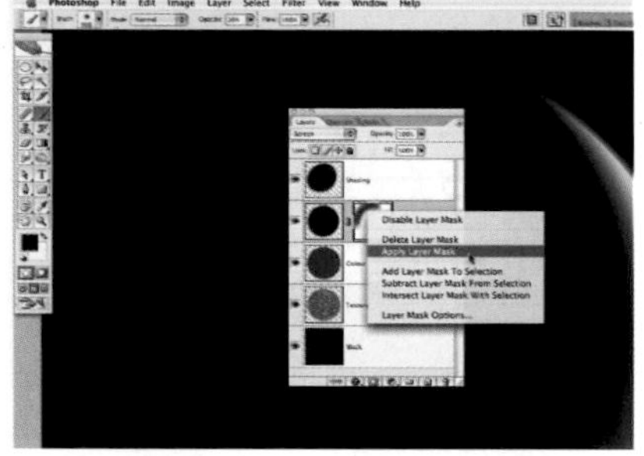

18 Mask the atmosphere Add a layer mask to the Atmosphere layer and use a soft black brush at a low (10-20%) opacity to gently remove most of the remaining glow on the top-right side of the planet. When you're done, Control- (Mac) or right- (PC) click the Layer Mask thumbnail and choose Apply Layer Mask. Drag the Texture layer above the Colour layer.

19 Forest moon Set the layer mode of the Texture layer to Screen and your planet will really start to come to life. You may want to decrease the saturation using Image> Adjustments>Hue/ Saturation to bring some of the blue colour back. Reduce the opacity of this layer to 33% and then duplicate it twice, set both of these copies to Screen as well.

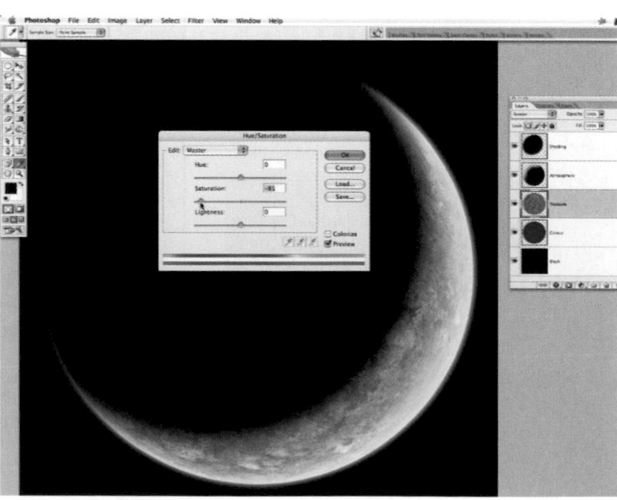

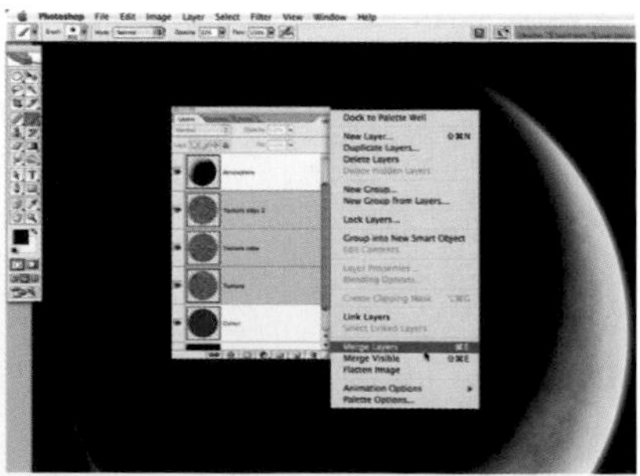

20 Tera-former Use the Free Transform tool to rotate each of these duplicate layers; the amount will depend on your texture, keep experimenting to find details you like the look of. When you're happy, merge the layers back together; keeping the result applied as Screen. You may then want to boost the contrast of the texture using Levels or Brightness/Contrast.

RING THEM UP

Make your planet spin

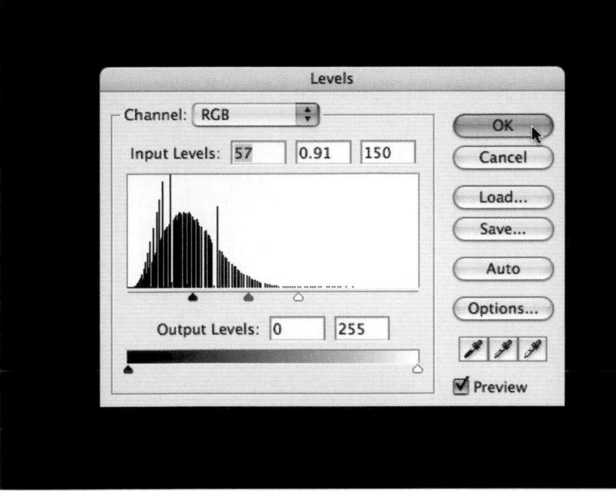

21 Weather man

Duplicate your texture layer again and set it to screen. Select Image> Adjustments>Levels and pull both the black and white triangles toward the centre (in this case the Input Levels were 57, 0.91, 150; this will create a hard clouds effect). Use the Free Transform tool again to rotate this layer until it gives the best effect.

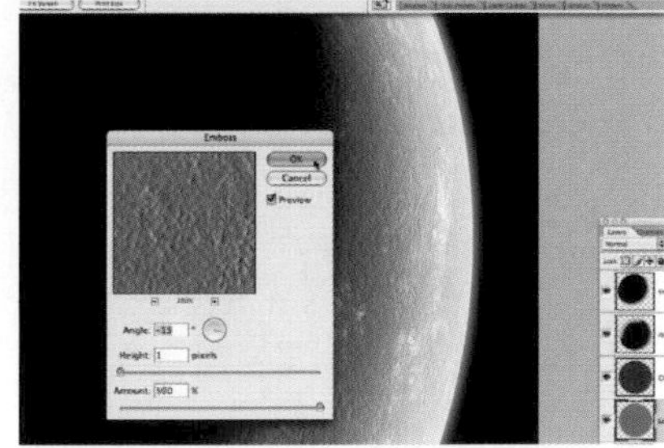

22 Give me relief

Rename this layer 'Clouds' and the original texture layer 'Land'. Decrease the opacity of your Shading layer to 95 so that more of the textures show through. Duplicate the Land layer and apply Filter>Stylize>Emboss with a Angle of -15, Height of 1 and the Amount right up to 500%. Duplicate this embossed layer and call one 'Land Highlights' and the other 'Land Shadow'.

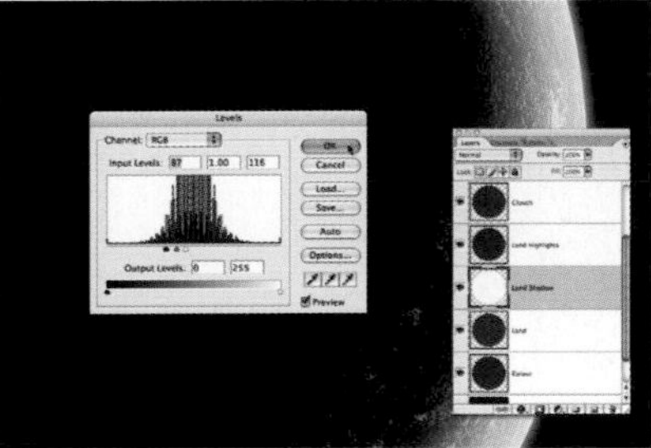

23 Leveller of worlds

With the Land Highlights layer active, open Levels. Type 145, 1.00 and 210 into the Input Levels fields and hit OK. Switch to the Land Shadow layer and do the same, but using the numbers 87, 1.00 and 116. Set the Highlights layer to Linear Dodge at 50% Opacity and the Shadow layer to Multiply at 70%. You might need to boost the brightness of the Clouds layer at this point. Your planet is now finished.

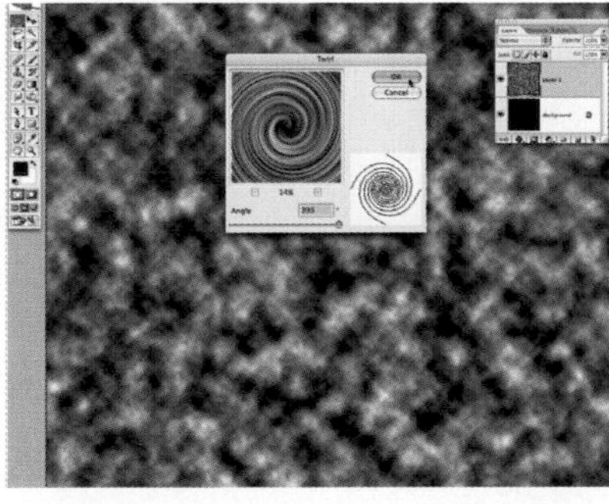

24 Spin the ring

No real planet is complete without rings, so make some. Create a new document, slightly bigger than your planet, and fill it with black. Create a new layer, and with black and white as your colours choose Filter>Render>Clouds. Open Filter>Distort>Twirl and apply it 999 degrees to give a spinning effect.

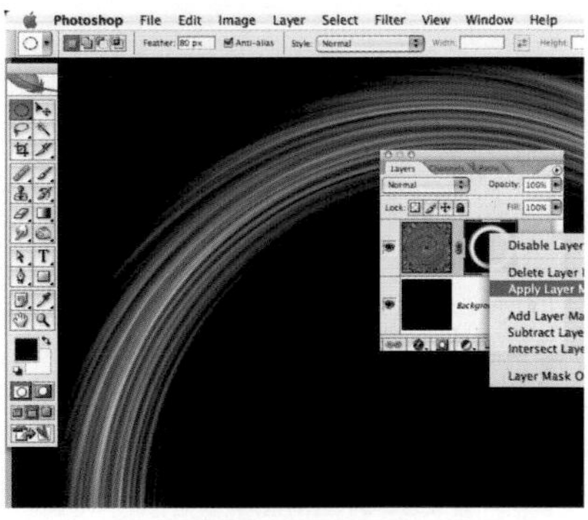

25 Ring of fire

Add a layer mask to the layer and make a circular selection. With the layer mask active choose Select>Inverse and fill the outer area with black. Make a smaller circular selection inside the twirl and fill it with black as well. Apply the layer mask from the contextual menu.

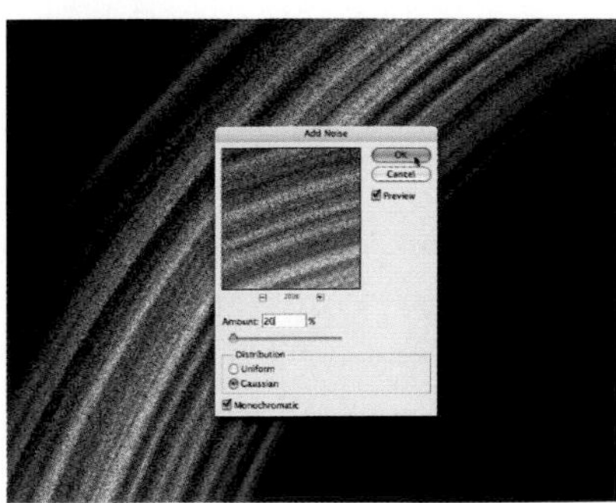

26 Noisy ring

To give the rings some grain go to Filter>Noise>Add Noise and apply a 20% Gaussian Monochromatic setting. Finally you can delete the background black layer. You're now ready to combine your images together so open up your planet file and the background star field you made earlier.

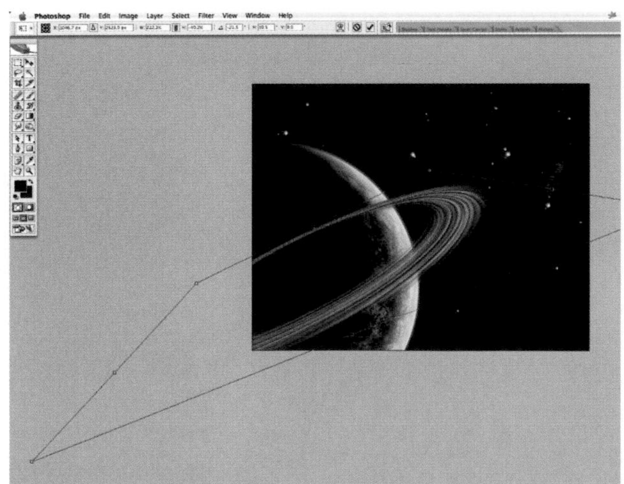

27 Get perspective

Using the Move tool, drag the planet onto the star field document; move it into position and scale it if necessary. Drag the rings into the document as well and switch to the Free Transform tool. Hold down the Option key (Mac) or Alt key (PC) and you can apply extreme distortions to each corner handle in turn. Here we've flipped it over, pushed the top corners in and down and pulled the bottom corner out and down.

Expert Tip

The masked hero of space

This tutorial makes heavy use of layer masks, and you may be wondering why they're used when the Eraser tool might very well do. The answer is that layer masks allow far more flexibility. Should you change you mind about something you've deleted you can go back to the mask and use a white brush to paint the element back in. You can also use filters on them for creative results; see step six.

Tool School

Perfect circles

When you're creating your circular selection in step 25 there's a trick to getting it just right. Instead of selecting from the top right corner and dragging down, use the twirl shape to help you. Look at the spiral and you'll easily be able to spot the centre. Select the Elliptical marquee tool and position your cursor at that point. Hold down Shift and Option-drag outwards (PC users Alt-drag), and the selection will grow from the centre.

MOVING ON TO THE NEBULA

The final addition to the space scene

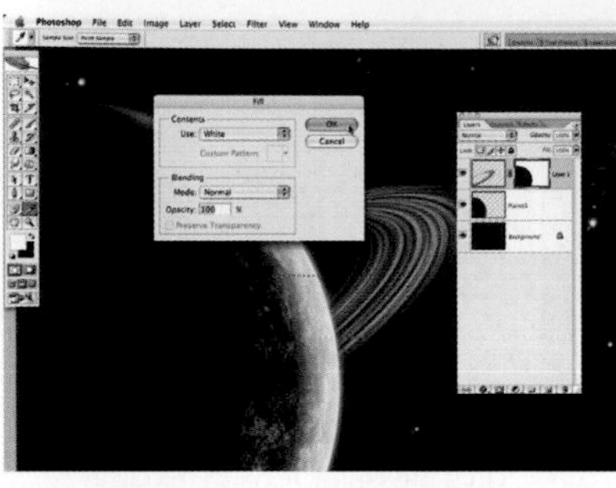

28 Mask the rings Add a layer mask to the rings layer and load the planet selection into it. Fill this with black. Draw a marquee around the areas of the rings that should be visible and fill it with white to bring them back. Click the chain symbol between the layer mask and layer thumbnails. This will allow you to reposition your rings later should you need to.

29 Finish it off Colourise your rings using Hue/Saturation and then duplicate the layer. Set both ring layers to Screen. Make the lower copy active and head to Filter>Blur>Gaussian blur to apply a reasonably strong blur and give the rings a soft glow.

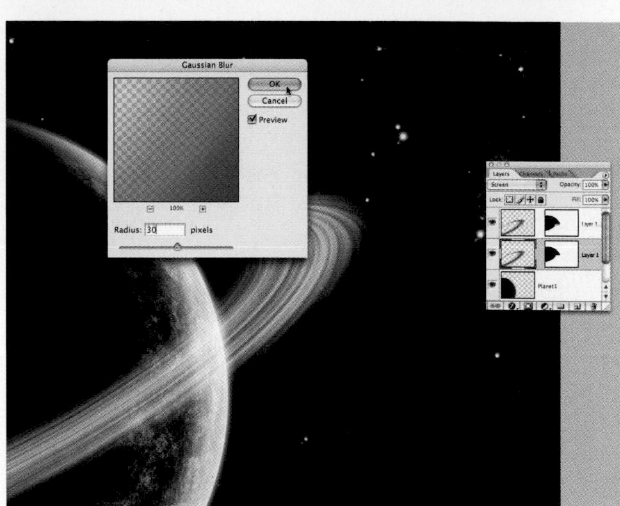

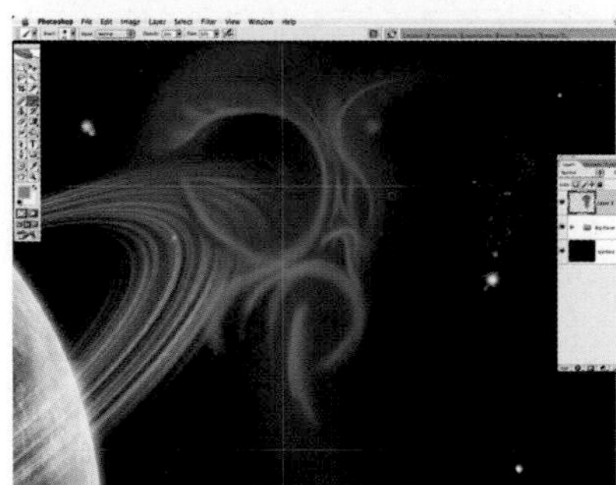

30 A word of warning One thing we've discovered about creating nebulas is that they start out looking awful. With that in mind, grab a 40-pixel soft green brush, at about 30% Opacity, 50% Flow, and on a new layer above the planet layer set, sketch a rough shape. When you're done, switch to a larger brush and add a haze around the shape.

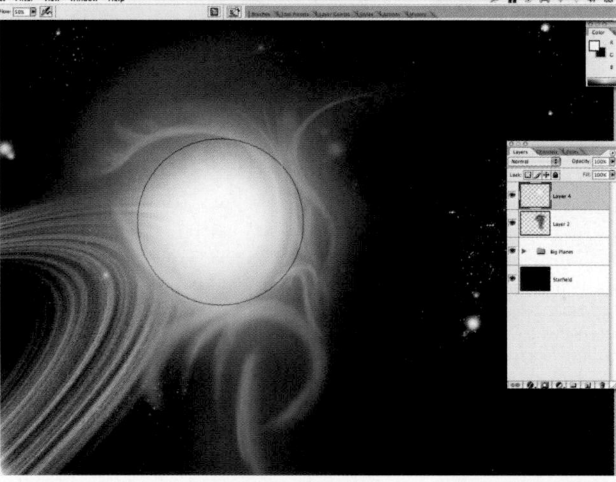

31 Bright light Increase the brush size to around 800 pixels, and switch the foreground colour to white. Create a new layer and click in the same place on your nebula a couple of times to create a highlight. Tweak the layer's opacity to your liking and then merge the two nebula layers.

32 Smudgy smudgy Now's the time to start seeing some results. Select the Smudge tool, with a size of around 50 pixels, and set the Strength to 50%. Now, starting from the white highlight, click and push the pixels out in flowing curves, so that the green and white mix and flow together. Think of this process as pushing wet paint around a palette.

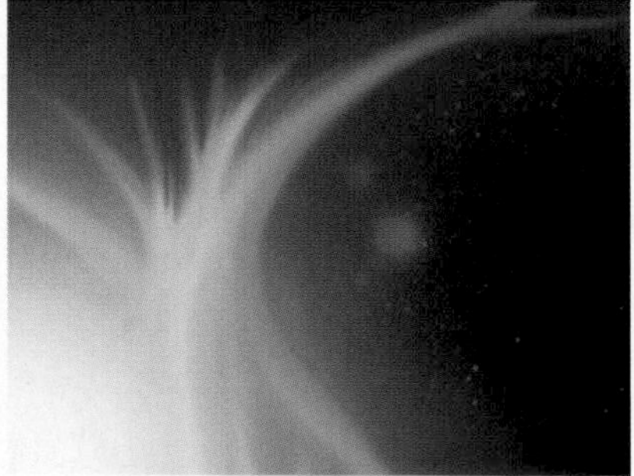

33 Add some detail When the paints are curving gracefully together, dial the Smudge tool right down to around 4 pixels, but take the Strength right up to 95%. Zoom in to the image and start feathering the swirls by pushing out from the edges – experiment with this technique and you'll soon get the hang of it.

SMUDGE YOUR WAY TO OBLIVION

Make the image work

34 Big it up Now increase the size of the Smudge tool to 125 pixels, but with the Strength still up at 95%, and perfect the shape of your nebula by nudging areas about so they seem to flow together naturally. Keep tweaking until you're perfectly happy with the result.

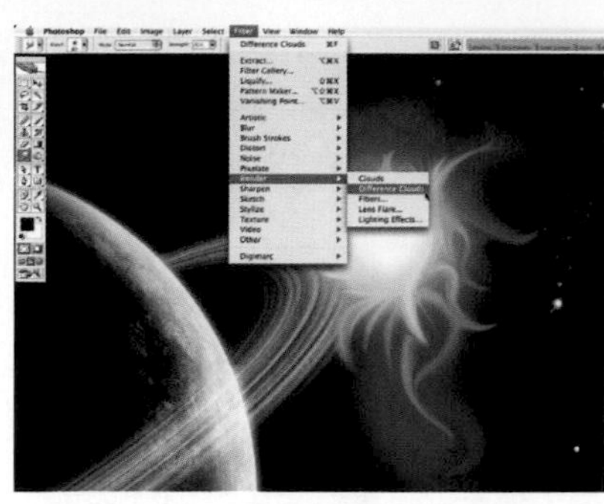

35 Spot the difference Your nebula will be looking more than a little flat and painted, so it's time to add a more realistic texture. Copy the nebula layer, ensure your foreground and background colours are set to black and white by hitting the D key, and from the Render section of the Filter menu select Difference Clouds.

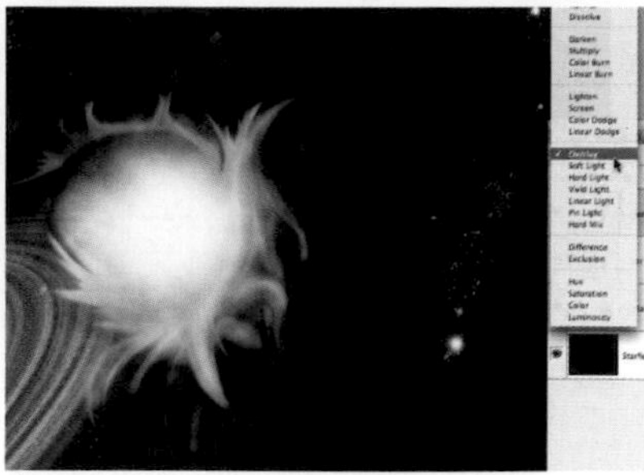

36 Whoa! Sure, the last step will give you a cloudy, smoky texture, but it will also give you some strange colour and no doubt almost completely obliterate your carefully-crafted nebula. Don't worry though; experimenting with blending modes and opacity settings can easily rectify this. In our case we simply switched the layer mode over to Overlay.

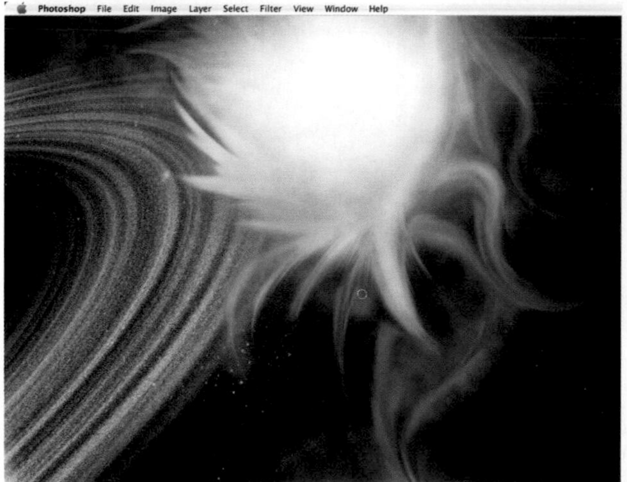

37 Smudge some more The cloud texture should look great, but probably more than a little artificial, so it's a good idea to switch back to the Smudge tool and smear the colours back along the curves again. This still retains the smoky feel in the background.

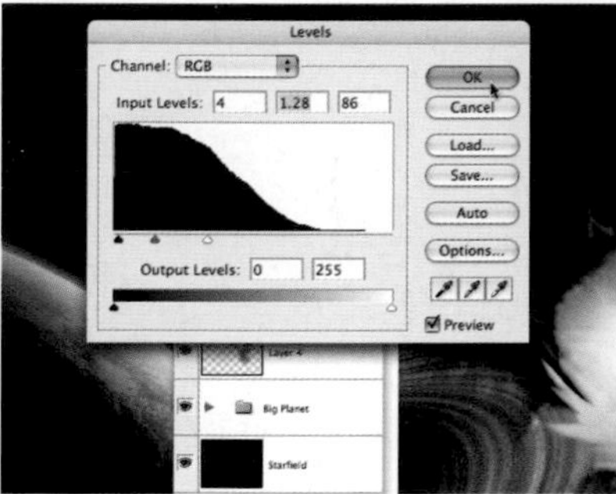

38 Dupe To start adding more contrast, duplicate the clouded nebula layer and switch the blending mode to Color Burn. Don't panic when this blacks out most of your image – choose Image>Adjustments>Levels and drag the white slider to the left past the middle point. Your nebula may not look great, but it'll look better.

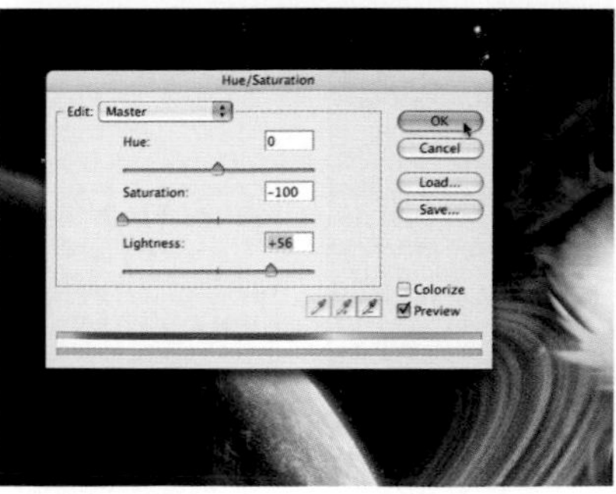

39 Hue and cry All it takes to get your nebula back to looking fantastic, is a trip to Image>Adjustments>Hue/Saturation. Leave the Hue slider alone, but drag the Saturation slider completely left to -100 and experiment with the Lightness to get the desired effect; in our case we dragged it up to +56.

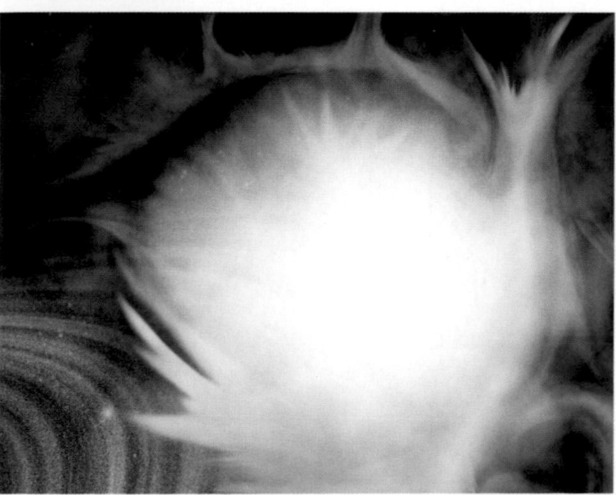

40 Let's smudge again Once again it's time to reach for the Smudge tool, and it's back to the 4-pixel setting at 95 percent. Work across both the clouded layers, pushing from dark to light and vice versa to build feathered, flaring detail into the image. It's the contrast between parts of the nebula that really give it depth.

Tool School

Paint with a soft brush

Many creatives shy away from hand painting, figuring that their mouse control isn't that great, but there's one secret to great results. Always work with a soft brush, set to a low opacity. Below 30% works best, but it can be much lower depending on your confidence. As you're building up colour instead of doing it in one stroke, any mistakes are harder to spot and instead you get a smooth and perfect finish – it just takes a little more patience.

Tip

Keep working at it

The steps printed here are a record of how we created our nebula, but it really is quite a random, organic process. Feel free to repeat any of the steps, building up multiple layers, trying different apply modes, smudge a copy of everything and generally have fun with it – the more time, experimentation and energy you put into it the better it will look.

GETTING CREATIVE

Colour and paint for effects

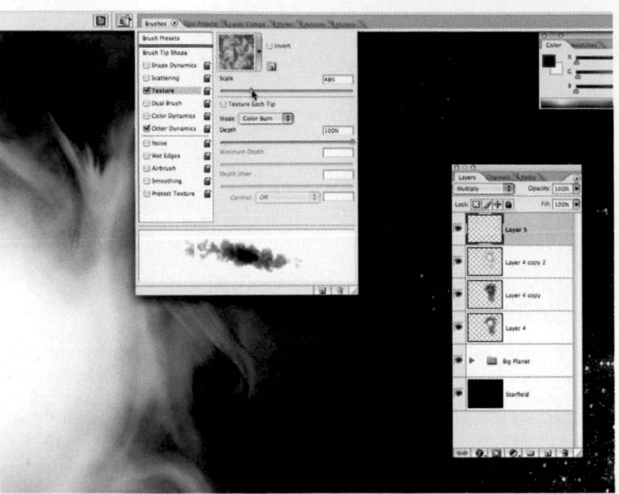

41 Build with brushes Create a new layer. Switch to the Brush tool, and open up the Brushes palette. Click on Texture, select Texture Fill from the thumbnail menu, and then the first texture in that set. Drag the Scale slider down to around 50%.

42 Paint effects With black selected as your colour, Flow set to 50% and the Opacity set to around 30%, carefully start painting some cloudy detail into the image. Do this by clicking the mouse, never dragging strokes. Again, your aim should be to build up contrasting areas, so work against the white.

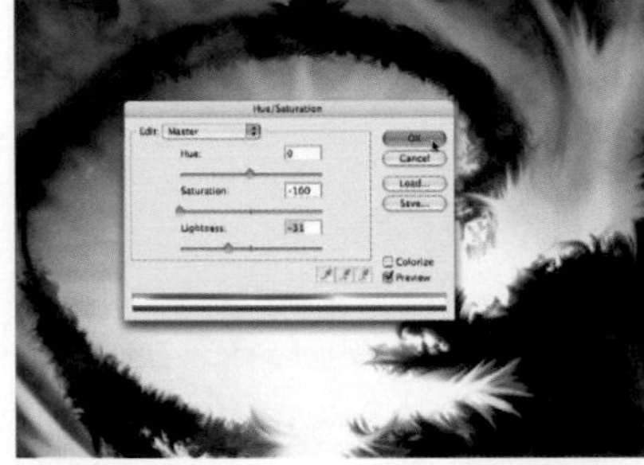

43 And repeat When you're happy with your contrasting shapes it's time to repeat a few steps from earlier. Begin by using the Smudge to tease out strands of black and break up the obvious edge; you can also reverse your strokes to great effect. Duplicate the layer, apply Difference Clouds, lower the Saturation and experiment with the Lightness. Set layer mode to Pin Light.

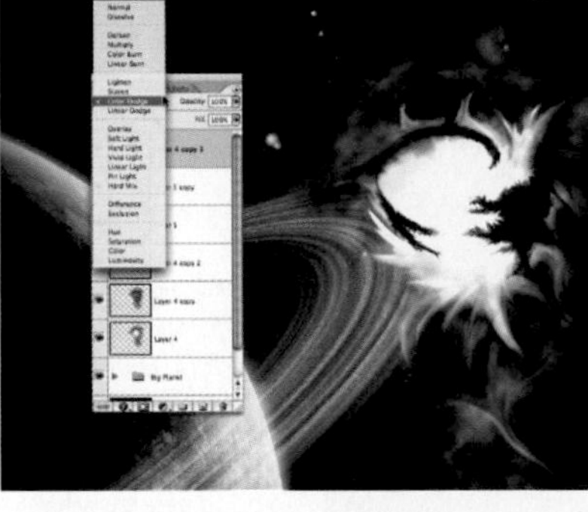

44 Experiment Now that the nebula is looking a bit healthier, it's a good time to experiment. Duplicate the main nebula layer (created in step one) and drag it to the top of the Layers palette. Repeat the Difference Clouds filter and set the layer mode to Color Dodge.

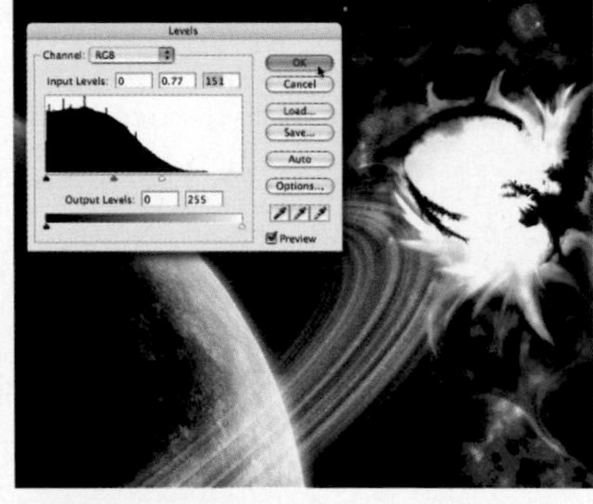

45 Highlights This should give you some pretty weird highlights. Emphasise these by opening Image>Adjustments>Levels and dragging the white triangle to the left, exaggerating the effect.

Expert Tip

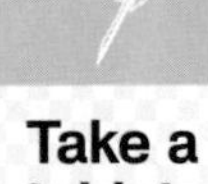

Take a tablet

It's probably the tip you'll find most repeated across the pages here, but it really rings true for this kind of work. If you can afford it, buy yourself a graphics tablet. For the kind of flowing brush work you'll need to replicate in this tutorial it really is a valuable asset. You can of course do it with a mouse, but it'll be much harder to get the same results.

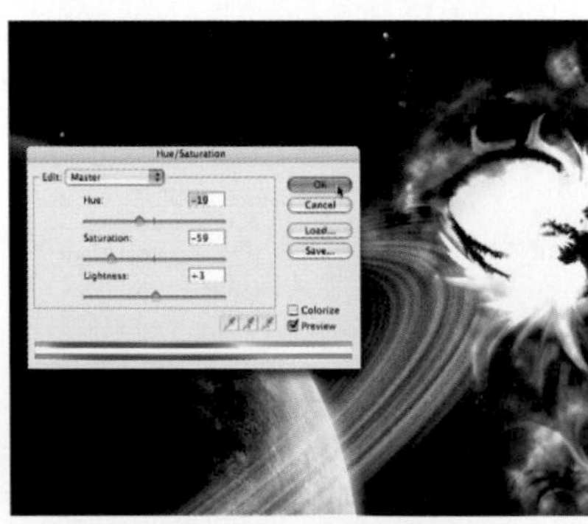

46 Seem familiar? Take a trip to Image>Adjustments>Levels again but this time, instead of desaturating the layer we're going to play with all three sliders. The aim is to create small light flares and highlights within the nebula. We set Hue at -19, Saturation to -59 and Lightness to +3.

47 Fix it The only problem with the previous step is that it may have introduced some unwanted and obvious highlights where you don't want them; particularly around the main flare. These can be easily dealt with by adding a layer mask to the Color Dodged layer and painting out any areas you dislike using a soft black brush.

SEND UP THE FLARE

Adding highlights for effect

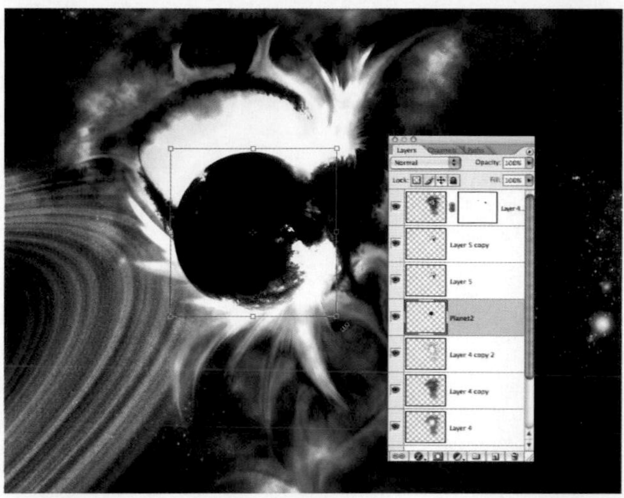

48 Creator of worlds Duplicate the main planet. Use Edit>Transform>Scale to resize it and position over the flare point in your nebula. Experiment with its position in the layer order until you find a combination that looks great. Repeat this step to create a few more planets to scatter about. Move the nebula layers under the main planet layers but above the starfield layer.

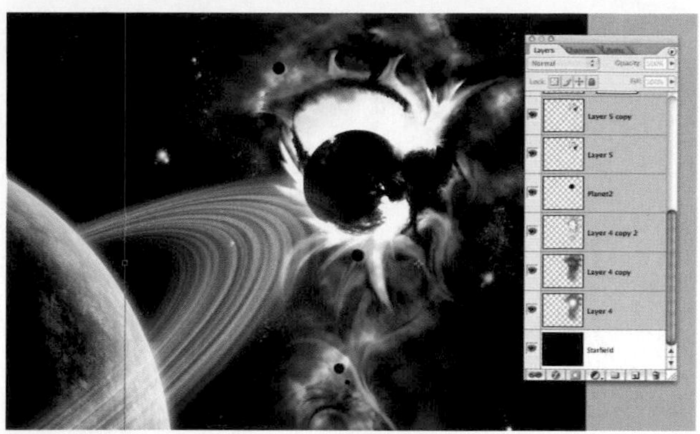

49 I like to move it The positioning of your nebula probably won't be spot on, as you've created it quite organically. Select or link all the nebula layers and experiment with moving it around the image until the composition works.

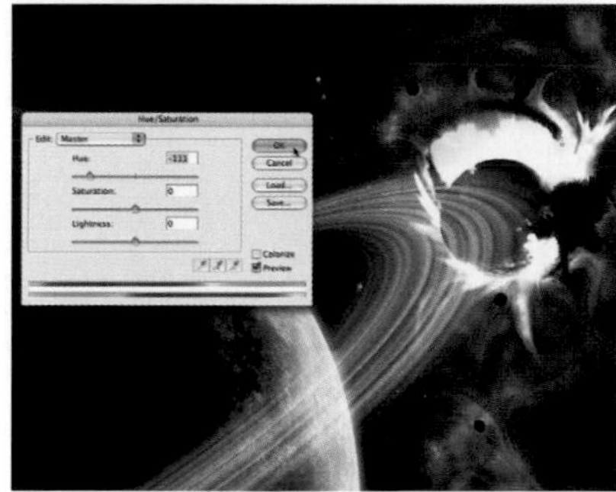

50 Colour shift A top tip for most Photoshop creations is to have a final experiment with colour before committing to an end result. Work through the nebula layer by layer using Hue/Saturation to tweak colour ranges until you find a combination you love. Ours took a red hue by taking the Hue slider right down to -111.

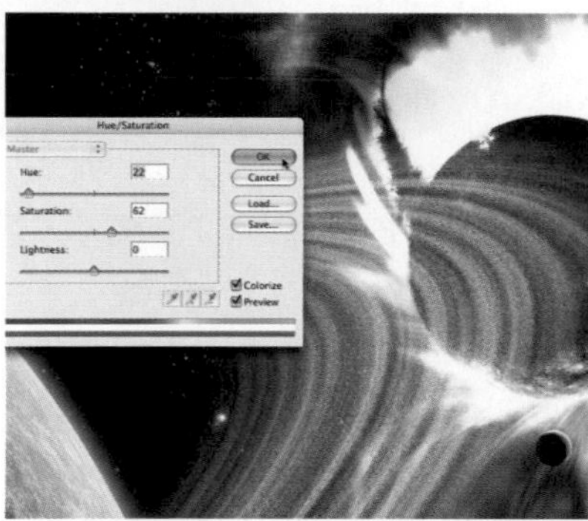

51 Colour the highlights When you're happy with the colour of the nebula, use Hue/Saturation again to tweak the colour of the planets so that they match. For the large planet in the nebula's centre it's also a good idea to push the saturation a little to give a strong coloured glow.

Out of this world

How our planets stacked up

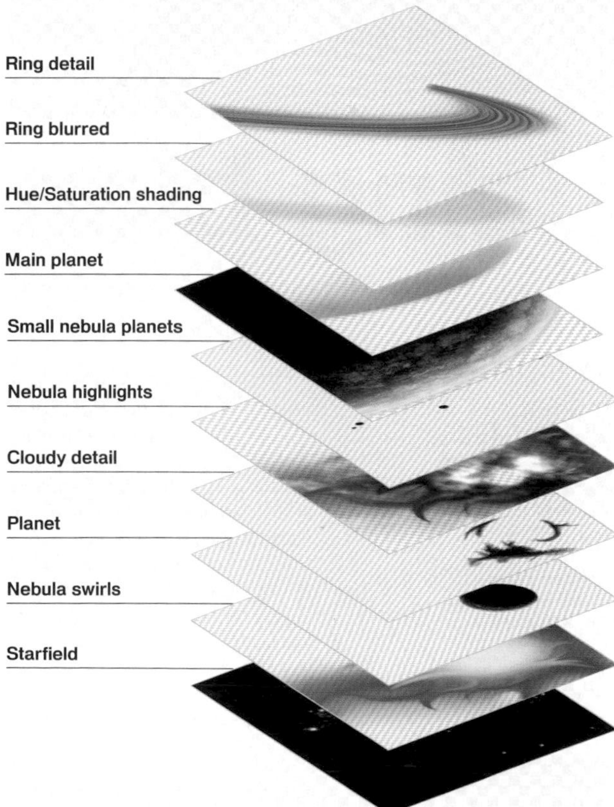

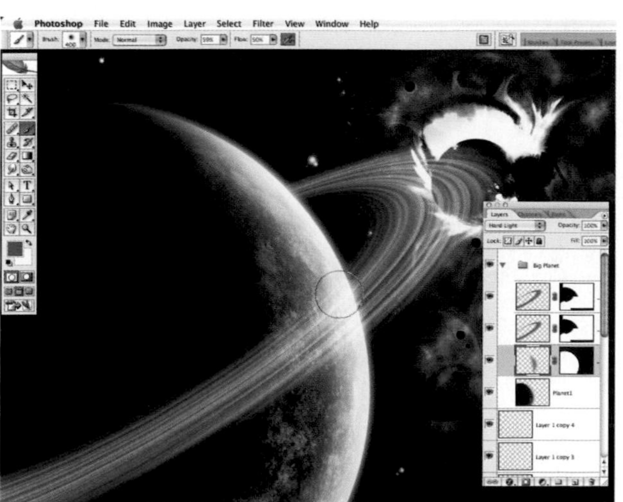

52 Sun burn Finally, to tie the whole image together, create a new layer in the Big Planet set, and create a layer mask using the planet as a selection (with the mask active, Cmd-click (Mac) or Ctrl-click (PC) the planet layer, select Inverse and fill with black). Pick a light colour from the nebula and with a huge soft brush at a low opacity, paint in a coloured highlight. The end result should look absolutely stunning.

Using blending modes

Blending modes are the perfect way of applying texture to your work. Here's a look at how to use them to add extra depth to your illustrations

essentials

SKILL LEVEL
Beginner
Intermediate
Expert

TIME TAKEN
About one hour

YOUR EXPERT
iLovedust

ON THE CD
Textures and starting images for tutorial

When an artist displays skilful use of texture in a painting or illustration, or retains light in an image, there is a notable contrast in the overall impact compared to a flatter, more 2D approach.

Texture can strengthen and support a simple image, drawing the eye into little unique details. A texture can make (or break) an image – initial attempts can look clumsy or disrupt a drawing, but with a bit of practice texture can soon become an integral part of the process of image making and bring your work to life.

Using the Photoshop software, digital work can incorporate textures with the same success. Blending modes can be applied using either an experimental or a controlled approach to achieve rich, unique artwork that lifts flat drawings off the page. Either way, the multitude of blend options available can bring depth to a graphic, almost providing a surface quality to your work. When applied to different layers in your Photoshop document, blending modes can play off each other and interact to produce a quality of light and colour that will transform a picture. Almost paint-like effects can be achieved if desired. But perhaps the most addictive attribute to blending modes is the element of surprise when you try different effects across different layers.

In this tutorial we will demonstrate the use of a handful of blending modes. We use a flat one-colour graphic, and then bring in textures on separate layers and transform the black-and-white graphic into a visual masterpiece. We apply blending modes to textures and also to flat colours and gradients, giving you a number of techniques that will allow you to duplicate the illustration we have made, and also enhance your own work.

You may find that halfway through the tutorial an incidental play-off between two layers takes your own work down a different route – if it looks good, go with it. The whole process is about building an illustration up until you are satisfied. However, we'd warn you off going too far, as there is nothing worse than artwork that looks like it has been churned through a million filters and tricks. Subtlety is the way forward and happy accidents are the key to enjoying the process and learning more.

PREPARE YOUR ARTWORK

Begin by gathering the material to use in your blending project

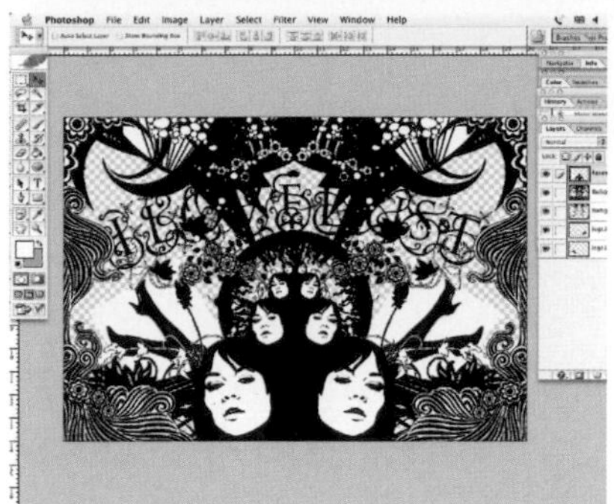

01 Illustration base To begin, import or open and compose an Illustration as simple or detailed as you desire. You could simply use a one-colour illustration, photographs or vectors, or use the sample files on the CD.

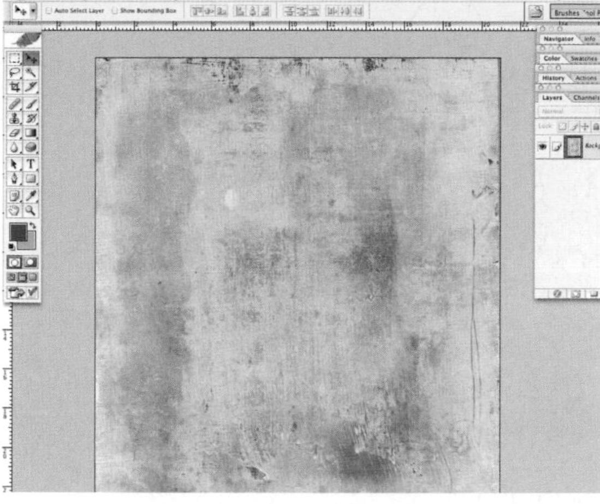

02 Choosing texture When you are happy with the graphics, it's time to start thinking about possible textures. We built up a painted texture to use in the illustration using acrylic paint and a screen-printing roller and a brush. After coating a piece of mount board with paint, we added new layers in different colours, occasionally using another bit of card or a rag to work the paint away in areas. When totally dry, we scanned it into Photoshop at 300dpi.

03 Prepare the textures The next step is to work digitally on these scanned textures. We simplified the painted texture by initially desaturating the texture; Image>Adjustments>Desaturate. The Desaturate command converts a color image to a grayscale image in the same color mode. For example, it assigns equal red, green, and blue values to each pixel in an RGB image to make it appear grayscale. The lightness value of each pixel does not change.

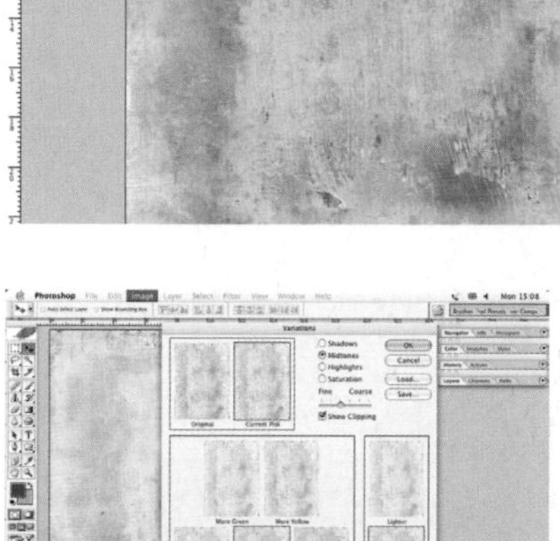

04 Variations You don't have to worry too much about what colour you paint your board because you can use variations: Image>Adjustments> Variations. From the options displayed we selected a more yellow and slightly darkened image variation. You can find the final texture on the CD ('texture.psd').

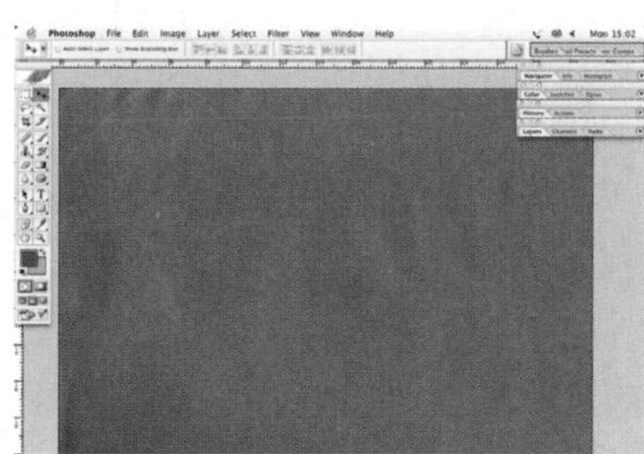

05 Paper texture We often scan various paper types to use in layers – it can provide a more natural printed look. It is good to collect a library of paper textures. Scan at 300dpi to use in your final illustration, but to reduce file size in previewing your work as you go, you could use a lower-res scan that you could later replace. This is also on the CD ('paper.jpg').

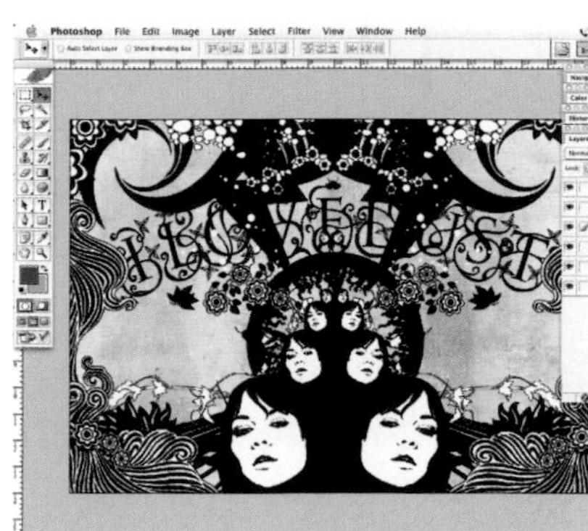

06 Add a texture layer The next step is to add the painted texture into the illustration file. Do this by simply dragging the texture into the separate file and then positioning it until you are happy.

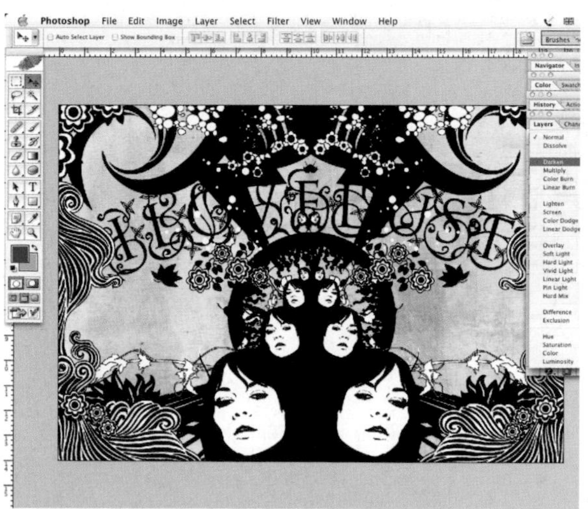

07 Adding a blending mode For this illustration we positioned the texture above the bitmapped images in the Layers palette. Within the Layers palette, choose Darken as the blending mode. This looks at the color information in each channel and selects the base or blend color – whichever is darker – as the result color. Pixels lighter than the blend colour are replaced, and pixels darker than the blend color do not change.

Blending Modes

As demonstrated in this tutorial, using textures and Blending Modes together can really enhance a flat graphic and produce some great, sometimes unpredictable results. When using Blending Modes it is worth experimenting with layer positions too, as this can totally alter the overall effect because one blending mode will react differently to what is beneath. Used carefully, whether on a simple illustration or a complex layered design, blending modes can enhance your work without causing an overly filtered look of some digital illustrations.

ALERT! | MAKE SURE YOU GET YOUR LAYER ORDER CORRECT OTHERWISE THE MODES WON'T WORK PROPERLY

Dusty example

The illustration in this tutorial is a good example of how blending modes can create some great effects. If you build up a library of textures, you will always have options when it comes to adding that certain something to the illustration. Scan in anything you see!

ADDING THE TEXTURE

See how the image builds up as texture is added

08 Peeping through Once you have applied the blending mode you will see the images in the layers below as if it was transparent, while exposing some of the lovely texture.

09 Mode to a paper texture Next simply drag or paste the paper file onto a new layer at the very top of the Layers palette. Go to the Blending Mode menu and then apply a Hardlight effect.

10 Hardlight The areas of black will pick up some of the paper texture, giving the illustration a completely new feel. The blending mode multiplies or screens the colours, depending on the blend colour. If the blend colour (light source) is lighter than 50% gray, the image is lightened. If the blend colour is darker than 50% gray the image is darkened, which is good for adding shadows.

11 Adding Brightness/Contrast At this point it may help if you add some brightness and contrast to some of the texture layers to draw out areas of the illustration.

12 Gradients The next step is to add some gradients of colour. This is a simple process and can be achieved very quickly. Begin by creating a new layer. Next, choose a colour, and hold down the Paint Bucket icon in the toolbox to reveal the Gradient Tool. From the gradient drop-down menu, choose the one that shows one colour fading out.

13 Applying gradients With a gradient selected, draw a line with the gradient tool from the top of the illustration to roughly a quarter of the way down.

14 Gradient blending modes Now, using the drop-down on the Layers palette, choose the Colour Dodge blending mode on the gradient layer.

15 Gradient merger Once the Color Dodge blending mode has been applied to the image, it will merge the gradient into the graphic elements that it overlays. The mode looks at the color information in each channel and brightens the base color to reflect the blend color by decreasing the contrast. Blending with black produces no change.

ADD MORE COLOUR

Colour at the bottom of the screen

16 Add a pink gradient We added another gradient at the bottom of the illustration, using the same technique as before but with a different colour. This time it was dragged from the bottom up.

17 Highlighting areas We then deleted areas of this gradient in order to expose the white details and highlights of the graphic below. On the graphic layer, use the Magic Wand to select areas of white (for instance the girl's face). Hold Shift while using the Magic Wand to select multiple areas.

18 Deleting selected areas When you have some areas selected, click on the new gradient layer with the selection still highlighted and simply delete the areas out of the gradient.

19 Light areas Carry this process on until you have enough white areas revealed. It's worth doing this because it helps prevent the image from looking like it's drowning in effects.

20 Adding an Overlay blending mode Once you have all the areas of white deleted from the gradient layer its time to apply the Overlay blending mode to this gradient layer. This multiplies or screens the colours, depending on the base color. Patterns or colours overlay the existing pixels while preserving the highlights and shadows of the base color. The base colour is not replaced but is mixed with the blend colour to reflect the lightness or darkness of the original colour.

21 Finished Illustration Now your illustration should look completely different from the original; the original composition and elements now have much more depth and texture.

The layer structure

A closer look at layers

Because blending modes are so dependant on the layer composition, here's a look at how the layers are positioned on this image

Turquoise gradient

Pink gradient

Paper layer

Bitmap faces

Darken Blending Mode

Painted texture

Background graphics

Legs

Legs

Background layer

TRACING THE BASIC COMPOSITION

Get some shapes on the canvas ready for paint

01 Inspiration source Open a new file in the horizontal format of the original and name it. As you will need to refer to Van Gogh's original painting throughout; go online and search for a large file of *Starry Night*. The higher quality will be of use later when zooming in for detail. Copy and paste the original into the main file. In the Layers palette, go to Duplicate layer>New.

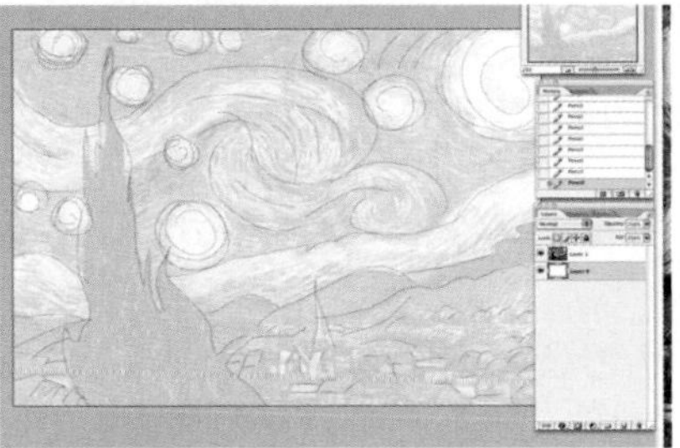

02 Guide drawing Choose the Pencil Tool and set to 4px, 50% Hardness and 100% Opacity. As you look at the original, use the pencil to draw outlines of the original composition. If you have no confidence in your drawing ability, there is an easier way. Set the painting layer's opacity to 30, select the drawing layer and use the Pencil Tool to follow contour lines, starting with well-defined areas.

03 Shadows and light To give the drawing more depth, we need to fill in the dark areas and highlight the brighter. Choose a 46px pencil at 50% Hardness and 30% Opacity, and start filling in the dark areas like tree and sky. You might find this task easier to execute with the Brush Tool, set to 55 and at 30% opacity. When you finish, turn off the original painting layer to reveal your filled-in drawing of *Starry Night*.

Using brushes to build up the image

A variety of brushes are used to get that Van Gogh style

Using the right brush is essential when trying to emulate a painting style, so it's worth putting in the effort to get things just so. Here's a look at the ones we used

Add depth Create the illusion of depth even before you add texture to the finished painting. Apply the main stroke, than select a shade slightly darker and apply to the edge. Here we have also used a stroke of white colour at the end of the green for the same effect.

House stroke Pastel Medium Tip is the brush used for the black lines around the houses. Any lightly textured dry brush would do, as well as oil with small tip. Sample the intense black from the original painting, and contour the lines of the scanned houses.

Strokes Stroke size obviously varies for different areas. The brush most widely used throughout was Wax Crayon, set to Depth of 40, Min Depth 100% and Depth Jitter at 10. Control is set to Pen Pressure and so responds to the pressure that's applied while painting.

Circular The paint is applied to the yellow lights in circular motion. Even when the strokes are straight, they are placed on the canvas in circular motion. You start from the centre heading outwards, with stroke colour eventually changing to dominant blue of the outside.

Expert Tip

Digital creativity does its best to imitate real life; it is therefore beneficial to examine various aspects of real life painting processes. Bear in mind that paintings are usually multi layered, with different colours and shades interacting with one another. This creates visual richness and also applies to Van Gogh's unique style. When using a digital paint application, always build up the image gradually. This will allow greater sensitivity and give greater dynamics.

NOTES | VAN GOGH ONLY SOLD ONE PAINTING WHILE HE WAS ALIVE

04 Get together Rather than search for a picture that matches Starry Night's composition, we have gathered several snaps as our source imagery. Each one contains items that loosely resemble the original (like trees and houses). Open the selected snaps from the CD and save each snap as a separate layer. Name each layer to describe snap content, bearing in mind that this is merely a temporary 'storage' file.

05 Compose yourself Some parts of our image will be painted directly onto canvas, where others are based on photographs. With a selection tool of your choice, select the houses in the snaps and paste into your main canvas. To access a layer without using the Layers palette, try selecting the Move Tool and press your mouse/stylus on the image. A list of layers appears for you to select one.

06 Transform Copy and paste the selection into the drawing in the main image, or simply drag your selection. Place houses loosely at this stage and save each transferred selection as a separate layer. Use the Transform Tool to create smaller houses and spread according to drawing lines. Great accuracy is not essential as these are going to be covered in thick paint.

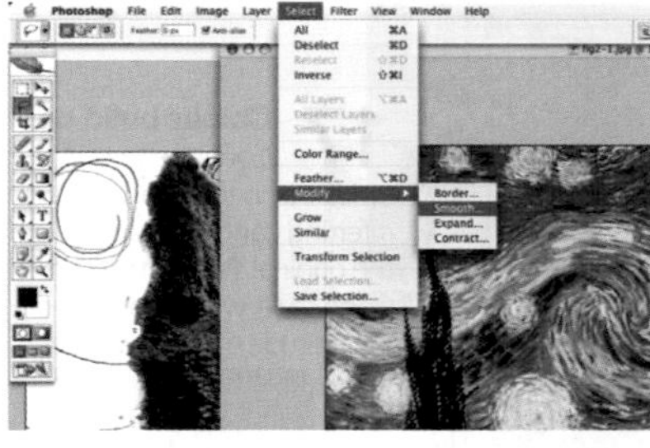

07 The tree The ominous tree adds eeriness to the image. Its prominent shape plays an important part in the composition so should be copied accurately. Use the Magic Wand Tool to select the tree in Van Gogh's original. Go to Select>Modify>Smooth, set the Sample Radius of 4 to smooth the selection out. Select the Lasso Tool and while pressing Alt, delete unwanted parts of the selection so only the tree remains.

08 Tree transformer Drag the selection onto the main drawing file. Go to Select>Transform>Selection and adjust the size and proportions of the selection to fit the original drawing guides. Save the selection and name it as Tree Selection.

09 Tree shape Copy and paste the tree snapshot into the drawing image. Adjust size to fully cover the drawn tree area. Go to Selection>Load Selection and choose the saved tree selection. With the tree snapshot layer selected, and the tree selection showing, go to Inverse, set a Feather of 0.2 and cut. You should now have the exact shape of the original tree.

10 A spot of colour It is time to add colour to the drawing. The end result will be made of several paint layers so this is the first of many. Use the original painting to source and sample colours. Select a brush and loosely apply paint to the drawing. Work methodically starting with the blue sky and cover all blue areas.

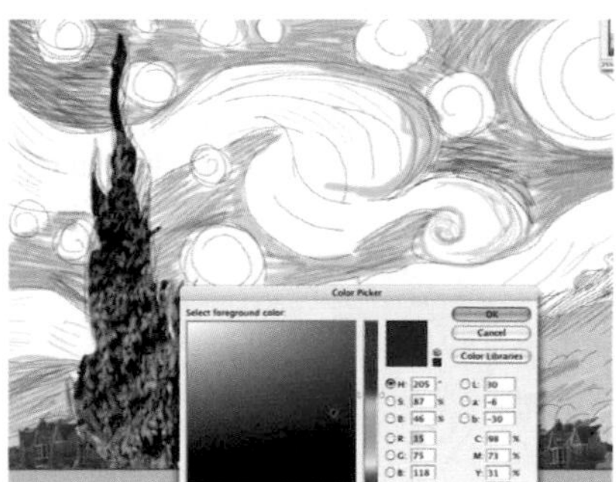

11 Colour palette Open the Color palette to choose darker shades of blue for darker areas. When you have finished covering blue parts of the image, use the Color Picker to sample yellow in the original painting and repeat the process. Again, start with pale areas and gradually move to darker ones.

Alternative painting method

We've used alpha channels to build up texture, but if you don't want to get involved with them, there is an alternative. Start with your main picture. Go to Layer>New Fill Layer>Pattern to create a Pattern fill layer. Set blend mode to Overlay. Make a ground layer which will be your canvas. Fill with white and turn the visibility off. Now make a new empty layer (this is your painting layer). You should have four layers: your original image, a pattern fill layer set to Overlay mode, a white layer with visibility turned off and a completely empty layer. Select the Smudge Tool and pick a natural media brush. Set Mode to Normal, Strength to 100% and make sure Use All Layers is on and Fingerpainting off. Paint away. To add texture, select the painting layer, create a new layer and merge. Desaturate, apply the Emboss filter and set blend mode to Overlay.

Working with light

When light falls on a subject, it creates many tones and subtleties. This means that lines are rarely rigid and uniform throughout. From the very beginning, draw and apply paint with sensitivity and dynamics. An insensitive application of pencil/paint tends to look like a child's drawing lacking nuance and variety.

PAINT TO CANVAS

With the outline in place, it's time to start filling with

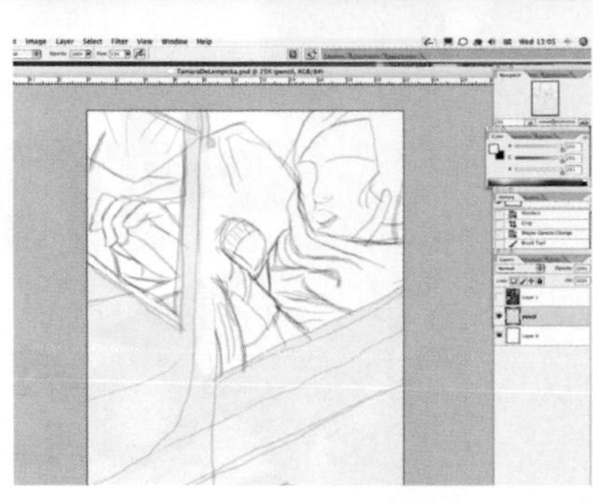

04 The green Bugatti Go to Brushes>Wet Media>Watercolour Light Opacity. Set Opacity to 50 and start applying colour to the car. Open the Color palette for the right shade of green, or sample from the original. Cover the entire car using a 200 brush for the main body and a small, 30 for the windscreen frame.

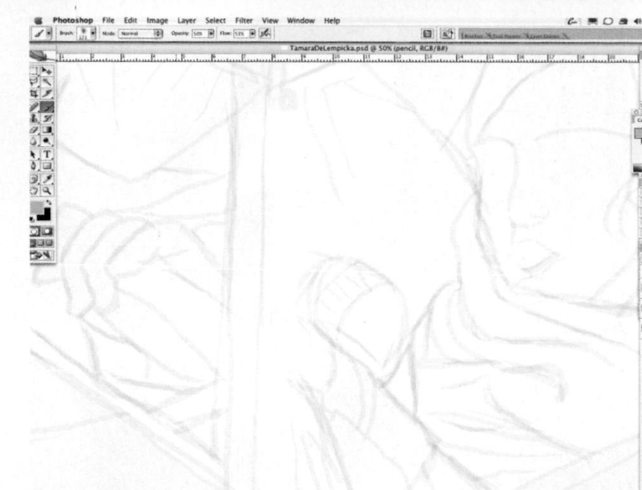

05 Elegant glove Sample the yellow/brown colour of the glove in the original and using the same Light Opacity, Watercolour brush, colour the glove resting over the wheel. As the colour of the glove is similar to the artist's face, you can safely cover that as well.

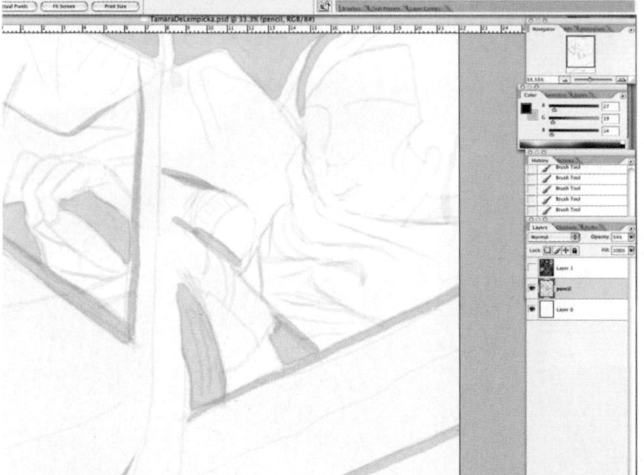

06 Dark areas The image has well defined dark areas, which sets the tone of the piece. Staying with low, 30 – 40 Opacity, fill in these areas. This all-over colouring is a rough guide, setting the scene for later stages. Use the brush to freely cover different areas but don't worry about getting the minute details to size.

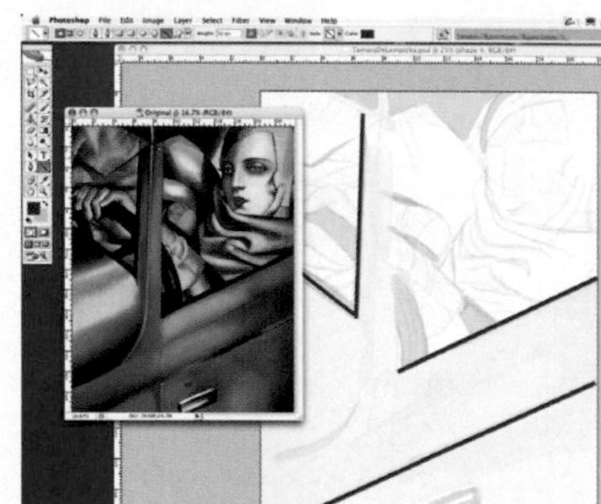

07 Straight lines Select the Line tool to inject colour into the straight lines you drew earlier. Sample dark green or brown from the original painting, or use the colour palette. Use a 30px line to cover the car's vertical lines on the door and also the windshield.

Tool School

Valuable tool

A graphics tablet is the single most significant tool you can get to dramatically improve your work. It will enhance every aspect of creative life and enable subtlety and control that are simply not available with a mouse. You use a pencil-like tool, controlling every aspect of the tool and its application, most notably, Pressure Sensitivity and Tilt. Check out **www.wacom.com** for some of the best.

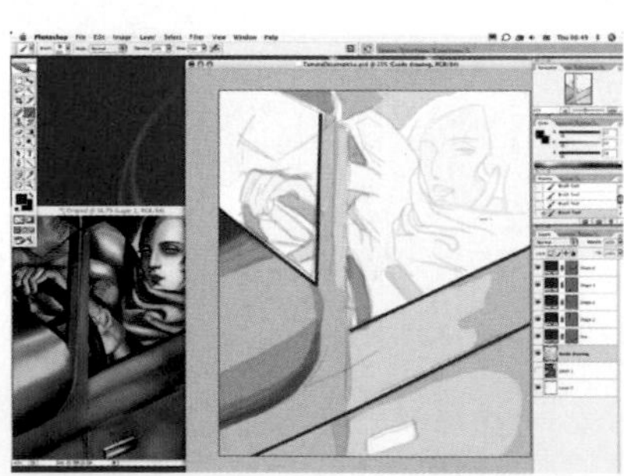

08 Setting the tone The car's body is made of many shades of green. Use the Color Picker to sample shades of green off the original. While closely observing the latter, apply lighter green first, gradually moving to darker. Use the Eye Dropper to sample different shades as you progress, aiming for gradual transitions of colour. These will be smoothed out later.

09 The face With a low Opacity of 11 and brush size of 91, trace the different shades of yellow/brown on the woman's face. Although just a guide layer, this is an important step as you familiarise yourself with the image subtleties. Even though this layer will be heavily blended with darker layers, as in the previous step, aim for smooth and clean transitions. Use long, soft strokes in line with the original.

10 Glove detail

Zoom in on the glove resting over the steering wheel. Move up to a 40% Opacity and apply the different shades of yellow/brown. Most importantly, observe the original closely for subtle changes in tone and lightness. Choose a starting point and paint the area, now use the Hand tool to drag the image along slightly as you move to the neighbouring one.

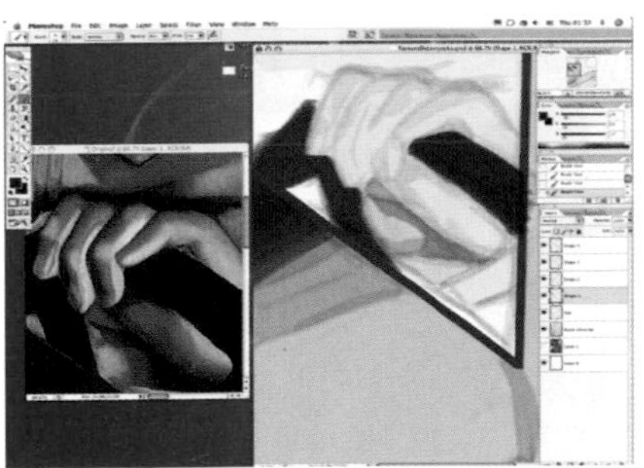

11 Surrounding area

The painting process is an organic one. Even though we are using a method to re-create the piece, a dynamic approach and sensitivity are the keys to a convincing artwork. As you work on a zoomed-in area like the glove, feel free to 'stray' to apply colour to surrounding ones. It will increase flow and ensure a more unified look.

12 Detail

This is the most demanding part of the re-creation – slowly applying stroke after stroke of paint to build up the image. Continue to zoom in on different areas of the image and apply a low opacity layer of paint. Pay attention to little details as you encounter them. Be dynamic and change brush size and opacity continuously, according to need. Name and save your brushes for simple loading every time.

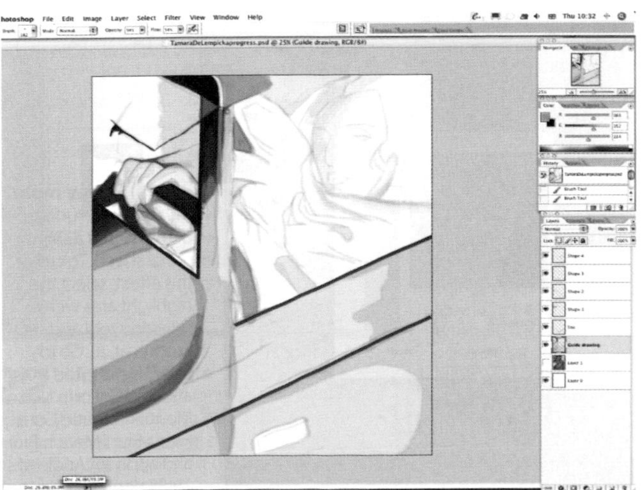

13 Step back

It is important to remember to step back and take a good overall look at the piece. Painters take a few steps back from their canvas to correctly assess progress. Do this regularly and you will be able to spot mistakes before it's too late. This is doubly important when working digitally as when you work at 100% magnification, other parts of the image are not in view.

PAINTING FABRIC

Apply natural light effects

Real fabric has flow and softness to it. It is made of a multitude of shades from dark black at the folds, to the bright highlights at the peaks. The darker areas usually create a shape where the fabric folds and shadow is cast. To create realistic fabric, the many midtones found in the peak and the heart of the fold need to be captured. These give the material its 3D look.

Any soft brush at minimum Hardness is ideal and Watercolour Light Opacity is suitable for fabric. Go to Brushes>Wet Media Brushes and select Watercolour Light Opacity. Set Hardness to minimum and you have a nice round and soft brush to work with.

After you trace the many contours of the material, mark the well defined shaded areas and fill them in. Turn to the midtones that are in-between the dark fold and light peaks and fill these in. Finally touch up the high peaks. Keep the strokes long and smooth to reflect the flow of the fabric in the original.

01 Brush settings

Set Opacity to 30. Following the drawing, start to fill in the shadow areas of the fabric. Work slowly, with sensitivity and long strokes. Follow the flow of the fabric.

02 Dark folds

Increase the Brush Opacity to 65 and go over the darkest areas again. When you finish this layer, increase opacity and mark the darkest black contour lines.

03 Everything in-between

It's time to fill in the midtone areas – those that are between the shadows and the light peaks. Apply with long strokes that follow the direction of the fabric.

Online Resources

Discover Monet's life

For a fascinating insight into how Monet himself saw life, go to **www.intermonet.com/biograph/autobigb.htm**. In this interview, originally published in 1900, Monet tells of days of poverty in London, and how dedicated the Impressionist painters were to the movement as a whole.

"England did not want our paintings and things were hard…" Monet says. The turning point was meeting Durand-Ruel, who represented them. "The 'pendulum was in motion," Monet writes, "today, everyone wants to know us".

THE FIRST STEPS

Time for the sketching part

01 Inspiration source Open a new file at 290mm high x350mm wide, and name it 'Monet'. You will need a copy of Monet's masterpiece to refer to. Do an online search for a large file of Water Lilies. Copy and paste the original into the Monet file. In the Layers palette go to duplicate Layer>New. You now have two copies of the original – one to trace from and one to refer to.

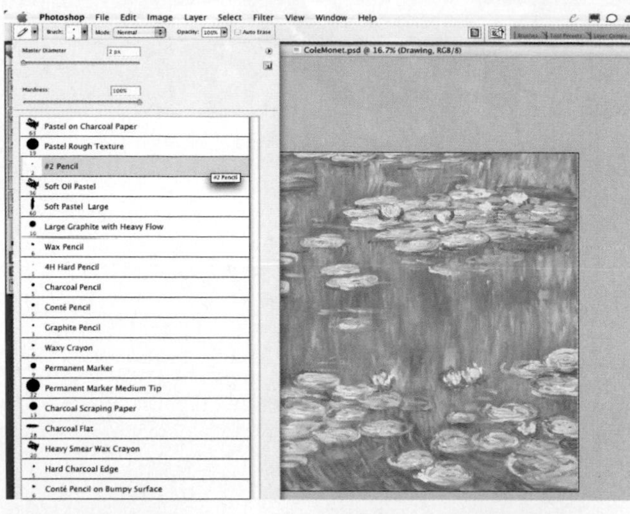

02 Guide drawing Create a new layer in the Monet document called Drawing. Choose the Pencil tool and set to 5px, 40% hardness and 100% opacity. Refer to the original and copy the outlines. You might find it easier to lower the original painting's opacity, select the drawing layer and use the pencil tool to follow the lines underneath. Remember to turn the original's layer off to assess the drawing as you progress.

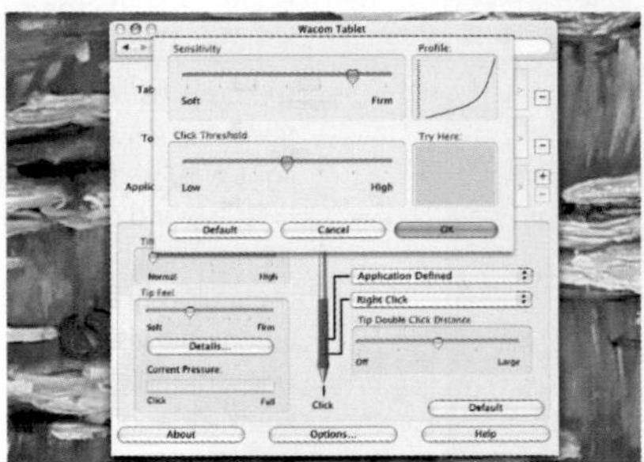

03 Graphics tablet Adjust your graphics tablet settings. If you are not using a tablet, make it the first item on your shopping list! It is the single most important item you could add to your setup. It is guaranteed to enhance your creativity, increase workflow and narrow the gap between traditional and digital creation. Set the Pen Pressure and Tilt to a level you feel comfortable with.

04 Turn into a sketch Continue to work on your black and white sketch on the Drawing layer. There are no bold and dominant objects in this painting to copy, and so the lines are short and strokes are brief. If you are not too bothered with creating the sketch from scratch, either paint freehand or turn the image into a sketch.

05 Colour With the Brush tool selected, click the down arrow in the Options bar and then click the right arrow to access different sets. Load the Wet Media Brushes and start applying colour to the black-and-white drawing. Oil Small Tip or Water Colour Light Opacity would work well here. Set your brush to low opacity, and while referring to the original, apply Monet's short strokes and curvy lines. Sample colours of the original as you go along.

06 White flower Open the water lilies photo and place as a separate layer in the Monet file. Use the Lasso selection tool or Magic Wand, to select one of the white flowers. Apply a feather of 12, copy and paste into the Monet document. To save time and effort at a later stage, be sure to give new layers descriptive names as soon as they are created.

07 More flowers Copy the flower several times and place each at different areas of the image. As you are still at early stages of applying colour to the image, bear in mind that this location is not final, and is likely to change later on. It is important to keep each flower as a separate layer.

08 Lilly pads Go back to the lilly pads photo and choose the Lasso selection tool. Select one of the flat green pads, and copy and paste several times onto the Monet document. Move the pads around the image to examine their position's effect on the overall composition. Refer to the main image for our placement.

EXTRA PADDING
Add foliage to the flowers

09 Water effect Place each pad underneath the previously created white flowers. Click on a lilly pad layer to select it, and on the Layers palette, make sure it is below all of the flower layers. Open the water lilies photo and choose the Rectangular Marquee tool. Select the clear water area at the top left of the image.

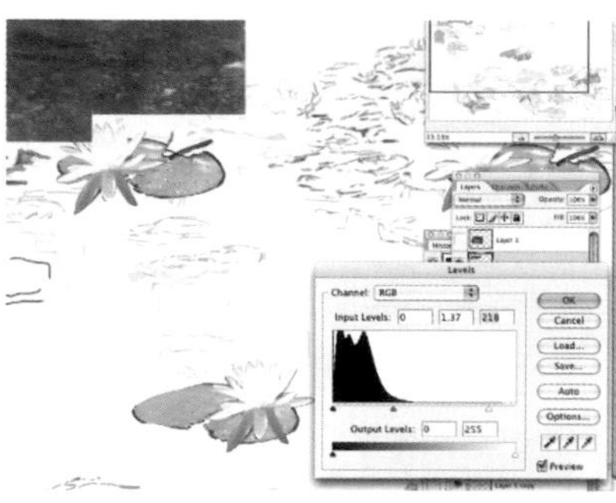

10 Levels Copy and paste your selection into the Monet document. We need for the water effect to show more clearly, and to adjust the colour slightly. For that we will use Levels, and Hue/Saturation controls. Go to Levels and set your mid slider to 1.37 and right slider to 218. Go to Image>Adjustment>Hue Saturation.

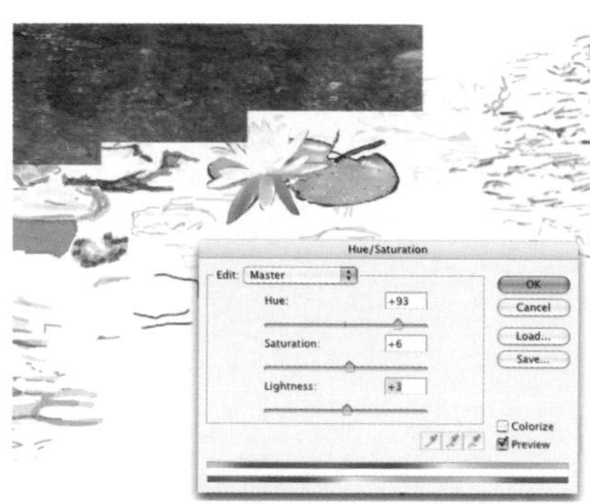

11 Hue/saturation Make sure Edit is set to Master and that the Colorize button is not selected. Push Hue level up to +93, Saturation up slightly to +6 and Lightness to +3. The water effect should now be clearly visible and water colour more in line with Monet's.

12 Watery rectangle With the water layer still selected, go to Edit>Free Transform and rotate the horizontal layer by 90 degrees to the right. Copy and paste this rectangle twice to create two new rectangle layers. You should now have three rectangle layers showing on your Layers palette.

13 Let the flowers show Nudge or use the Move tool to join the water rectangles. Make sure their layers sit above that of Drawing. Reduce their opacity to 60 or under, just enough for the drawing layer to clearly show underneath. Use the lasso tool to cut out the flower areas. You will be left with a white patch surrounding the flowers and lily pads.

14 Rough pastels Apply more guiding colour to the Drawing layer. We applied pink red to the flowers. Select one of the flowers and go to Filter>Artistic>Rough Pastels. Try the following settings but do feel free to experiment, Stroke Length 8, Detail 9, Texture Canvas, Scaling 73 and Relief 43.

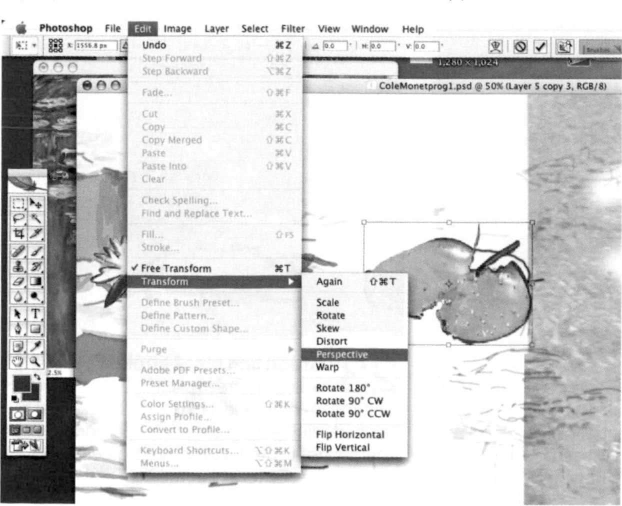

15 Perspective Select one of the green pads. Go to Edit>Transform> Perspective and pull the two lower points outwards, and two upper ones inwards. The angle will change considerably. Adjust the angle until it looks right for the overall composition.

16 Build up colour Continue to build colour on the different layers. You can now increase brush opacity and choose a more textured brush. Work at 100% and aim to copy stroke feel and detail with accuracy.

Online Resources

The history of the lilies

Monet painted tens of paintings of his water lilies, as seen at different times of day, and throughout the year. The water lilies have become a precious testimony of Monet's last years in his Giverny garden, with failing eyesight and old age. Painted during the last 20 years of his life, they lead Monet on a journey of exploration and a looser style of painting. Go to **http://www.expo-monet.com/1_4.cfm** for a list of images by the artist and be inspired by Monet's very different views of the beautiful plant.

Expert Tip

Forewarned is forearmed

Instead of finding your colours as you go along, you can plan your colour theme before you start work on your painting. Create an artist's palette that includes the colours to make your piece. Go to Brushes and select a medium-sized brush. Choose a colour to go in your palette and apply a dab of it to the new palette. Continue to build a selection that will serve you throughout. You can use any brush as well as any dab shape to create the palette.

SEEING CIRCLES

Carrying out the background detail

17 Pink circle The pink/red circle behind the cat's head plays an important part in the overall composition. Create a new layer for the circle and name it. Select the Elliptical Marquee tool, and while pressing Shift, create a perfect circle around the head. Set the pink colour, go to Edit>Stroke and set a 5px width on the outside.

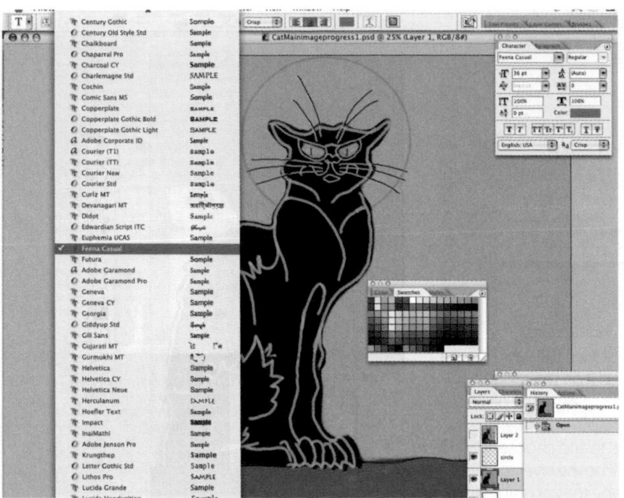

18 Type 1 Many Art Nouveau fonts exist that imitate the period's style. You can select a ready-made font to achieve the period poster effect. Open the long Photoshop font list and examine the samples. We experimented with Sarah Caps (from **http://eksten.net/webgraphix/fonts/s/sarahc.html**) and Feena Casual (from **www.1001fonts.com**). Both are free.

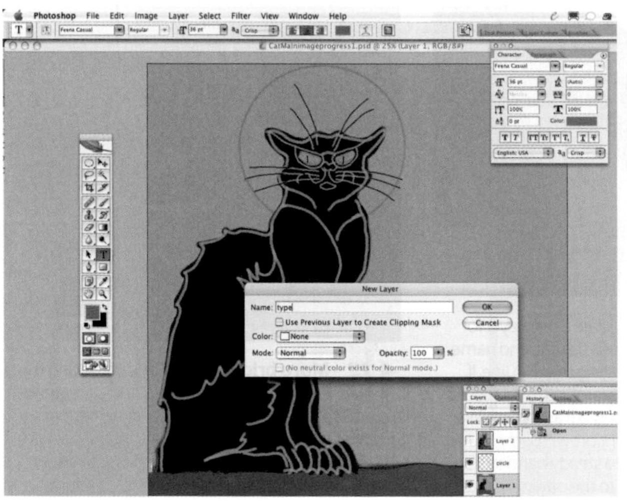

19 Type 2 We will not use a ready-made font, here, but use a brush to draw the writing in. First create a new layer. Now set a small brush size (use the same watercolour brush as before). In the Brushes palette, select Shape Dynamics, set Fade in the Size Jitter Control drop-down menu to 100, and experiment with Minimum Diameter Level in order to get the smaller, fading ends of letters right.

20 Type 3 Start drawing the brown letters. If you think the brush is too big or too thick, adjust the size. There's no right or wrong way of doing this. Add in all of the text.

21 The tail The cat's tail is missing. Again, start by creating a new layer and naming it. Choose the same Watercolour brush used for the cat's body, sample the same black colour and carefully draw the shape. If you chose to complete the text in an earlier step, use that as a positioning guide. Draw the thin contouring line around the tail to match the body.

22 Type on the stand Carefully sample the colour of the original text and draw the remaining type on the pink stand. The text on the original poster has almost fully covered the area around the cat, but we've opted for the popular present day version. Place a low opacity version of the original over your text to check on progress.

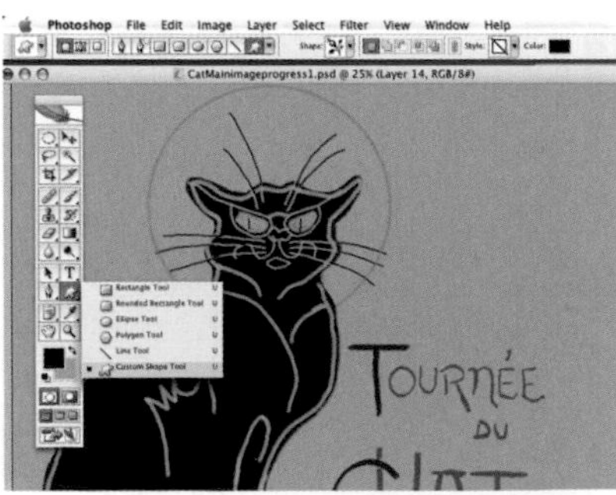

23 Pattern In order to create the Art Nouveau feel, we designed a pattern to fill the circle over the cat's head. In the toolbar, click on the Shape icon and select the Custom Shape tool. In the Options bar, make sure Shape Layers is selected. (First square shape on the left next to the Custom Shape icon.)

CONTINUE THE BACKGROUND

Things are shaping up nicely

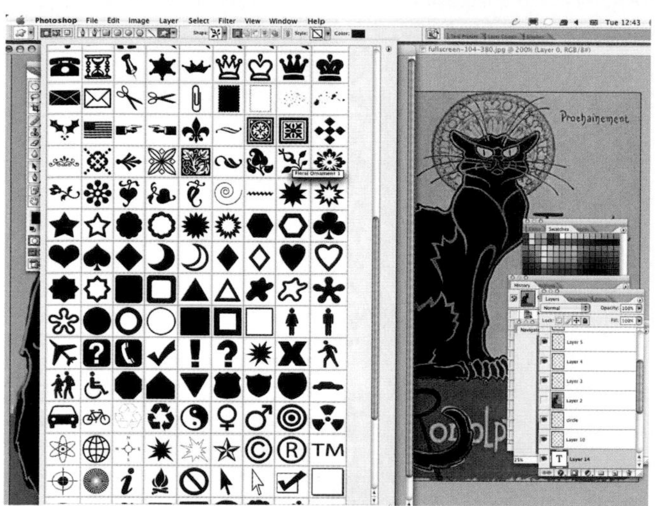

24 Ornaments In the Options bar, open the Shapes selection and click on the little triangle on the top right. From the list, hit Select All to display all the shapes on offer. We chose Floral Ornament 1, but any of the floral ornaments will suit this decoration.

25 Transform the ornament Sample pink from the original or use the colour picker. Drag the Shape over the image until you reach the desired size. Create several copies. You might wish to change the direction of some. To do that, go to Edit>Transform and adjust accordingly.

26 More ornaments Create three copies of the original pink circle and use the Transform tool to adjust size according to the original. Use a small smooth brush to freely create letters around the head. Adjust the angle of your hand as you go along. Finish with a pattern drawn freely, or choose a ready-made shape.

27 Smoothing and fine-tuning Use the Eraser tool as well as the Cloning tool to clean up the image. Lose any 'leftovers' and smooth imperfect lines. You might find it easier to create a flattened version of the image to do this, but please keep a layered version as well!

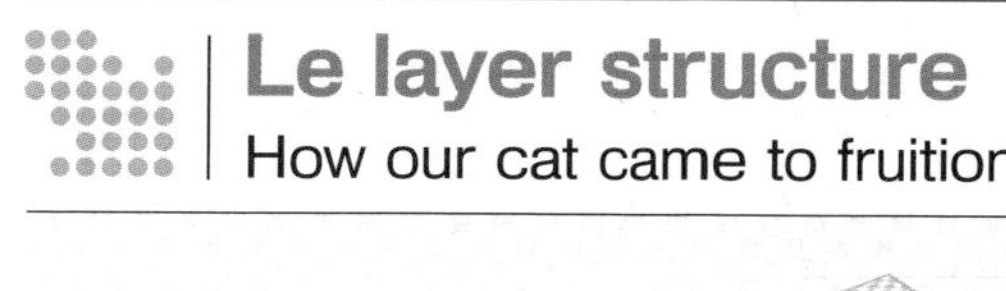

Le layer structure

How our cat came to fruition

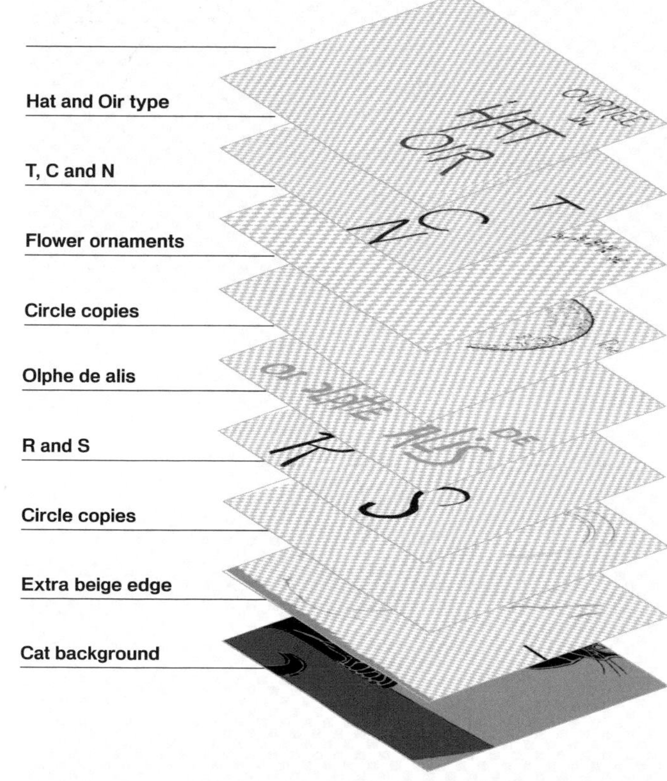

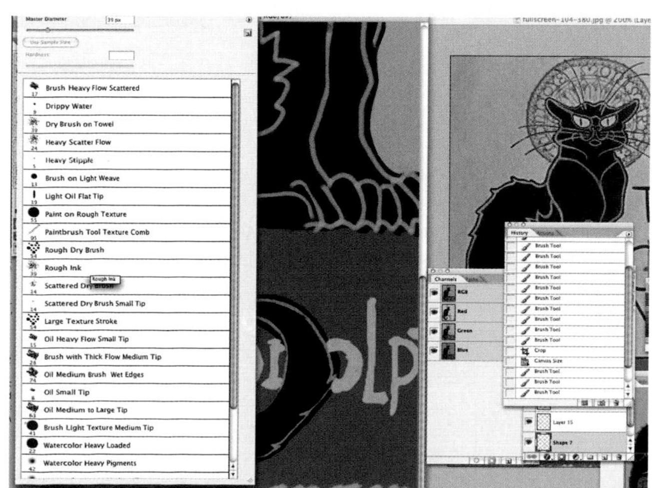

28 Rough Ink The bottom of the pink stand is made of inward brush strokes. Use the Rough Ink or Rough Dry Brush (in the Wet Media brush set) to re-create this effect. Apply one stroke and adjust brush size accordingly. Make sure you cover the entire length of the stand.

GET CREATIVE WITH TEXT

Grab the reader's attention with a unique look

The Type tool gives you a multitude of choices to help get your typography up to scratch. Here's a look at how to use some of them…

essentials

SKILL LEVEL
Beginner
Intermediate
Expert

TIME TAKEN
20 minutes

YOUR EXPERT
Mark Shufflebottom

ON THE CD
Original image

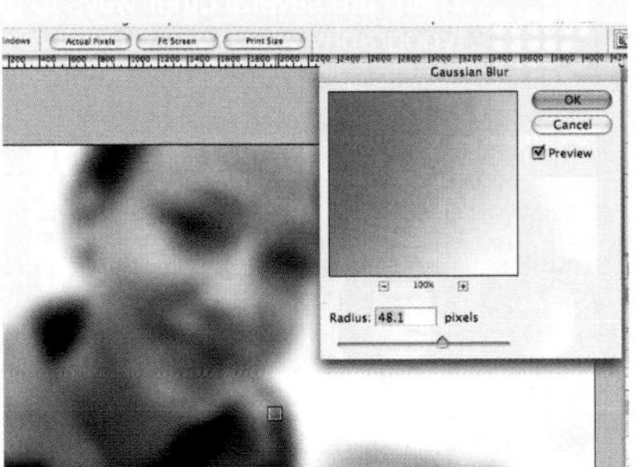

01 Starting the project Open the image 'starting.jpg' from the CD. Go to Image>Rotate Canvas>Flip Horizontal. Now go to the Filter>Blur>Gaussian Blur menu and add a 48-pixel blur to the image. Use the Eyedropper tool to select a dark brown colour from the image. This will now become the foreground colour.

02 Adding text Select the Text tool and change your font to a calligraphy font; here we've chosen Bickham Script Pro but any similar font will be suitable. Make the font size 500pt and then add the word 'Art'. Position the curve of the letter 'A' over the chin as shown in the screenshot above.

03 Draw a path Open the Paths palette and click the icon at the bottom of the palette to create a new path. Select the Pen tool from the toolbar and then draw the shape of the curve on the screen that follows the natural curve of the shoulder and around the chin to the letter 'A'. It should look like a big and small hill.

04 Text on the curve Add a new layer and change the foreground colour to white, then select the Type tool. Change the font to a thin clean one such as Arial Narrow, and the font size to around 60pt. Click on the path with the Type tool and add the text as shown. Change the blending mode of this layer to Overlay.

05 Smaller text Create a new layer and choose a light grey as the foreground colour. Select the Type tool again and change the font size to 30pt. Add the text as shown above, and drag a guide down from the top ruler to the bottom of the text. Change this layer blend to Screen. To see the rulers, go to View>Rulers.

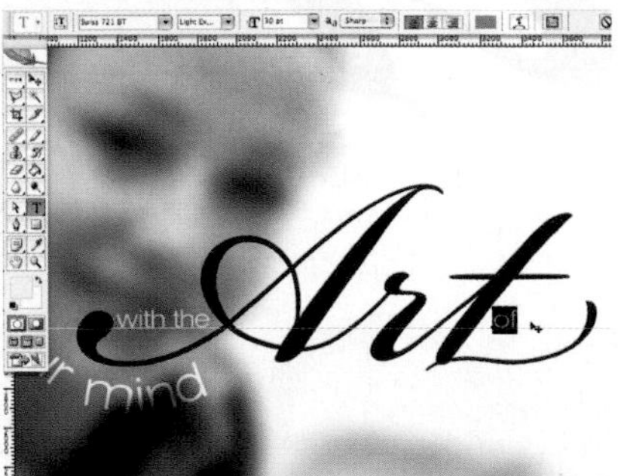

06 Another word Use the Type tool to add the word 'of' on the guideline, just after the word 'Art' as shown above. This time do not blend the layer as in the last step, or the text will become invisible. You can, however, change the blending mode of the Art layer to Multiply.

Type composition

Balancing the design

When you create a composition or add typography to an image, the position of the elements that go into the piece are important to the artistic balance of the design. In our example, we've created the background features a girl who's positioned to the left. The right of the background is quite plain and white. This immediately helps decide how we'll position our text. The word 'Art' is placed here to help balance the image – note how the colour of this word also balances the dark jacket of the girl. As we arrange the other typography elements around this, you can see the empty space in the top right is a contrast to the dark colour in the bottom left. The space in the top left is balanced by a similar small space in the bottom right. Next time you're adding text, look at how you can balance the design and bring unity through the text.

A different hue

Experiment with colour schemes

Colour schemes have come about through the study of colour theory. In our tutorial, we used an Analogous colour scheme for our design – which is choosing a hue and selecting similar hues either side of it. You can experiment with other colour schemes by trying the Complementary scheme, which uses the opposite colours on the colour wheel – using blue shades instead of beige/brown, for example. Alternatively, what about trying Split Complementary, which takes the two colours either side of the Complementary – so instead of blue, use midnight blue and cyan. Avoid using oversaturated hues, because this doesn't look great.

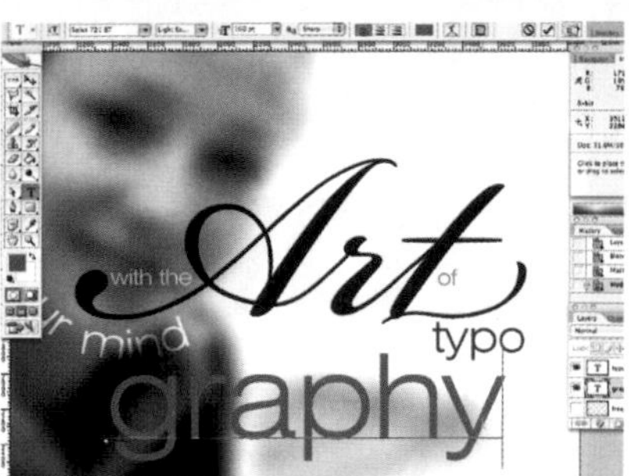

Tip

Guiding paths

Adding guides to your page is very useful in aligning different text elements. Just click on the rulers, either horizontal or vertical, and with the mouse still held down, drag the guides onto the document. If you haven't got any rulers in your document, go to View>Rulers to bring them up.

07 A little more text Use the Eyedropper tool to select a dark brown/beige colour from the shadows of the girl's face in the background and add a new layer. With the Text tool, increase the font size to 60pts and then add the half-word 'typo', positioning this just under the main 'Art' text as shown in the screenshot above.

08 Typography conventions As you can see from the text we've added so far, we have followed the conventions of typography as found in traditional text. By this we mean the flow of the text moves from left to right and top to bottom, so that as the reader tries to follow the text it is still easy to read.

09 The last word Select the Eyedropper tool and grab a mid beige colour from the girl's face in the background. Add a new layer, select the Text tool and increase the font size to 160pt. This will be for the final word, so click on a new spot on the document and add the remainder of the word 'ography', as in 'typography'.

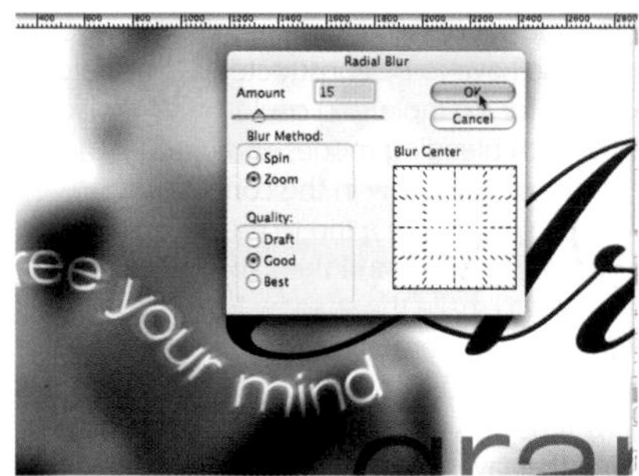

10 Position the text Using the Move tool, change the position of the 'ography' word so the ascender on the 'h' letter is directly under the 't' of the 'typo' word. It may be necessary to move both pieces of text in order to get it aligned properly, in which case just select the appropriate layer and move it.

11 Change the mode Select the 'ography' layer and change the blending mode to Multiply, then change the opacity of the layer to 80%. Select the type layer which is along the path, and drag this onto the New Layer icon in the Layers palette to create a copy of the layer. Now choose Layer>Rasterize and Type.

12 Blur the text With the copied layer selected, go to the Filter>Blur>Radial Blur menu. Change the blur type to Zoom and change the blur amount to 15 pixels, then click OK. This just adds a little movement to the type along the path in order to add more interest. Save the document to finish.

Vertically challenged

Changing the orientation of text

If you hold down the Type tool in the toolbar you will see from the flyout menu that besides horizontal text and the Type mask, there is also vertical text. Selecting vertical text is useful for emulating signs where the flow of text is top to bottom instead of left to right. When typing vertically down the page, the distance between the characters is not line height, as you may be fooled into believing. Instead it's the space between characters horizontally, which controls the vertical spacing. This can obviously cause a little confusion.

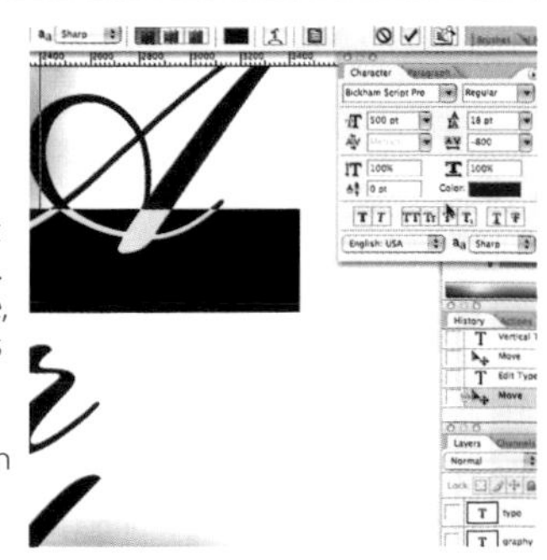

In the mix

Playing with blending modes

Being familiar with blending modes is essential for creating any composition, and is useful with typography. The blending mode decides how the colour of a layer reacts with those in the layers below. This is very useful with type, as this is an area of flat colour which can look more interesting if it blends with existing colours. When selecting a blending mode, ensure the text is still legible after the blend. The human brain is very good – if it can see half the word or shapes of letters, it can fill in the rest. Darken, Multiply, Color Burn and Linear Burn darken colours, while Lighten, Screen, Colour Dodge and Linear Dodge lighten already light hues. Blending modes are easy once they're understood!

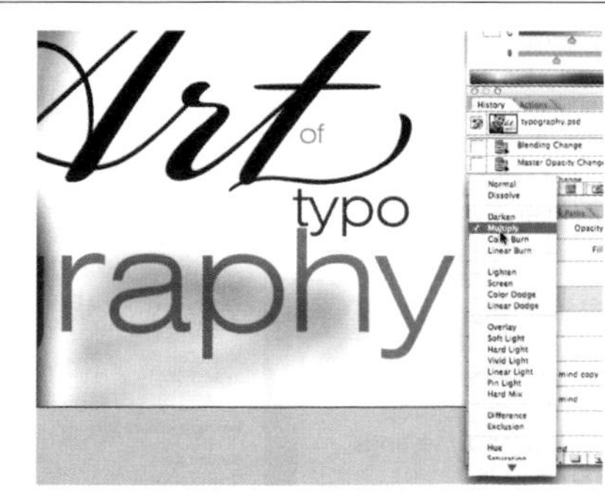

Bevel and Emboss

As we continue our tour around the Layer Styles neighbourhood, we drop in on the Bevel and Emboss command

Photoshop is a 2D program, so you are obviously working in a flat environment. Most of the time this is fine, but there may be occasions where you want an object or shape to stand out from the rest of the page furniture, or maybe you are working with text and want it to have a bit more 'zing' than the rest of the elements. In these occasions, it's worth paying a visit to the Bevel and Emboss Layer Style. These two help create a feeling of depth by adding highlight and shadow to layer shapes. Depending on where these highlights and shadows are placed, a 3D effect can be quickly generated.

The bevel effects make an object look as though it has been chiselled away, and is great for giving hard, sharp edges. The emboss options are a bit softer and make objects seem to rise out of the document or look as though they have been stamped into the page. In addition to deciding on a bevel or emboss, you also have control over the size of the effect, the direction of light and shadows and the shape of the edges. The option to apply a texture is also worth investigating and opens up even more options.

On these two pages, we're going to look at where all the different options for bevel and emboss live and what they can be used for. As with everything to do with Photoshop, the best way to learn is to experiment for yourself, but at least these pages will get you started!

Pick the style

The bevel or the emboss?

With the Layer Style window open and the Bevel and Emboss checkbox checked, go to the Style drop-down menu in the middle section to pick whether you go for a bevel or an emboss. The Technique menu allows you to choose the type of chisel effect you fancy. We used Chisel Soft in our snowflake example.

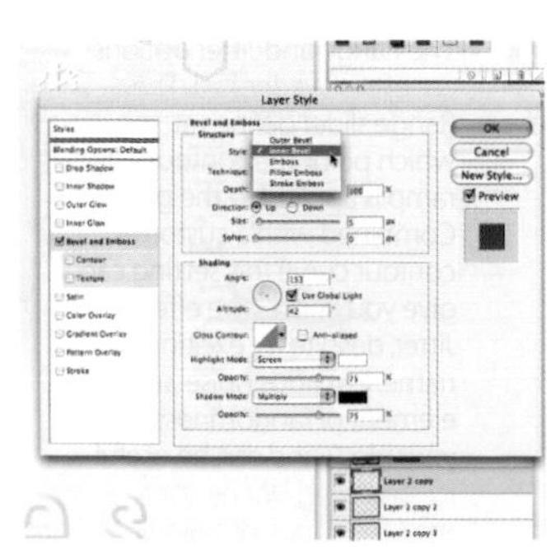

Depth and Shadow

Alter the spread of the effect

Depth controls how much highlight and shadow are offset. The higher this is, the more the effect will spread out. The Up and Down buttons switch the highlights and shadows, while Size affects the size. The Soften slider tones down the shadows and highlights.

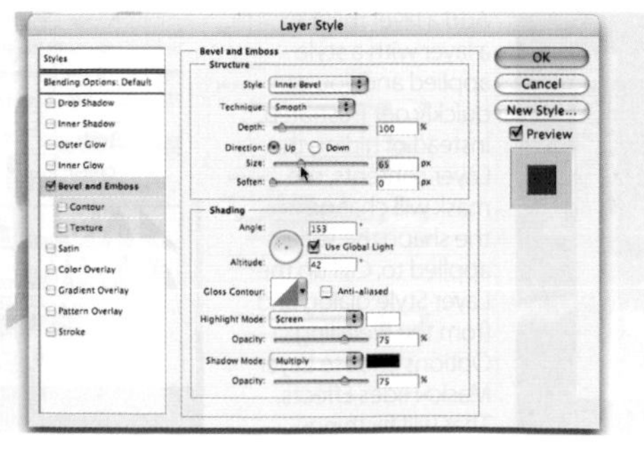

Tip

Not just shapes

You can apply Bevel and Emboss effects to text layers as well as shape layers. In fact, the effect is probably most successful with text, especially the emboss options.

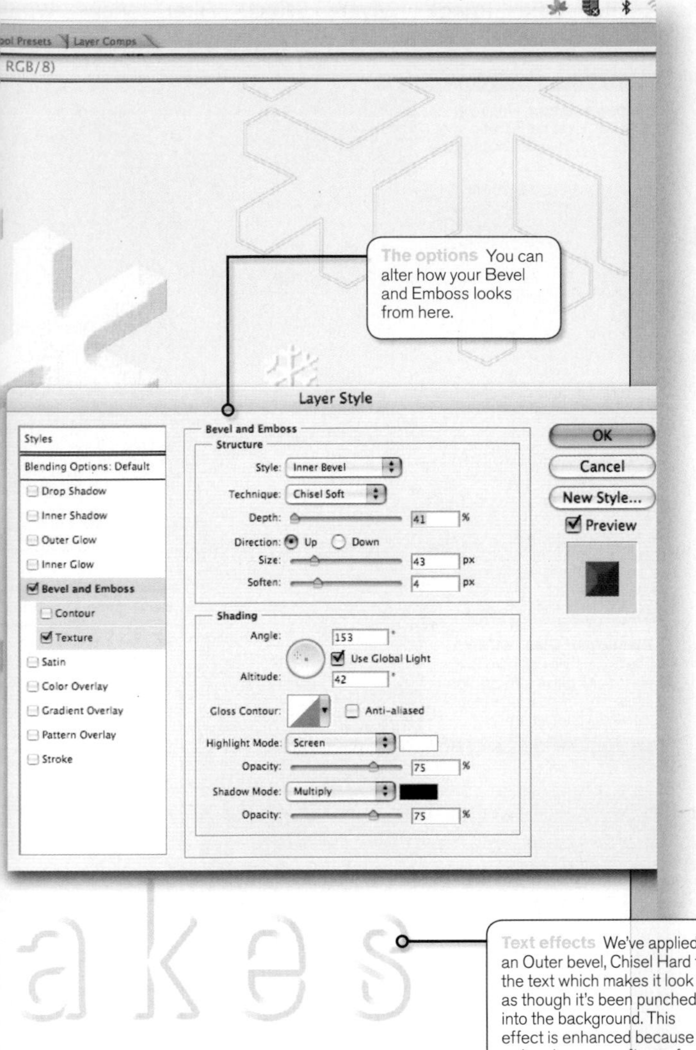

Tip

Keep it all together

When you're applying a texture to a bevel or emboss, you can select the Link with Layer checkbox. This allows you to move the texture and layer in complete unison.

Add texture to your layer's shape

The Bevel and Emboss options do a pretty good job of accenting an object, but for even more impact, try adding a texture to the shape…

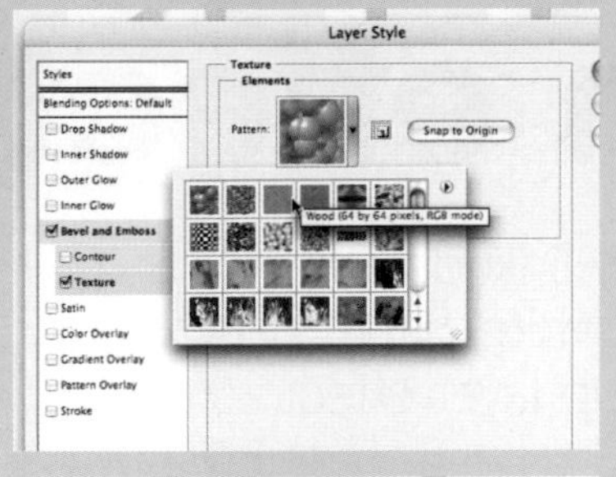

01 View the textures To get to the textures, you need to click the Texture box at the left side of the dialog box and then click on the word Texture. Click the arrow to see all the different textures. You'll notice these are pattern files.

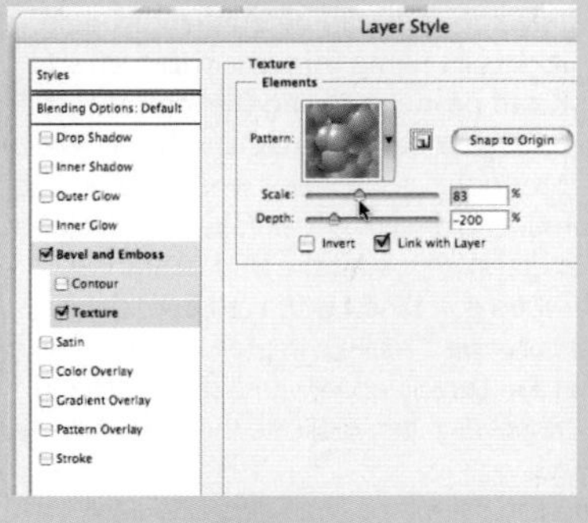

02 Alterations You can adjust the scale of the texture or alter the Depth setting to adjust the contrast of shadows and highlights in the pattern. This is achieved by using the sliders.

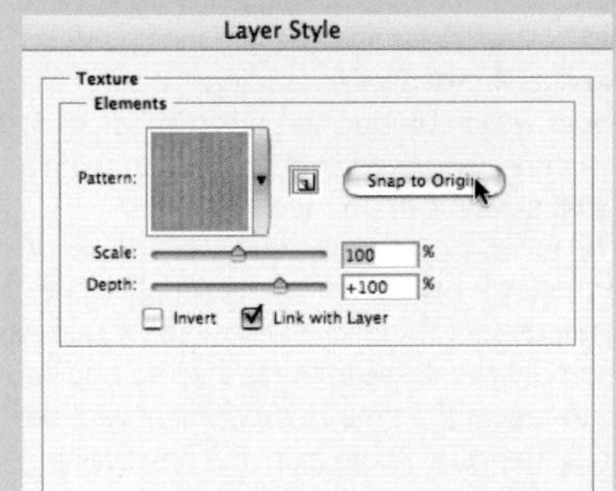

03 Reposition You can drag the texture about in the shape to alter the effect. If you click the Snap to Origin box, you can realign the pattern to the upper-left corner of the image. When you're happy, click OK.

The right angle
Sort the light source

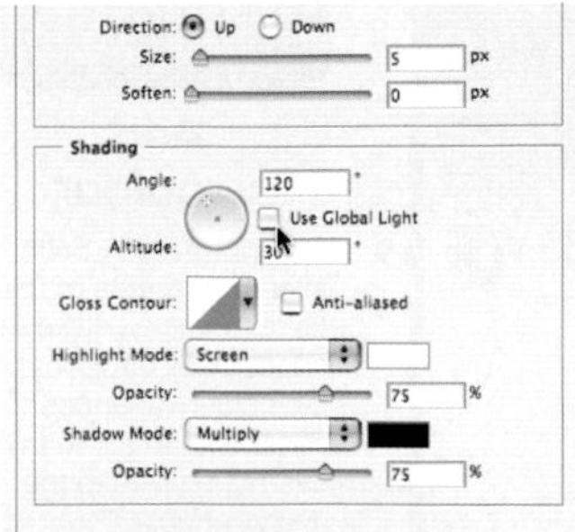

The Angle and Altitude settings let you set the location of the light source. The light source affects the highlights and shadows of the effects and it's important to get it right. Unless you have a special Global Light setting, it's best to uncheck the Use Global Light box.

Contours
See to the edges

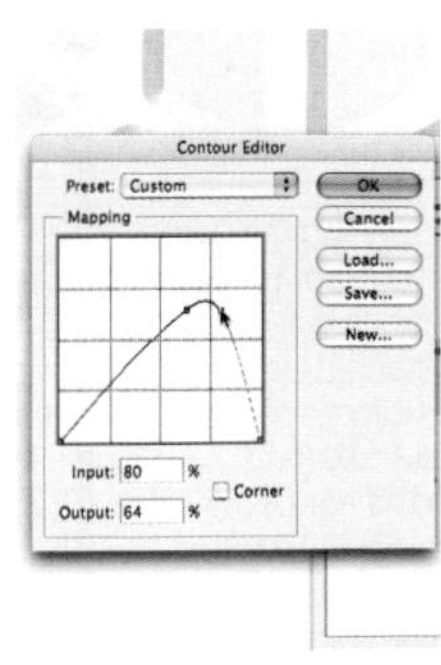

Click the Gloss Contour arrowhead to adjust contours. Contours affect the fade on a drop shadow or the highlight on a bevel and can influence how an effect looks. For example, you can take the cone contour and make the Bevel and Emboss look carved.

Tonal control
The highlights and shadows

The bottom part of the Bevel and Emboss window deals with editing the shadows and highlights. You can alter the mode of the shadow or highlight, which allows you to have the same control as if you were using layer blending modes. If you click on the colour swatch, you can also decide on a new colour for the highlight or shadow. We used a grey in our example here.

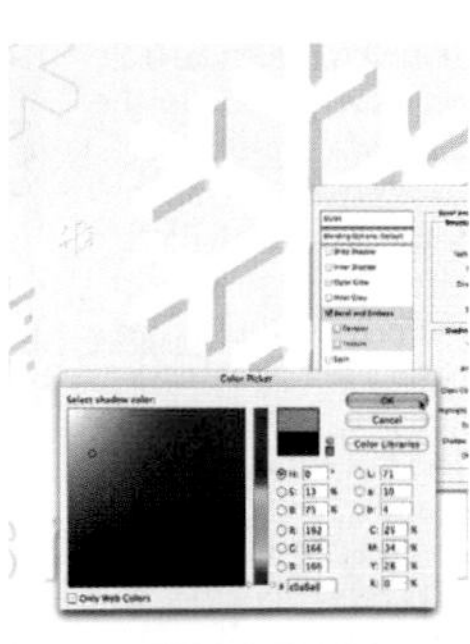

Using the Satin effect

Most commonly linked with bedding and the colour white, Satin is also a very handy Photoshop layer effect

The Satin style can be quite misleading. Yes, it gets its name from the sheen effects it can produce; giving the look of soft folds of material across an object. But its uses don't stop there – when applied in its harsher variations it could have just as easily been named the chrome or metal style; giving the kind of distorted reflections that when combined with hard bevels and gradient effects can give a realistic impression of chiselled metal. When used in combination with a soft bevel and flowing shape, however, it can replicate the look of melted metal or mercury.

Another common use of the Satin filter is to add refractions to plastic and glass effects; the banding effects produced by the filter are perfect for adding the soft colour variations that work well in producing buttons, glass, plastic or jewel effects such as the green oval example to the right.

Like all layer styles, Satin can be used with any combination of shadow, glow, bevel, overlay or stroke and then saved into the Style palette for one-click application to any layer. It's this degree of flexibility and editability that has made the addition of layer styles to Photoshop so popular, and why it's worth the taking the time to experiment with the settings. As with all things in Photoshop, the best way to get your head around how something works is to read these pages and then have a go yourself…

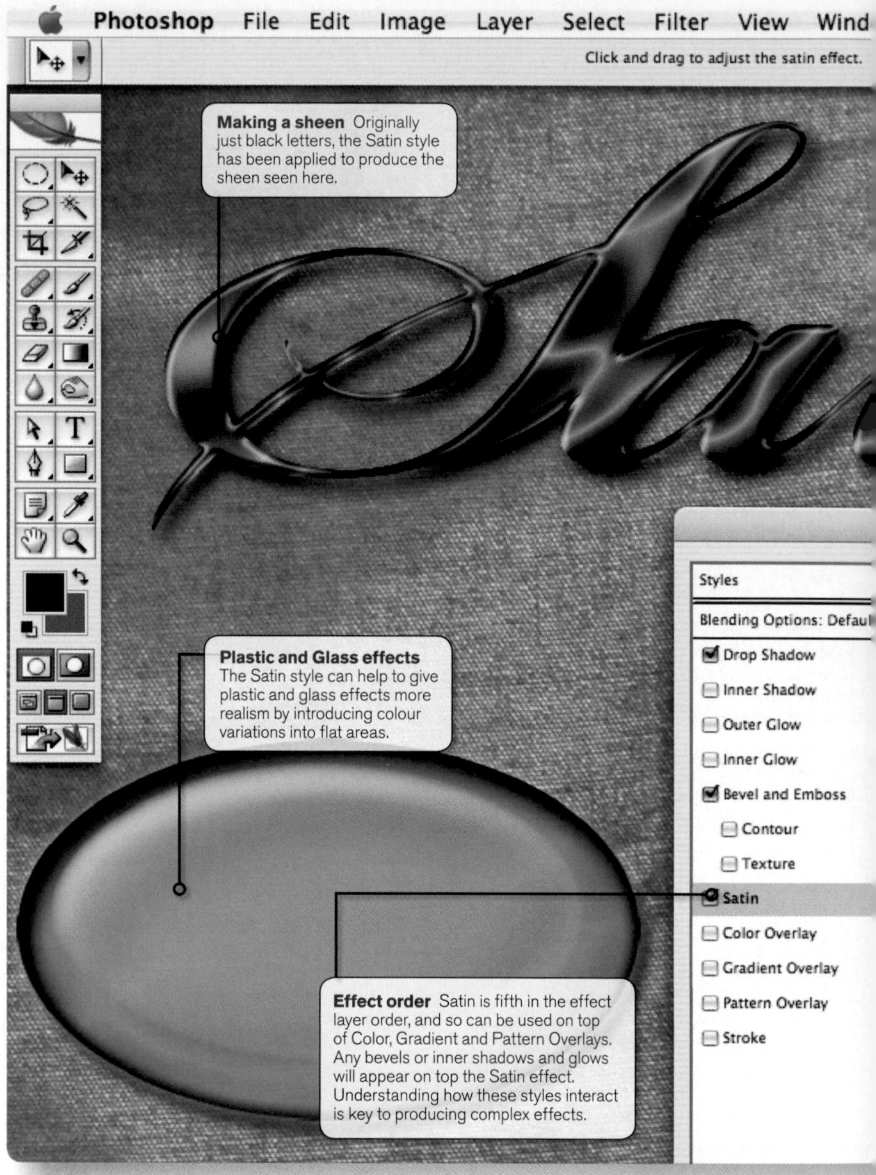

Making a sheen Originally just black letters, the Satin style has been applied to produce the sheen seen here.

Plastic and Glass effects The Satin style can help to give plastic and glass effects more realism by introducing colour variations into flat areas.

Effect order Satin is fifth in the effect layer order, and so can be used on top of Color, Gradient and Pattern Overlays. Any bevels or inner shadows and glows will appear on top the Satin effect. Understanding how these styles interact is key to producing complex effects.

Work all the angles

Turn it around

Spinning the Angle dial allows you to control the direction of the colour bands that make up the Satin effect. With most elements you'll find that there is usually one particular angle that will look the most natural. This dial is the same as in shadows and bevels, but controls the direction of banding, not the light source.

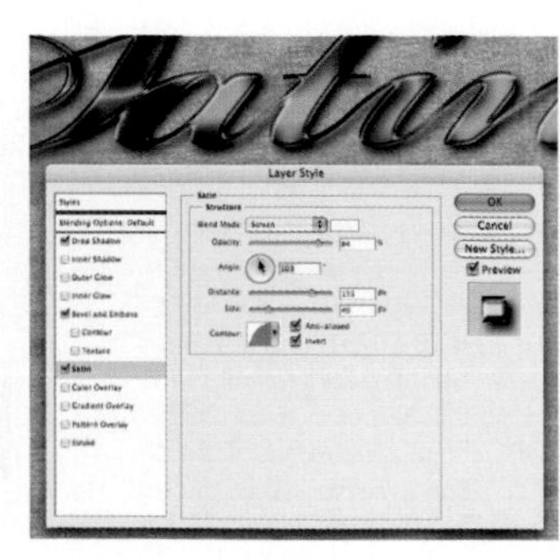

Keep your distance

Stick to the edges

Although the colour bands produced by the Satin filter may seem almost random, they are in fact produced by a combination of the Contour setting and the shape of the object you are applying the style to. The Distance slider controls the contour's distance from the edge of the object, moving the bands nearer the centre as you drag it to the right. Low settings work particularly well in conjunction with the Bevel styles, producing complex effects.

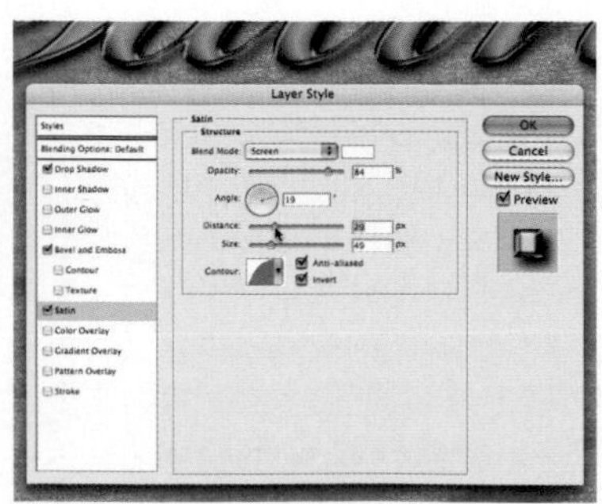

Tip

Add colour

Try applying the Satin filter to elements of flat colour that you'd like to appear less cartoony; the colour variances will soon add a healthy dash of realism to the overall effect.

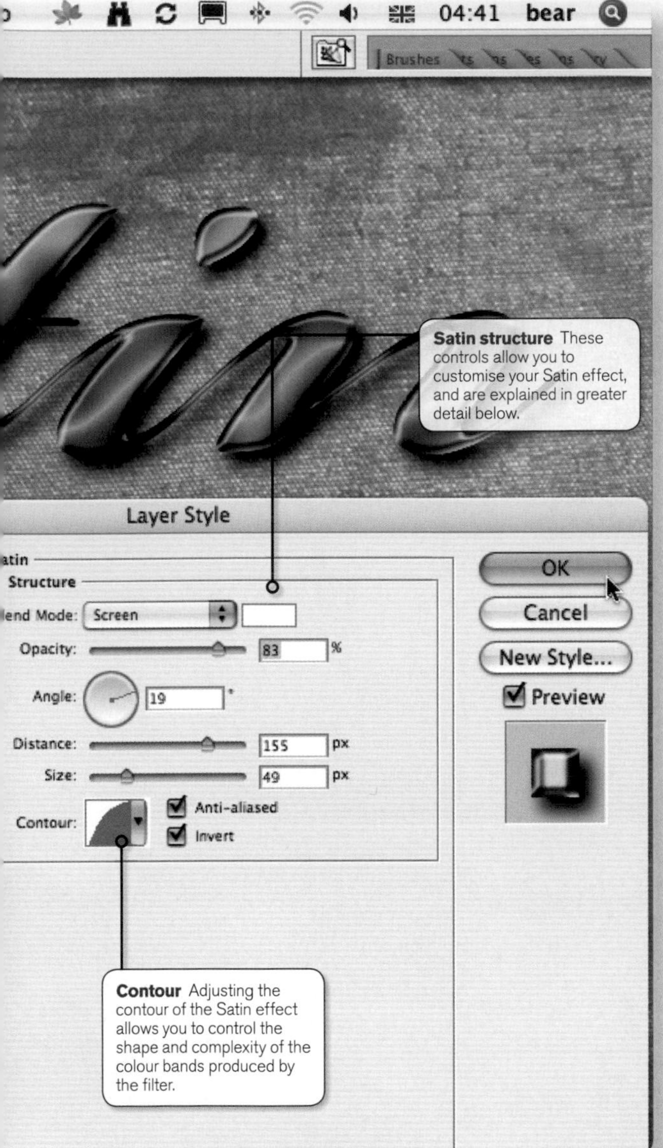

Satin structure These controls allow you to customise your Satin effect, and are explained in greater detail below.

Contour Adjusting the contour of the Satin effect allows you to control the shape and complexity of the colour bands produced by the filter.

Tip

Click and drag

As is the case with the Drop and Inner shadows, you can control the distance and angle of the Satin filter by clicking and dragging in the document window, outside the Layer Style dialog window.

How contours affect the Satin layer style

Contours control the shape of the banding applied by the Satin filter. Avoid anything too complicated unless you want a very definite look.

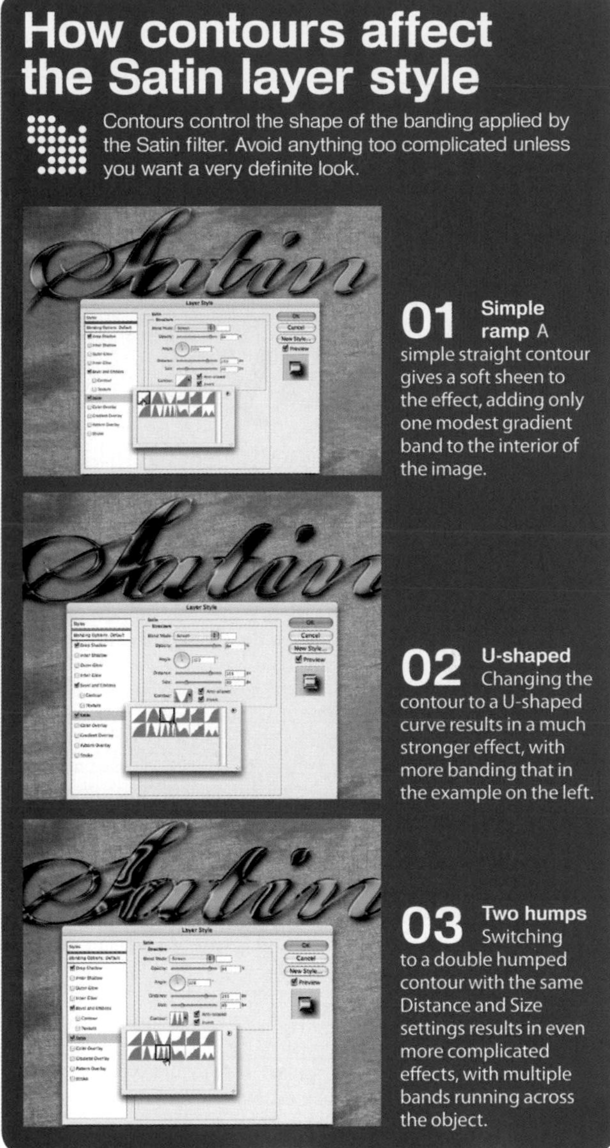

01 Simple ramp A simple straight contour gives a soft sheen to the effect, adding only one modest gradient band to the interior of the image.

02 U-shaped Changing the contour to a U-shaped curve results in a much stronger effect, with more banding that in the example on the left.

03 Two humps Switching to a double humped contour with the same Distance and Size settings results in even more complicated effects, with multiple bands running across the object.

Customise contours

Make it yourself

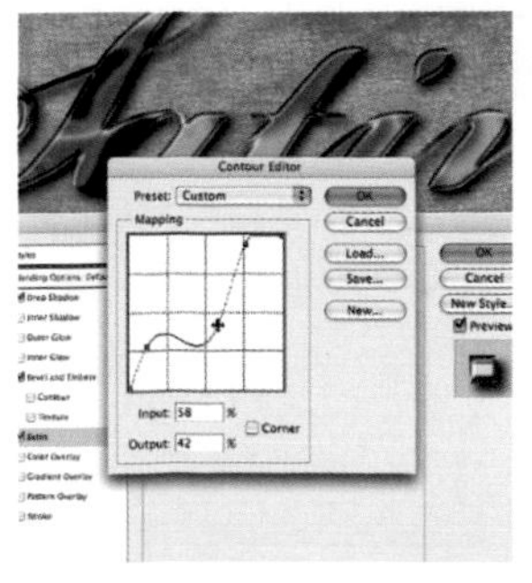

Clicking the Contour thumbnail will open a dialog window to create your own bespoke contour. Click and drag any point on the line to add a control point and move it into a different position; the line will curve gracefully to accommodate it. The more complicated the line, the more complex the Satin effect. Take a closer look at this relationship in the box to the left.

Size it up

Little or big?

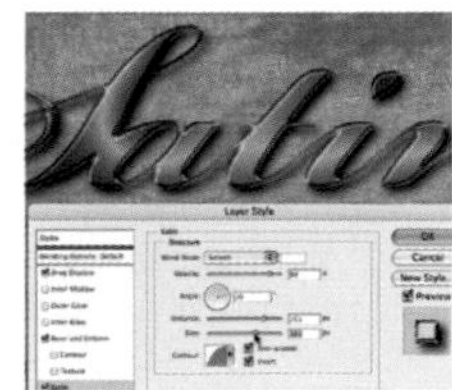

Dragging the Size slider to the left or right gives you complete control over the size of the blur, softening the contours that produce the banding effect. Smaller settings will give you a harsher more obvious effect, which are best used for metal and chrome effects. If you go for larger settings, you will produce subtler sheens that are slightly pillowy in appearance, as shown above.

Save your effects

Create a lasting style

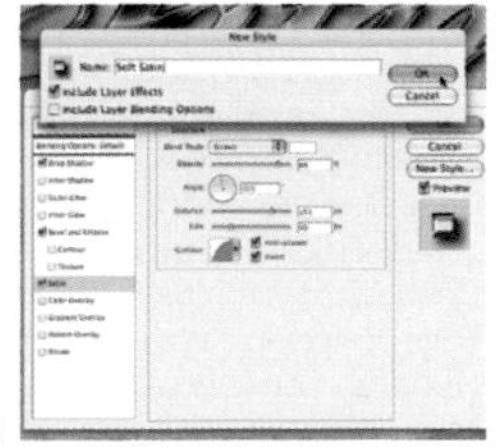

If you have produced a layer style that you're particularly happy with, you can create a New Style and save it to use again. A saved style can be a combination of any of the individual styles, as well as any layer blending options you have sprinkled in for good measure. Just hit the New Style button and then choose which options to save and give the style a name in the resulting dialog. Saved styles appear in the Layer Styles dialog for one-click application to any layer in any future document.

Color, Pattern and Gradient Overlays

Be imaginative with the three Overlay layer styles and transform text, photographs and illustrations

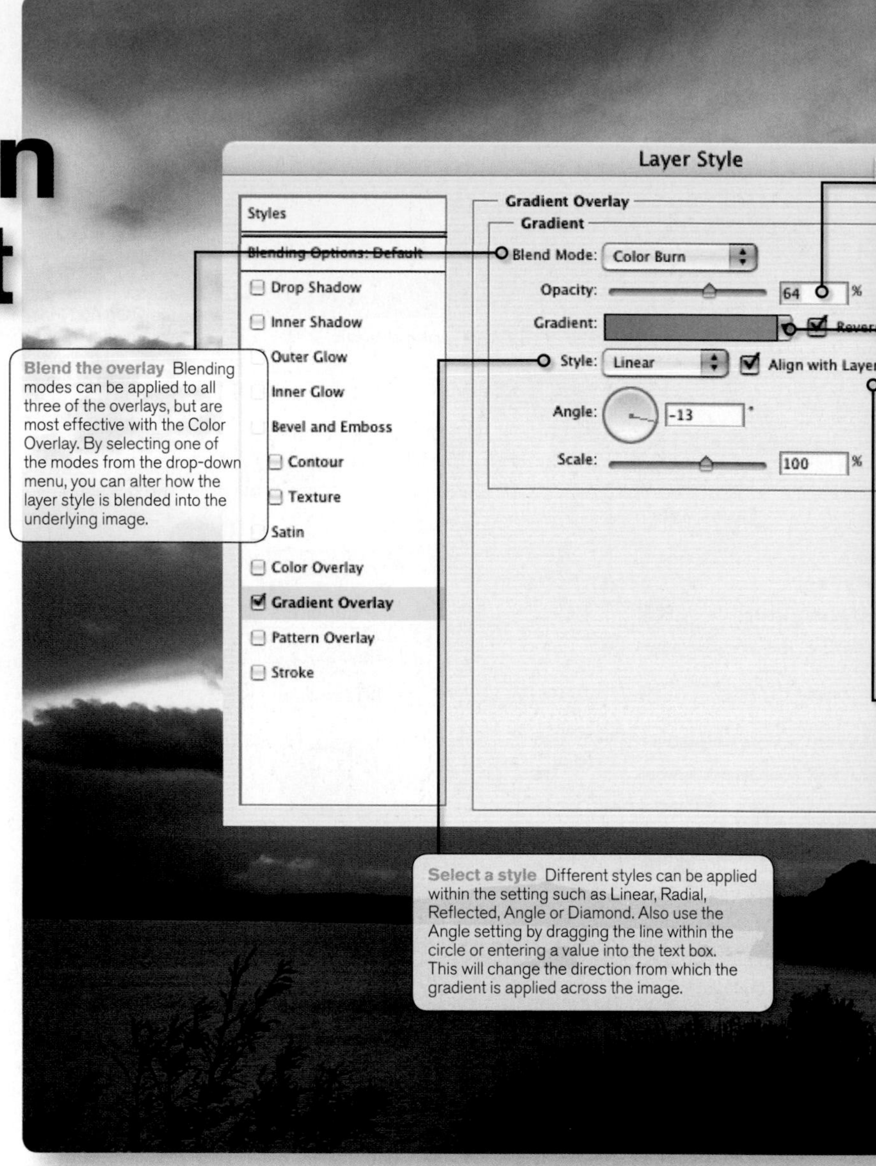

Blend the overlay Blending modes can be applied to all three of the overlays, but are most effective with the Color Overlay. By selecting one of the modes from the drop-down menu, you can alter how the layer style is blended into the underlying image.

Select a style Different styles can be applied within the setting such as Linear, Radial, Reflected, Angle or Diamond. Also use the Angle setting by dragging the line within the circle or entering a value into the text box. This will change the direction from which the gradient is applied across the image.

Now we have to admit something – before writing these pages we had never really investigated the Overlay effects. But after spending some time with the Color, Pattern and Gradient Overlay layer styles, we're delighted to report that they open up a whole range of new design possibilities. The overlays do pretty much what their name suggests; a Color Overlay applies a layer of your chosen colour; Pattern Overlay fills whatever is on the layer you are working on with pattern; and the Gradient Overlay lets you choose from a selection of gradient styles and colours to apply. Different overlays can be applied to separate layers of your image, which is great for building up a composition. It is also possible to apply an overlay to selective parts of an image. Combining different layer styles together, such as Bevel and Emboss, Color Overlay and Gradient Overlay often produces the best effects. The application of an overlay can also be fine-tuned using Align with Layer to control whether it will snap to the origin. The concept of the three overlays is very simple yet the results you can produce can be extremely dramatic, so have fun experimenting with the settings.

Color Overlay

Change the entire mood of an image

As the name suggests, Color Overlay covers a layer with your chosen hue. For example, you may have some text on a layer and want to see what it looks like with different colours without changing its original values. To apply, simply select Layer>Layer Styles>Color Overlay. When you originally bring up the Color Overlay it will wipe out whatever you have on screen with a solid layer of red, the default colour and opacity setting. This is only temporarily masking it, and can be easily adjusted. Experiment with colour change by clicking on the red colour box and then selecting from the Color Picker. Because you don't want to blast the image with colour, adjust the Opacity slider to reveal the image underneath.

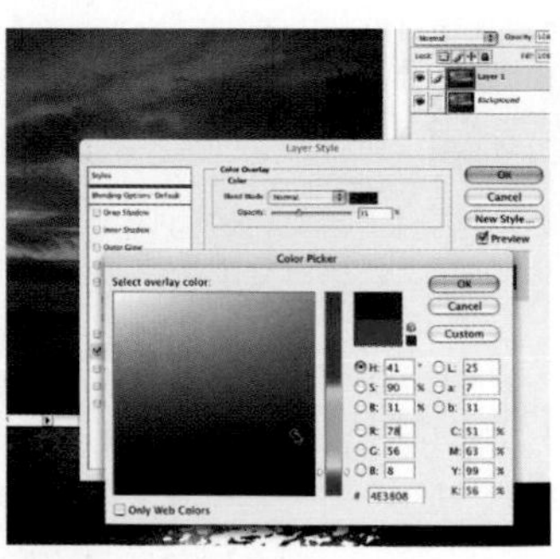

Pattern Overlay

Not just limited to filling custom shapes

When applying a Pattern Overlay, you are quite simply adding a specific patterned fill to the layer or image you are working on. If you want the overlay to be aligned with what is on the active layer, check the Link with Layer box. Patterns are really good for adding texture. For example, to make a photograph look like an embroidery, apply a suitable Pattern from the Artistic Surfaces set over a photograph and then lower the Opacity to around 30%.

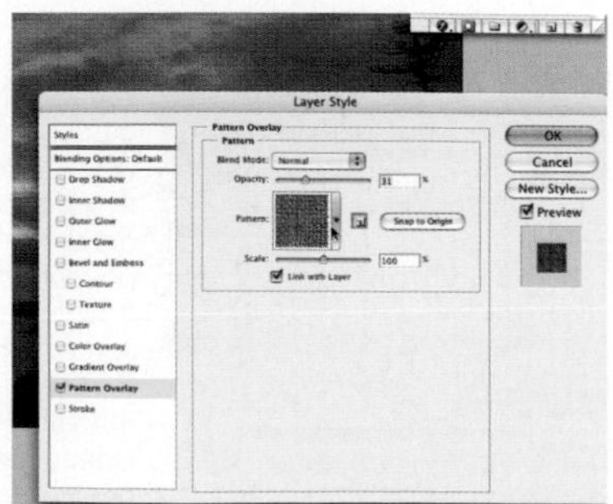

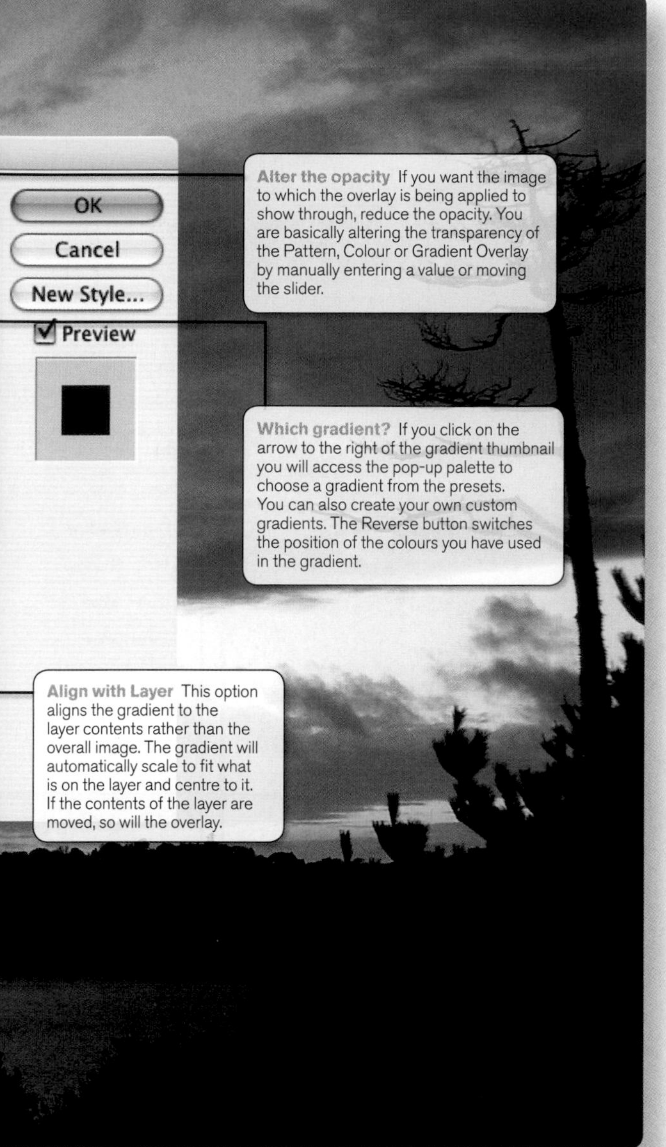

Alter the opacity If you want the image to which the overlay is being applied to show through, reduce the opacity. You are basically altering the transparency of the Pattern, Colour or Gradient Overlay by manually entering a value or moving the slider.

Which gradient? If you click on the arrow to the right of the gradient thumbnail you will access the pop-up palette to choose a gradient from the presets. You can also create your own custom gradients. The Reverse button switches the position of the colours you have used in the gradient.

Align with Layer This option aligns the gradient to the layer contents rather than the overall image. The gradient will automatically scale to fit what is on the layer and centre to it. If the contents of the layer are moved, so will the overlay.

Tip

Custom overlays

If you do not want to use the default presets for your overlays, you can create your own. Create a folder and begin collecting your favourite overlays. Select New when in the Overlay dialog and a new custom preset will be created. Choose a name for your style and begin adjusting the different settings. Once in a new image or layer, select Window>Styles and your saved Color, Pattern or Gradient Overlay will appear within it. To apply the style again, simply drag it onto the layer you are working on.

Combine layer styles

Build up a more interesting effect

Using Overlays with other effects is a good way of getting that 'wow' factor. Try Bevel and Emboss and Drop Shadow styles with Gradient and Color Overlay.

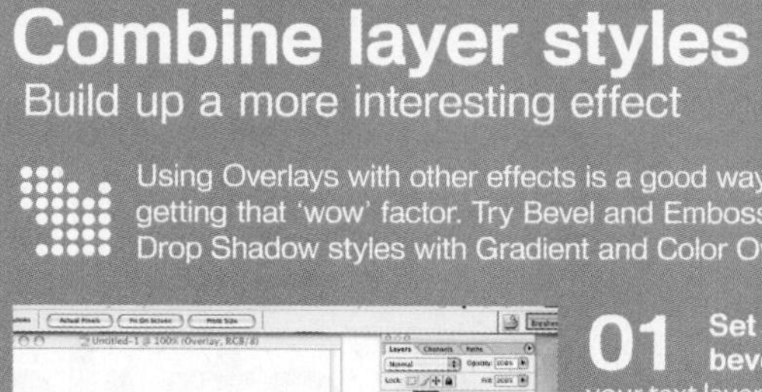

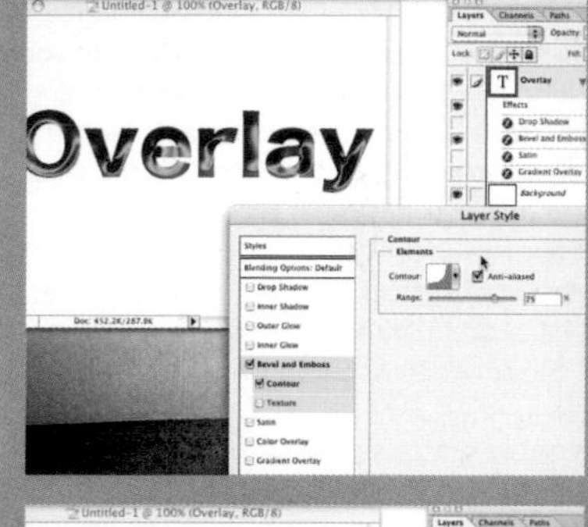

01 Set the bevel With your text layer all ready to go, move to Layer>Layer Styles>Bevel and Emboss. Apply an Inner Bevel. Select Drop Shadow from the Layer Styles pull-down menu to give the text a bit more body.

02 Contour time Within the Bevel and Emboss section, select the Gloss Contour icon and pick the most raised type. Click the Contour section to add reflection to the bevel. This can be enhanced by selecting the Satin layer style and applying a contour to suit the lettering style.

03 Metal touch Select Gradient Overlay from the Layer Styles and choose the gradient style that has a few alternating bars. Choose a dark and light yellow for the two colours to be used in the gradient and the text will appear metallic gold.

Gradient Overlay

Use subtle gradients to finish off artwork

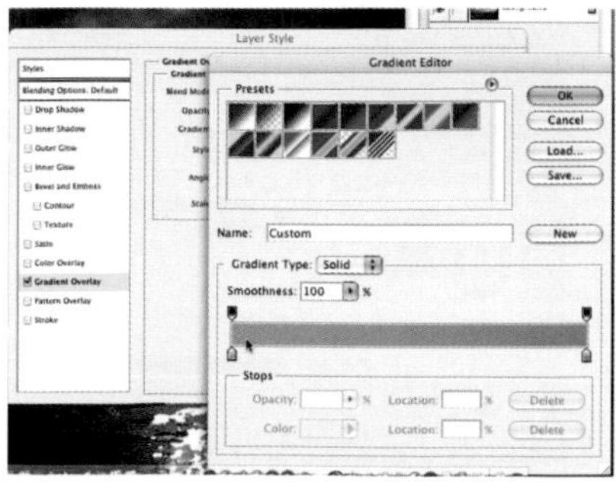

Gradient Overlays are fairly simple effects. As with Color and Pattern Overlay, they are constructed by combining the filled layer, a blending mode and an opacity setting. Use the small arrow on the right to bring up a window, where you can choose a gradient from. You can also use this window to begin creating your own custom gradients by clicking on the right-pointing arrow. By selecting different opacities and blending modes you can achieve some very diverse results. Click the gradient pattern to bring up the Gradient Editor, which allows you to specify Gradient Type, Presets, Smoothness and Colour. Gradient Overlays are particularly good for enhancing skies.

Magical blend modes

Achieve some fantastic results

Experimenting with the various blending modes allows you to alter how a specific colour, pattern or gradient blends into whatever is on the active layer. To use the feature, simply click the arrow next to Blend Modes to see the selection from the pull-down menu. These options instruct Photoshop on how to blend the Overlay with the colours of the active image (in the example here, Color Overlay). Applying the Color Burn blending mode with red overlay created the image on the top-left , while the other used a green overlay with a Hard Mix blending mode set to an Opacity of 40%. Blending modes are a quick way of getting great results.

Stroke style

Whether you need to enhance text or create easy borders, Stroke is the layer style for the job. Here's how it works…

When you talk about stroking an image or selection, it isn't anything to do with some kind of weird computer worship. Adding a stroke basically means you add an outline to whatever is active on the selected layer. You can alter how drastic the stroke is by using the Size adjustment that appears in the Stroke dialog box. It is also possible to create a stroke effect by selecting Edit>Stroke, but you should be aware that this doesn't give you as many options to tailor the stroke as is found within the Layer Styles palette.

Although the Stroke effect is most commonly used with text, it can also be applied to graphics and photographs. One thing worth mentioning is that you must ensure the object you are applying the stroke to is surrounded by transparent pixels. Although it is possible to stroke an entire layer, it can also be used for individual objects. If your chosen object is not separate from the background layer you will need to select it and then paste it onto a new layer. A stroke can also be used to paint a coloured border around a selection, layer or path. The stroke style is not limited to block colour as it is also possible to apply a gradient or patterned stroke, which opens up more variations on styles. Before beginning to apply the stroke, always remember to make a copy of your image onto a new layer so the original is protected.

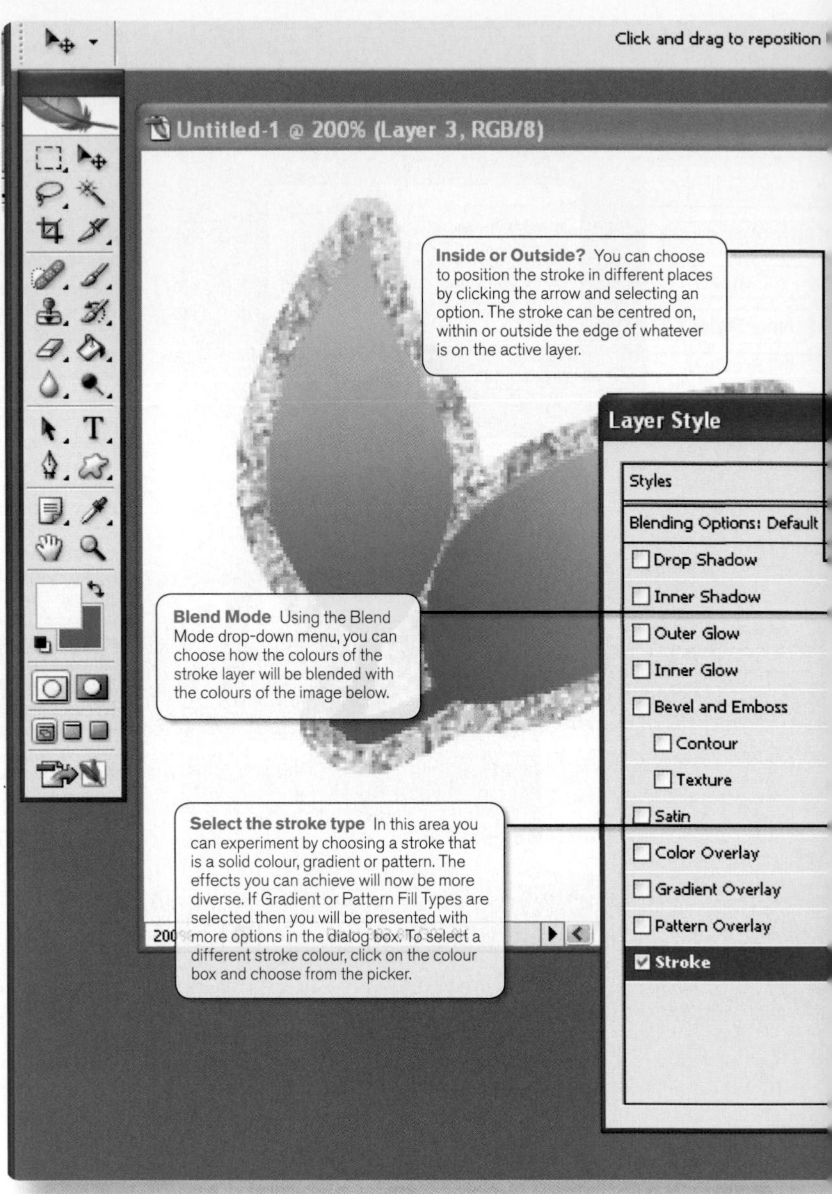

Inside or Outside? You can choose to position the stroke in different places by clicking the arrow and selecting an option. The stroke can be centred on, within or outside the edge of whatever is on the active layer.

Blend Mode Using the Blend Mode drop-down menu, you can choose how the colours of the stroke layer will be blended with the colours of the image below.

Select the stroke type In this area you can experiment by choosing a stroke that is a solid colour, gradient or pattern. The effects you can achieve will now be more diverse. If Gradient or Pattern Fill Types are selected then you will be presented with more options in the dialog box. To select a different stroke colour, click on the colour box and choose from the picker.

Position is key
Where to place the stroke

Applying a stroke will automatically add an outline to an edge. You can choose what area of the element's edge it falls on, which also changes the way the effect is created. The stroke can be applied to the outside or inside of the content's edge or centred on top of its edges. By applying the stroke to the outside of the edge, a layer is created below the selected layer. The fill is slightly larger than the contents of the layer above. Setting the Stroke Position to Inside uses the opposite method, as the layer is added on top of the contents layer and filled so it overlaps the shapes slightly. If you are positioning the stroke in the centre, it will be placed directly over the edges it is applied to and the layer effect is below the contents layer.

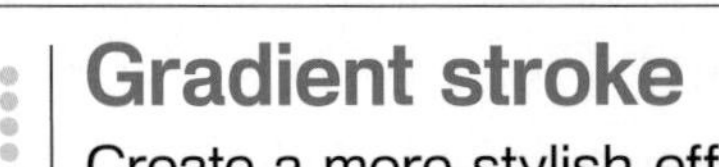

inside

centre

Gradient stroke
Create a more stylish effect

When adding a Stroke layer effect, you get to choose from several fill types. Gradient is a good one to pick, because you get to choose various styles such as Linear, Radial, Angled, or Shape Burst. You can then select the colours used in the gradient and reverse them by ticking the Reverse check box. It is also possible to align the gradient with the layer and alter its scale. To alter the Angle of the gradient, either enter a value or move the angle manually.

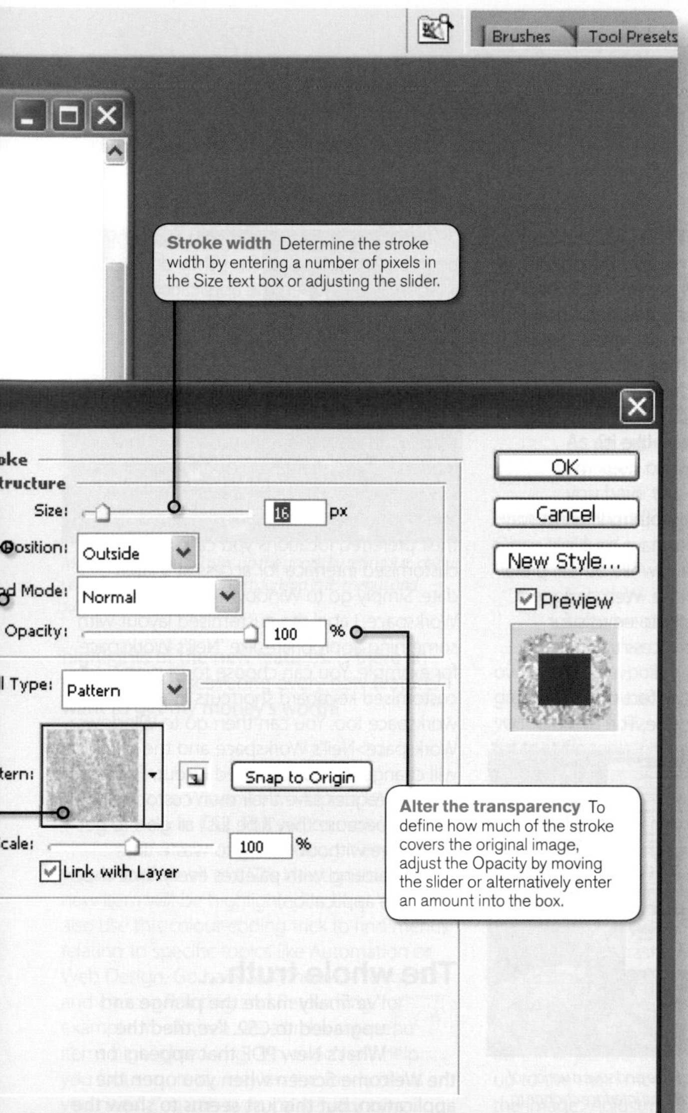

Tip

Double strokes

If you do not want to use the method we have described to create multiple strokes, apply an Outer Glow to your first stroke. Set the Blend Mode to Normal and the Opacity to 100%. You can then play with the size and spread to get the desired effect.

Tip

Tone down

You may find the stroke you have applied too drastic, so to lessen this select Layer>Layer Style>Scale Effects. This can be applied to all of the layer styles and allows you to rescale them without having to manually re-enter the Layer Style dialog box.

Double-stroke your text

The quick route to a more graphic effect

A thin stroke can help enhance the definition of text, but sometimes it needs even more impact. Reusing the Stroke layer style can be just the ticket

01 Type away Choose File>New. Select Transparent from the Background Contents pull-down menu. This creates a transparent document, which is essential for the stroke to work. Type your text.

02 Start to stroke Make sure the type layer is active and go to Layer>Layer Styles>Stroke. You can now alter the way your stroke appears by adjusting the colour, angle, size and type. We have chosen a solid colour for this exercise.

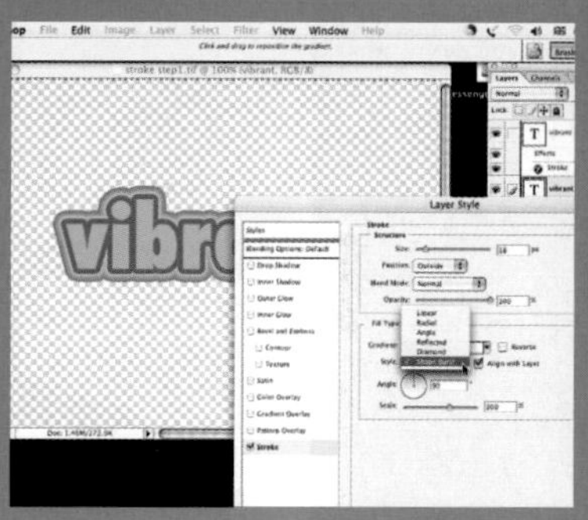

03 The double stroke Drag the stroked layer onto the New Layer icon. Select the bottom of the two layers and choose Layer>Layer Styles>Stroke. Now increase the Size to make the stroke appear around the edges of the top one.

Easy borders

Frame an image

Strokes have lots of uses. For example, if you have an image that you would like to frame, flatten the image (if it has multiple layers) and then apply a stroke. Make sure the stroke position is set to Inside. You can now adjust the size of the stroke and see the effects as you alter the border. Experiment with using the Pattern and Gradient strokes to create more innovative borders. Combine with the Bevel and Emboss effects and make full use of the Contour options for getting different looks to the border.

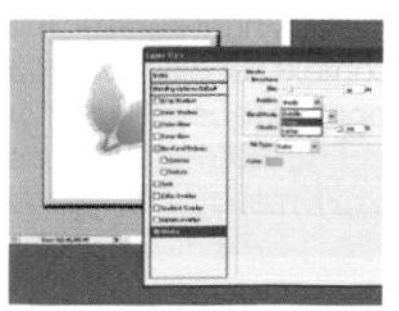

Use patterns

Be adventurous

In addition to solid colour and graduated strokes, you can also create a patterned stroke. If the Fill Type is set to Pattern, the dialog box will present a greater number of adjustment settings. Once the stroke has been applied, try experimenting by adding other layer effects. For this leaf graphic we selected from the Rock Patterns list to apply as a stroke. As with the Gradient stroke, you will find many presets already in Photoshop, but if you want even more patterns, just check out our CD-ROM.

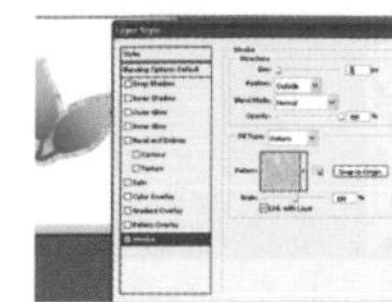

Stroke Emboss

Add more body to a stroke

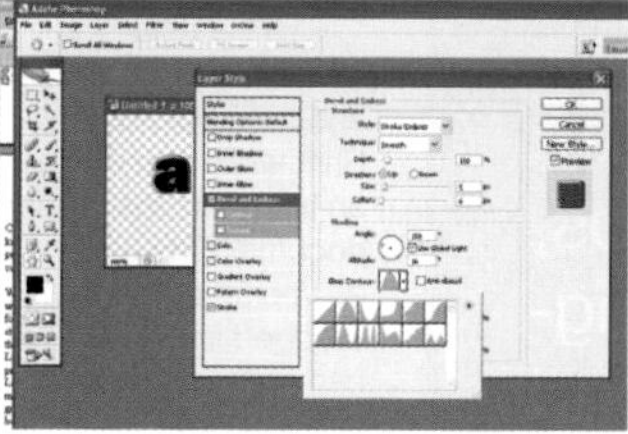

As with all the layer styles, strokes reach their full potential when applied alongside another style. Bevel and Emboss makes a particularly good partner. Make sure that you set both styles to the same size for them to work in unison. If working with text, the best setting for the Bevel and Emboss is Stroke Emboss. This makes the text appear rounded. When combining layer styles such as these it is often difficult to see them in detail. To draw attention to them, click on the Blending Options box in the top right of the Stroke dialog box. Once within this area, reduce the Fill Opacity to fade out the text or image that you are applying the styles to.

KEYBOARD SHORTCUTS The Undo commands

	PC	Mac
Undo	Ctrl + Z	Cmd + Z
Step Forward	Ctrl + Shift + Z	Cmd + Shift + Z
Step Backward	Ctrl + Alt + Z	Cmd + Option + Z
Fade	Ctrl + Shift + F	Cmd + Shift + F

ISOLATING COLOUR

Get picky about elements

Q What's the easiest way to select and isolate a specific colour? I'm trying to create a shot where a model's coat is in colour and the rest of the image is in monochrome.
Michael Bradshaw

A Photoshop is such a powerful package that there are many ways to select and isolate colours. You could try using the Magic Wand and Shift-click to add the desired colours to the selection. Another effective but more advanced method is to use the Color Range option.

01 Duplicate the layer Before editing an image's colour information, create a duplicate of the main layer (in case things don't work out as planned). Then go to Select>Color Range. Select the Eyedropper Tool. Click on the colour you want to select. All similar coloured pixels in the selection will appear as grey or white.

02 Add to the selection To fine-tune the selection increase the Fuzziness slider. Try and get it to look as white as possible. Areas outside the selection show up as black. Change the Selection Preview to Grayscale to get a better look at the sampled white areas. Use the Add to Sample Eyedropper to include areas of colour that have been missed.

03 And invert When you're happy with the preview tap the OK button. The 'marching ants' will indicate the selected colour. Go to Select>Inverse to select the background and pick Image>Adjustments>Desaturate to lose every other colour in the image.

the package's existing keyboard shortcuts and even assign shortcuts to menu items that don't have any.

CS users can go to Edit>Keyboard Shortcuts and assign their own shortcut to menus that don't have one. The Application Menu section lists all the menu commands. Simply scroll down to a command like Brightness/Contrast and click in the Shortcut column. You can then assign your own keyboard shortcut to that menu item. Your shortcut must include either Control (Command on a Mac) or an F key to be valid. If you chose a shortcut that's already been assigned to another menu item, a warning will appear. You can pinch this shortcut and apply it to your chosen menu item instead or look for something unique.

In CS2 go to Windows>Workspace> Keyboard Shortcuts and Menus. This works in the same way as the Keyboard Shortcuts menu in CS, though it has the additional option of letting you make menu items invisible. This is a great way of creating a lean and mean streamlined interface. This will give you less menu choice to wade through when looking for specific items in the future (a bit like deleting the shopping channels from your TV freeview box to avoid wasting time channel hopping). Spending a bit of time customising Photoshop's menus and shortcuts will greatly speed up your workflow.

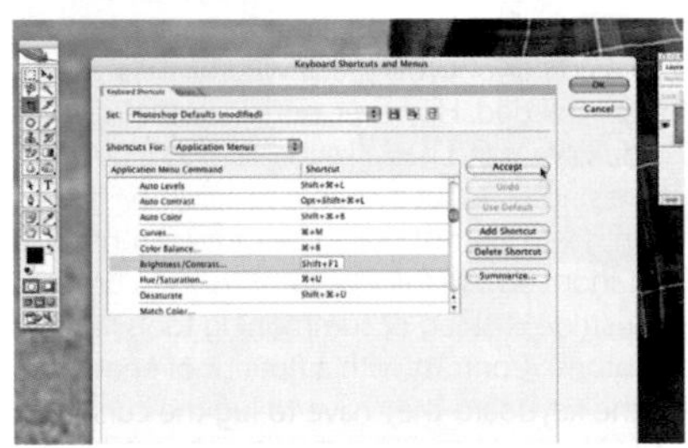

Customise your keyboard shortcuts and even assign shortcuts to menu items that don't have one by default!

Clipping paths

Q I use the Pen Tool to draw paths around objects so that designers have the option of easily isolating the subject from its background. I'd like to share these paths with clients when I mail them the images, but as I have to compress my PSDs down to .jpg files the paths disappear. Is there any way to store paths in a .jpg?
Laurence Postgate

A Paths are very handy tools for designers to use as they allow them to quickly isolate specific objects from a scene. Fortunately you can store your paths in a .jpg file by converting them to a clipping path. Use the Pen Tool to draw the path as normal. Once the path has been created go to the Path options menu in the Paths palette and choose Save Path. In the Path options menu set the Flatness value to 1. Flatness adjusts the way the clipping path follows the curves you've created. A value of 1 will make the

Layers tip

Quick opening

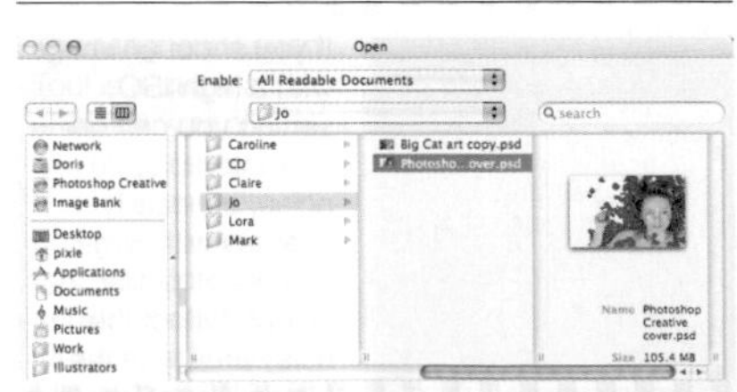

The downfall of layered files is that they can take aeons open up. To look at a file without waiting for the layers to load, go to File>Open and then navigate to the layered file. But before you click Open, hold down Shift+Option (Mac), Shift+Alt (PC). This opens a flattened version of the image.

RAM tip

Purge your contents

If it feels like your version of the Photoshop software is crawling through treacle, it may be time to do some purging. Go to Edit>Purge and then choose either Undo, Photoshop's Clipboard, History States or All. Hopefully that will sort out your RAM dilemma.

Make your .jpgs more functional by embedding a clipping path inside them. This will allow other people to use the path to make a selection

clipping path faithfully follow the path's curves, while higher values will be less accurate. Click OK. When you save the file as a .jpg the path will remain intact, allowing other designers to access it. Don't use the Save for Web option though, as this will create a jpg without a clipping path. If you save your document as an EPS file, then packages like QuarkXPress and Adobe Illustrator can also use the embedded clipping path to make a selection.

Colours from photos

Q **Sometimes I can't find the colour I want in the Swatches palette to match up with an image. Is there any way I can quickly create some hues that fit in with a photo? I've tried using the Eyedropper tool but that's only good for one colour.**
Jimmy Ragge

A There is indeed a way for you to create swatches of colour from a photo. This is worth doing if you have to create supplementary boxes such as frames around the image and makes sure all the colours work well together. With the image open in the Photoshop software, go to Image>Mode>Indexed Color. A dialog box will pop up. Choose Local (Perceptual) frm the Palette list and then set Colors to 256, Forced to None, Dither to None and then click OK. Now go to Image>Mode>Color Table to see the colours sampled from your image. Click Save, give your swatch a name and save to the Photoshop>Presets>Color Swatches folder. To load, go to the Swatches palette, pick Load Swatches from the menu and select Color Table from the Files of Type list. Now just click on the one you've saved and then click Load.

If you can't find the colour that you want, you can save a colour swatch from one of your photos

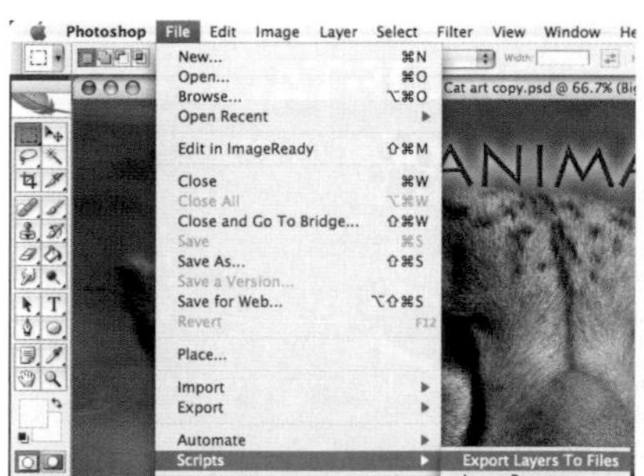

You can easily turn your layered files into separate documents by having a little route around the options in the Scripts menu

Separate out layers

Q **I've got some layered files that have elements on that I want to use in other illustrations. So far I've been selecting the layer and then copying and pasting it to another document, but this is getting very tiresome to do. There must be a quicker way.**
Abigail Fleck

A Ha ha, yes there is. You can get the Photoshop software to quickly sort out your layered files into separate documents, so you can then save these documents somewhere and always have an image's layers to hand. Open up the layered file and then go to the File menu. Navigate down to the Scripts option and pick Export Layers to Files. After a bit of shimmying about, all the layers will appear as separate documents.

Opacity tip
Perfect slider control

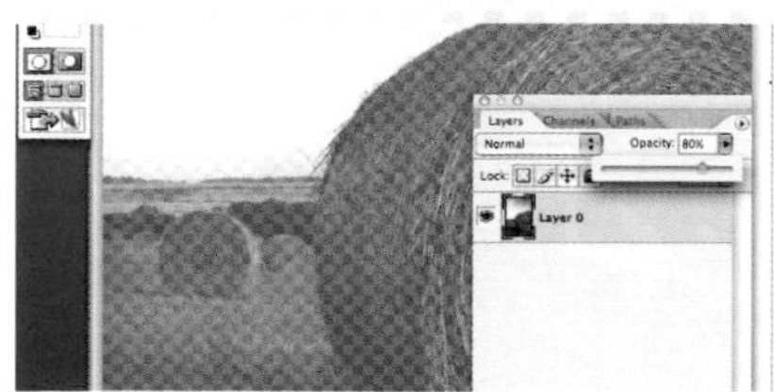

You can control the Opacity slider in the Layers palette with the keyboard rather than fiddling about with the mouse. Click the arrow next to the Opacity field and then use the Left and Right arrows to move 1% at a time, or get the Shift key involved to move 10% at a time.

Function tip
History lesson

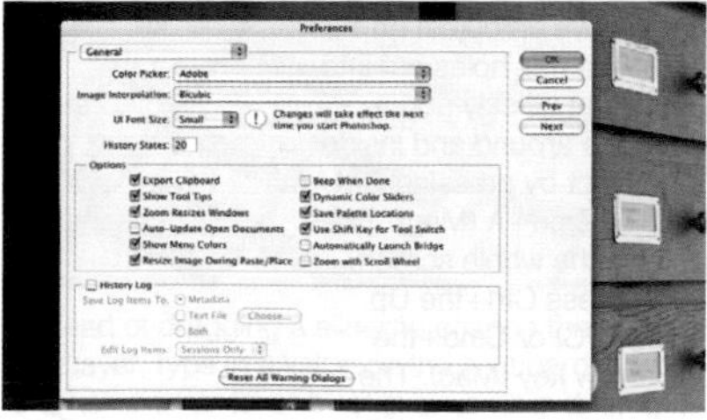

Experimenting is easy because you can retrace your steps if things go wrong. This is because the last 20 things you've done are recorded. You can increase the number of History States in the General Preferences window.

Tool tip
Brush up on your skills

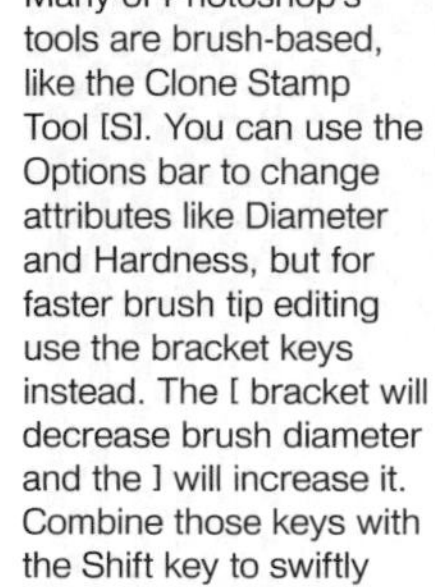

Many of Photoshop's tools are brush-based, like the Clone Stamp Tool [S]. You can use the Options bar to change attributes like Diameter and Hardness, but for faster brush tip editing use the bracket keys instead. The [bracket will decrease brush diameter and the] will increase it. Combine those keys with the Shift key to swiftly increase or decrease brush softness.

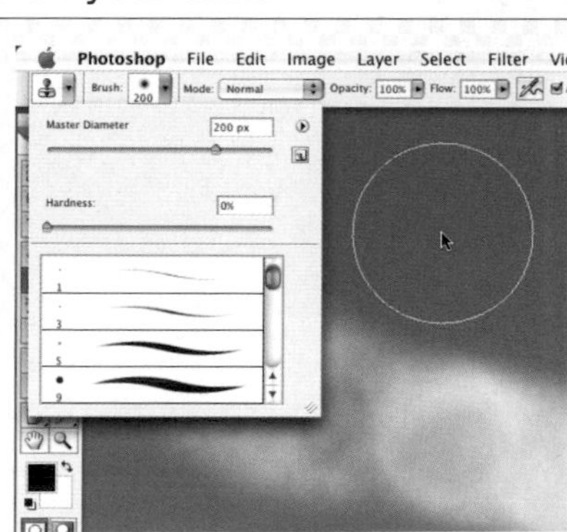

KEYBOARD SHORTCUTS Tool presets

Tool	PC	Mac
Magnetic Lasso tool	L	L
Magic Wand tool	W	W
Crop tool	C	C
Spot Healing Brush tool	J	J

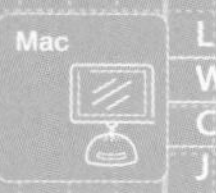

FIT THE FRAME

Create true works of art

Q I'm trying to create a birthday card for my daughter. She wants to be a painter when she grows up, so I'd like to place her work on the wall of a famous gallery to create a mock-up image of her as a painter. How can I do this?
Rebecca Havers

A This sounds like a straightforward job for Photoshop's pixel-pushing Transform tools. Follow the steps in our mini walkthrough to distort any source image so that it will fit the frame of a picture hanging on the wall of a famous gallery.

01 Pick a gallery You'll want to use your own source image to fit in the frame, but feel free to practise with Source.jpg from the CD. Open the gallery shot too (Gallery.jpg). Select the source image, Edit>Copy it and Edit>Paste it onto the galley document as a new layer.

02 Target the Source layer Change the opacity of the layer to 40% so that you can see the background too. Press Ctrl+T (PC) or Cmd+T (Mac) to activate the Free Transform tool. Handles will appear around the image. Hold Shift and drag a corner handle inwards to scale the image down.

03 Final fittings To make your picture fit the frame hold down the Control/Command key. Drag each corner of your source image and make them align with the corners of the frame. A Brush filter like Accented Edges can add a suitable painterly finish to any source photo.

Marvellous monochrome

Q I'm a keen portrait photographer and like to work in monochrome. I can get Photoshop to turn colour shots to black and white, but how do I tweak my shots to get a decent monochrome shot that has a good range of blacks, midtones and whites?
Paul Steinway

A Many folk probably think that to turn a shot to black and white they need to go to Image>Mode>Greyscale. This technique will work, but it limits your creative options. If you go to Image>Adjustments>Desaturate you get an identical-looking monochrome image, but you can add a hint of colour later to create a cool or warm monochrome shot. Simply removing the colour information is not enough to get a well-balanced monochrome shot. The shadows often aren't black enough and the highlights are grey instead of white. Luckily it's a simple matter to create a striking black-and-white image with a good tonal range. Convert your shot to monochrome. Now go to Image>Adjustments>Levels to open the Levels window. We've split our example image into two sections. On the left you can see the histogram for the image that we desaturated. Note that there isn't much graph information contained in the highlight section. This shows that the monochrome image doesn't have

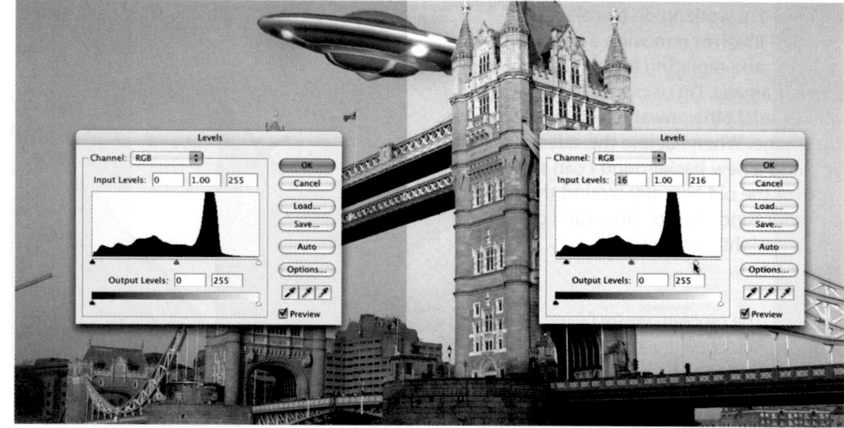

Restore washed out whites and get striking blacks by playing with the Shadow and Highlight sliders in the Levels window

One at a time

Don't overdo the effects

Some of Photoshop's dialog boxes (like the Bevel and Emboss layer style window, or some of the Filter menus) have a great many attributes that you can edit to control the way a tool, filter or layer style behaves. While this is obviously good because you get to enjoy complete control over a setting, it does mean that things quickly stack up. To avoid getting confused and overwhelmed by the amount of editable options available, change one thing at a time and see how that affects your image. This will help you learn what each slider or attribute does and will be far more helpful in the long run.

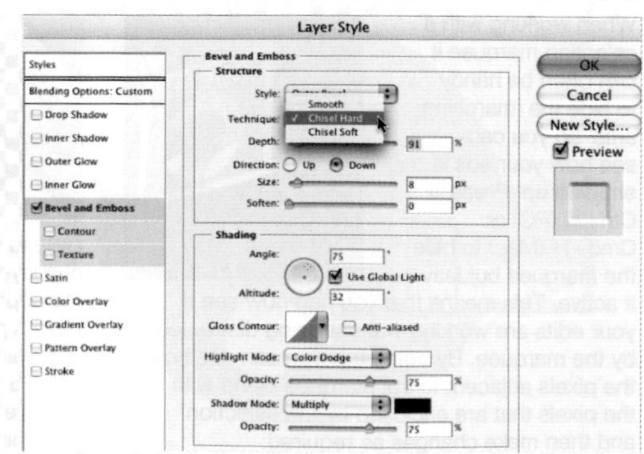

KEYBOARD SHORTCUTS Tool presets

	PC	Mac
Brush tool	B	B
Clone Stamp tool	S	S
Gradient tool	G	G
Blur tool	R	R

bright enough highlights. To sort out this type of problem drag the white highlight slider to the left. This remaps the brightest pixels to a value of 255, which is pure white. Pure black is 0, and you can make the darkest parts of a shot blacker by dragging the black slider towards the right. After a couple of tweaks with the histogram you can soon get a well-balanced shot with black blacks and white whites.

Faking filters

Q I'm a fan of shows like *Top Gear* because of the slick look of the footage. How can I fake the effect of gradient filters and vignettes in Photoshop?
Denise Crawley

A Photoshop has all the tools to re-create the look of in-camera filters. The sky in our original powerboat source image was flat and bland, as you can see from the left half of the screenshot. We tinkered under the bonnet of the Gradient tool and used it to make the sky darker at the top. Here's how you can achieve the same effect.

First of all activate the Gradient tool in the toolbar. Click on the Gradient Editor in the top Options bar and select the Foreground to Transparent preset. Click on the Foreground Color icon in the toolbar. Choose a dark blue, and make sure that it is darker than the blue sky in your source image. Create a new layer in the Layers palette. Select the Linear Gradient option and draw upwards on the new layer to add a gradient to it. All being well, the sky will

You can easily create a dark and moody sky with a little help from the Gradient tool

now darken moodily towards the top of the screen.

You can fake the effect of other filters by changing the gradient type. The Radial Gradient on a Foreground to Transparent setting makes the image go darker around the edges, creating a vignette effect.

Have the last word

Q I'm trying to promote my photography by mailing it to various companies. Have you any tips on making it easier for viewers to find out more about me?
Darren Eldred

A The best way to get a potential employer to associate your work with your good self is to talk to them. How? Well for starters you'll need to have a microphone plugged in. Open the image you want to share and hold down the mouse over the Notes tool icon in the toolbox. You'll get a pop-up menu showing the Audio Annotation tool. Select that tool and click anywhere on the main image. The Audio Annotation box will appear. To record a message for your potential employer click the Start button and start chatting. Press Stop when you're done. You'll notice a little yellow speaker icon is visible on your image. Click this to hear your message!

You have to save a file as a PSD or a TIF. Make sure you tick the Annotations box in the Save Options section. If you save your file as a JPEG the annotation won't be included. To see audio annotations in action, open Audio.tif on the CD. Click on the audio icons to hear the dulcet tones of George Cairns. Because annotations are part of Photoshop's Extras, their little icons won't appear on any prints that are made of your images.

Make yourself heard wherever your image ends up by leaving an audio annotation lurking around the file!

Online Resources

If there's something you want to create in Photoshop but you're not sure of how to go about it, pay a visit to the Photoshop 101 website. In addition to free tutorials, you'll also find a damn fine selection of tips that will help you in your endeavours. Head over to **www.photoshop101.com**

Clashing preferences
Let everyone play nicely

If you run two versions of Photoshop (like CS2 and Elements 4.0 for example), then you might find that CS2 will refuse to open. This is due to a clash of preference file settings. But not to worry, it isn't a permanent hassle. You can solve the problem by holding down Ctrl+Shift+Alt (PC) or Cmd+Shift+Option (Mac) when you open CS2. You'll see a dialog box appear that will ask you if you want to 'Delete the Adobe Photoshop Settings File'. Click the Yes button and the package will open, though you need to be aware that you will lose any of your saved workspaces.

Play it straight
Get in line

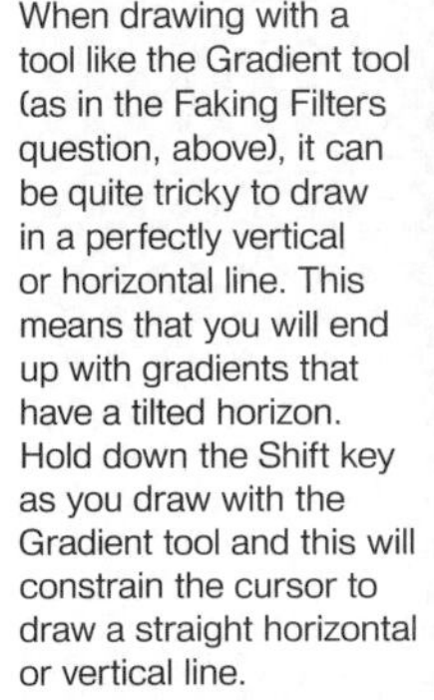

When drawing with a tool like the Gradient tool (as in the Faking Filters question, above), it can be quite tricky to draw in a perfectly vertical or horizontal line. This means that you will end up with gradients that have a tilted horizon. Hold down the Shift key as you draw with the Gradient tool and this will constrain the cursor to draw a straight horizontal or vertical line.

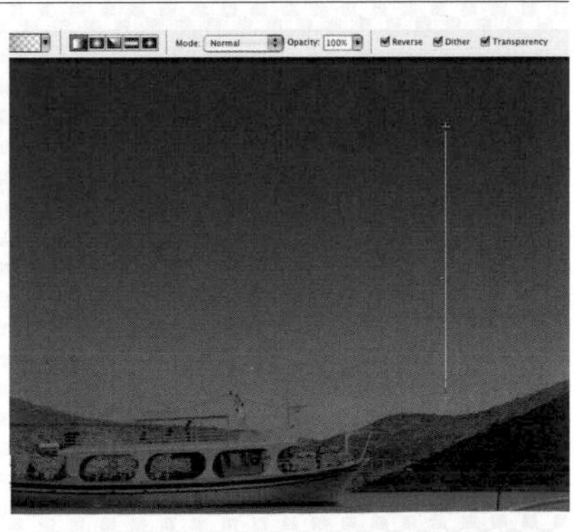

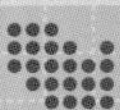

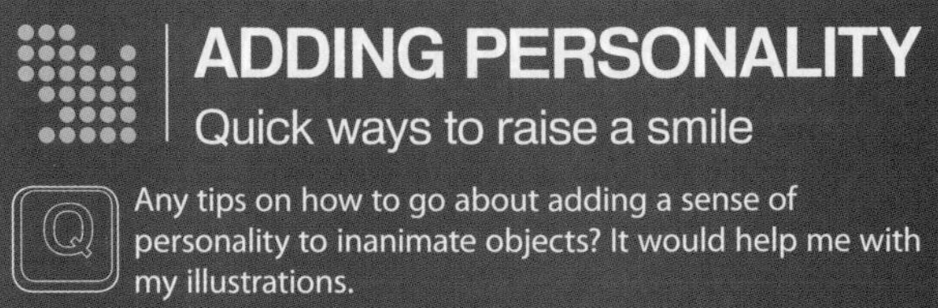

KEYBOARD SHORTCUTS Palettes

	PC	Mac
Show/hide	Shift+Tab	Shift+Tab
Show/hide Brushes	F5	F5
Show/hide Layers	F7	F7
Show/hide Actions	F9	Option+F9

ADDING PERSONALITY
Quick ways to raise a smile

Q Any tips on how to go about adding a sense of personality to inanimate objects? It would help me with my illustrations.
Michael Campbell

A Thanks to Photoshop's pixel-pushing powers it's possible to quickly bring inanimate objects to life. The Liquify filter enables you to keep your image looking photo-real while distorting solid objects to make them smile or frown. Here's how we made this letterbox look happy to collect your mail!

01 Suitable source Open your source image. Choose an object that has the potential to have its existing components converted into a recognisable facial feature, like this letterbox's 'mouth' for example. We shot the letterbox face on to the camera to make our image-editing task easier to perform.

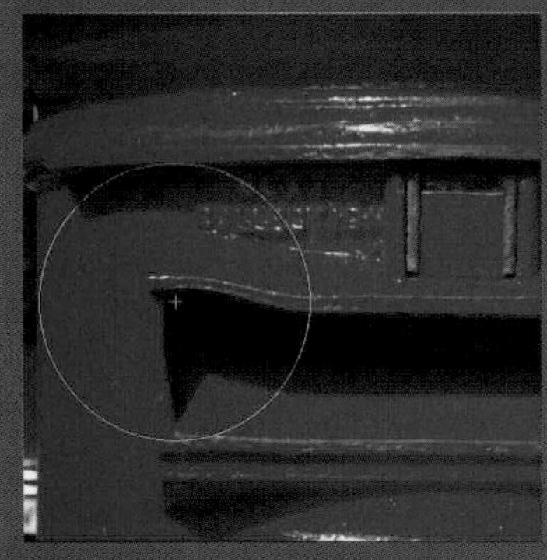

02 Liquify Go to Filter>Liquify. Select the Forward Warp tool from the toolbar (or press W) In the Tool Options pane, make the Brush Size large enough to cover the area you need to manipulate. Reduce the Brush Density so that you need to perform several strokes to move your chosen pixels. This will make the editing more subtle and effective.

03 Smile please Try to restrict your warping to the area with the facial feature (the 'mouth' in this case). Warping other parts of the image will draw attention to the fact that the image has been liquified. If you push things too far use the Reconstruct tool (R) to retrace your steps.

the Warp tool's selection handles were. You can even place the warped Smart Object in an Illustrator or InDesign document and then edit the original Photoshop file at a later date. Any changes you make to the Smart Object's warp will be updated in both the Illustrator and InDesign document.

Protect your copyright

Q I mail images to clients. They know who the image belongs to, but once it's been passed on I have no control over who uses (or abuses) my work. I've tried adding annotations to my files so that people can see who they belong to. However it's easy to miss an annotation if the Extras are turned off (or even deleted). How can I assign copyright to my images?
Martin Eldred

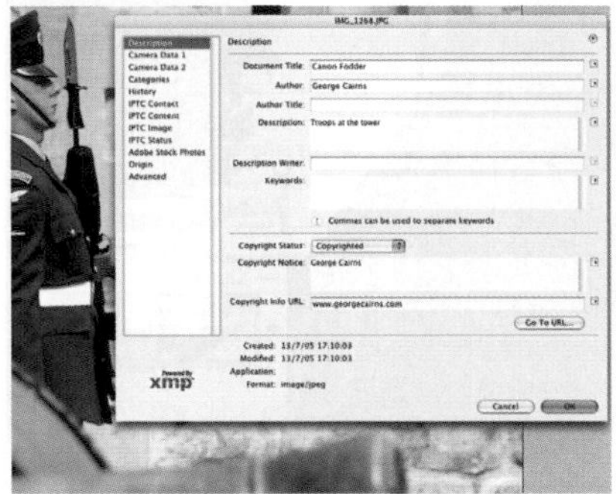

Protect your images from getting lost and misused by assigning copyright to them and adding a URL link

A It's a simple matter to assign copyright to your images by using Adobe's XMP-powered File Info menu. XMP (or Extensible Metadata Platform if you want the full title) is an easy way to assign metadata to any of your Photoshop files. As the data is embedded in the file itself there is no danger of it becoming separated from the image. You can even add a handy URL link to your images so that potential clients can access your site with the click of a button.

Go to File>File Info. In the File Info dialog box select the Description category and click on the Copyright Status pop-up menu. You can change the status of your image from Unknown to Copyrighted. In the box below you can add additional information about the image's copyright status (like limits to how it can be used, for example). There's also a useful Copyright Info URL box. Type your website address in this box and viewers of your image can click on a button to take them straight to your site.

The File Info dialog box can be used to add lots of other handy metadata to your image. In the IPTC Contact section, for example, you can add more information about the photographer who owns the image including work and email addresses. Once you've added your desired copyright and other metadata information, click OK. Now when people view your file they'll see a little © symbol appear by the file's name, prompting them to check out the metadata to see who owns the image content and you'll hopefully avoid any image theft.

Time-saving tip
Recycle your settings

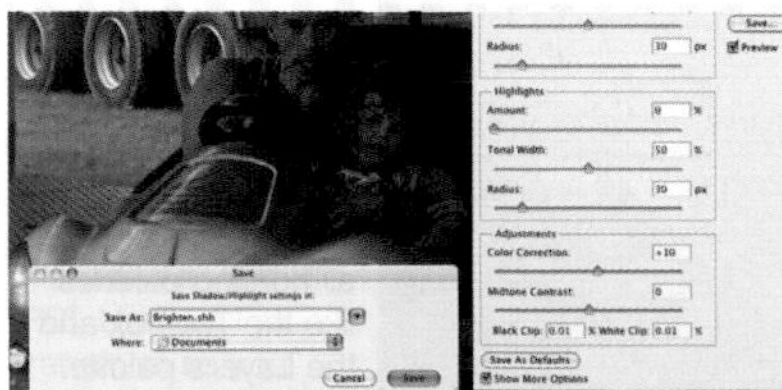

When you perform image-editing tasks like using the Shadow/Highlights menu, you can save your settings for future use, saving you from repeating the same procedures over and over again. Click the Save button. This will enable you to load in the same settings and apply them to a new image.

DVD menu tip
Design for TV screens

TV screens have a lower resolution than a PC monitor, so fiddly serif fonts could buzz or vanish when displayed on a TV screen. When designing a menu in Photoshop remember that the user will be using a remote control from several feet away. Make your fonts big enough to read.

KEYBOARD SHORTCUTS Clipboard

	PC	Mac
Cut	Ctrl+X	Cmd+X
Copy	Ctrl+C	Cmd+C
Copy Merged	Ctrl+Shift+C	Cmd+Shift+C
Paste	Ctrl+V	Cmd+V

Creative cookie cutting

Q: I've just bought Photoshop Elements and am working my way through the different features. I was wondering if you could give me a quick idea about how the Cookie Cutter tool works. I can't see why it would be of any use.
Ron Bellmam

A: The Cookie Cutter tool is unique to Elements 3.0 (though like other Elements tools it could end up being promoted to a future version of Photoshop CS, as we saw in the case of Elements' Healing Brush tool). It works much like Photoshop's Custom Shape tool, but has the added ability to mask out a photo so that it only appears within the shape you select. In our example we chose a comic-book style 'thought bubble' shape from the Options bar and used that to cut away the rest of a source photo. We scaled down the thought bubble and added it to a cat photo to create a frame from a photo-real comic strip. We then added a Bevel layer style to the shape to give it a slightly raised 3D edge.

Use Elements 3.0's Cookie Cutter tool to quickly knock up components for your photo illustrations

Square pixels

Q: I'm using Photoshop to design DVD menus. My menu looks fine on a computer monitor, but when I watch it on my widescreen TV it looks squashed. This is especially noticeable with shapes that should be perfect circles – they become elliptical ovals. How do I get the circle shapes to look identical on both PC and TV screens?
Tania Darwood

A: For a successful menu design you need to be aware of a few differences between computer monitors and TV screens. One important difference is the shape of the pixels. Pixels are the building blocks of colour that make up our onscreen image. A computer monitor's pixels are square. The pixels on a TV screen are rectangles. When your DVD menu is shown on a TV, the square pixels are stretched horizontally to become non-square. This is why perfect Photoshop circles become elliptical when seen on TV.

Photoshop CS2 is designed to help you create images that will display correctly on TV screens. When creating a DVD menu set up the new file so that what you see on your monitor will match what you'll see on a TV screen. Go to File>New. In the Preset pop-up menu scroll down until you find TV screen presets. For content designed to be displayed on a widescreen TV choose Pal D1/DV, Widescreen (with guides). Notice that the Pixel Aspect Ratio changes from Square to 1.422. Photoshop scales the document's square pixels to match the non-square pixels of a TV screen. Because a TV screen has a lower resolution than a computer monitor your Photoshop design will display as such. Create a perfect circle and it will appear to have a jagged edge to it. However it will appear as a perfect circle when you view the design on a widescreen TV. If you want to view your Photoshop DVD menu design at a higher quality setting on your PC, go to Image>Pixel Aspect Ratio>Square. This will make a circle appear to be squashed inwards as the rectangular pixels become squares. Once the squashed circle appears on a widescreen TV the image will be stretched horizontally to turn it back into a perfect circle.

These two circles are the same, but are being previewed using different Pixel Aspect Ratios

Reset tip
Don't cancel a thing

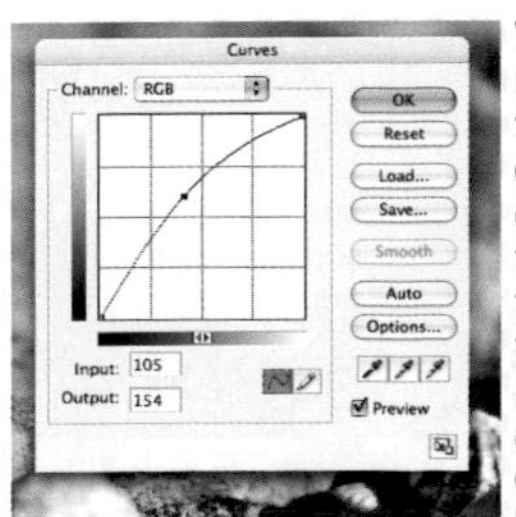

When you're making changes from within a dialog box, it can soon get frustrating having to keep clicking the Cancel button. However, there is a better way. Hold down the Option key (Mac) or the Alt key (PC) and then take a look at the Cancel button. Lo and behold, it's turned to a Reset button. Click this to reset the dialog and pretend nothing ever happened.

Transparency
Change the view

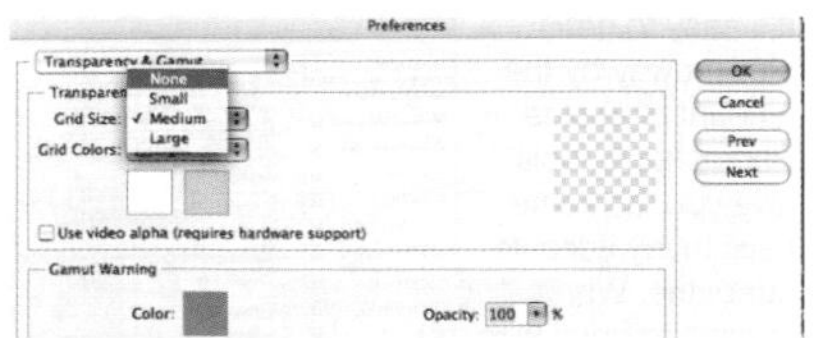

Whenever you create a new layer, a chequered pattern will be placed behind transparent pixels. This can be turned off, though. Mac users need to go to Photoshop>Preferences>Transparency & Gamut. PC users should go to Edit> Preferences>Transparency & Gamut. Once there, turn Grid Size from Medium to None. Now you'll see white instead of chequer.

Tool tip
Lovely labels

If you are unsure about the identity of a particular tool or the name of a brush preset, for example, let the cursor hover over the icon in question. After a second or two, a little label will appear displaying the name of the tool. However, if you find these notes annoying, you can turn them off by visiting Photoshop's General Preferences menu.

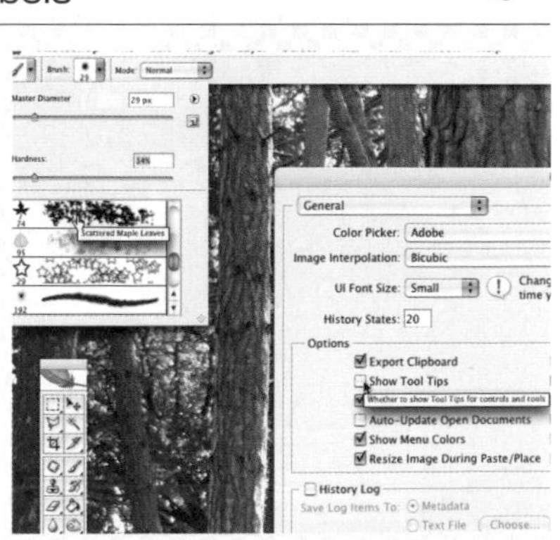

KEYBOARD SHORTCUTS Arrange layers

	PC	Mac
Bring to front	Ctrl+Shift+]	Cmd+Shift+]
Bring forward	Ctrl+]	Cmd+]
Send to back	Ctrl+Shift+[	Cmd+Shift+[
Send backward	Ctrl+[	Cmd+[

FAKING DEPTH OF FIELD EFFECTS

Q I'm not too confident on using my camera's aperture settings to create shots with a shallow depth of field. How can I fake different focal points in an image using Photoshop? Is it even possible?

Patricia Wilson

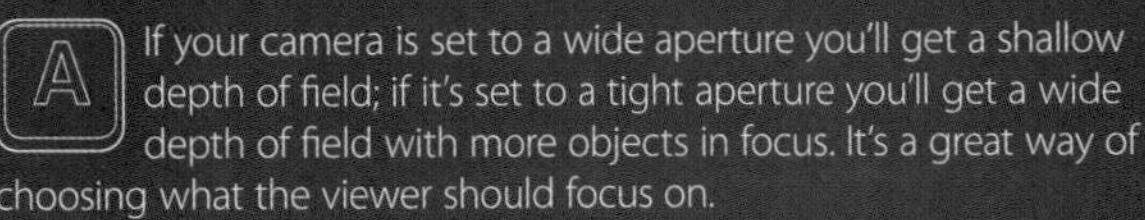

A If your camera is set to a wide aperture you'll get a shallow depth of field; if it's set to a tight aperture you'll get a wide depth of field with more objects in focus. It's a great way of choosing what the viewer should focus on.

01 Duplicate and then blur Start off with a shot that has everything in focus. Ideally it will have objects in the foreground and background. Duplicate the Background layer. Go to Filter>Blur>Gaussian Blur and blur the duplicated layer.

02 Magnetic lasso Hide the blurred 'soft focus' layer for the moment. Target the original layer. Select the Magnetic Lasso tool. Set it to a Feather of 3 pixels. Use the lasso to select the object in the foreground.

03 Add layer mask Turn on the hidden blurred layer, select it and add a layer mask to it. This will use the lasso selection to punch a hole in the foreground layer. You'll now see the blurred foreground object against a sharp background.

Magnetic Lasso is great for quickly selecting objects against a contrasting background, but it's not so hot when it comes to dealing with finer details like fur. Use the Extract Filter instead. This powerful tool is geared up to selecting objects that have hair or fur around their edges. Go to Filter>Extract. Press 'B' to select the Highlighter tool (or click on its icon in the Extract filter's toolbar. Use this brush-based tool to draw around the edge of the animal (or person) you want to isolate. You can increase the brush size using the Tool Options section of the menu, or use the left and right square bracket keys to increase brush size interactively via the keyboard.

Alternatively turn on the Smart Highlighting option. This causes the brush size to increase or decrease automatically as you draw round the edge of your furry subject. The Smart Highlighting option also makes the Highlighter tool behave like the Magnetic Lasso, causing it to stick to the edge of your subject as you draw around it. Make sure that all the hairs are selected as you draw and you'll soon end up with a green line outline around your pet. Once you've draw round your subject, select the Fill tool and click once inside the green outline. This will fill the selection with a purple colour, telling Photoshop which part of the image you want to keep.

Use the Extract filter to make sure you don't harm a single hair on your subject's head when making a selection.

To see how your selection is shaping up, hit Preview. The filter will go to work and show you the selected object against a transparent background. It's unlikely that the Highlighter tool will have made a perfect selection first time round, so reach for the Cleanup tool. This makes the mask around the subject transparent, so it's handy to remove parts of the unwanted background that remain visible. It works in a similar way to painting a black brush on a layer mask. You can change the pressure of the Cleanup tool by using the number keys. Hold down the Alt key (PC) or Option key (Mac) to make the Cleanup tool restore missing pixels. Another handy tool is the Edge Touchup tool. This is especially useful when restoring detail to wispy areas of hair and fur that have been masked. Once you've tidied up your mask press OK and the tool will remove the unwanted background.

In synch?

Q I've just bought the whole Creative Suite and although I haven't had it very long I can tell that I'm going

Blending modes

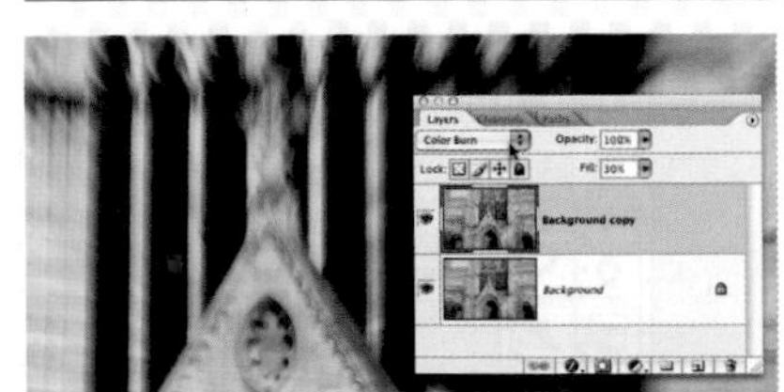

Experiment with blending modes by cycling through them. A quick way of doing this on a PC is to click on the blending mode icon in the Layers palette and use the Up and Down arrow keys to change them. Mac users need to hold down Shift and press the + or – keys.

Help yourself

It's there for you...

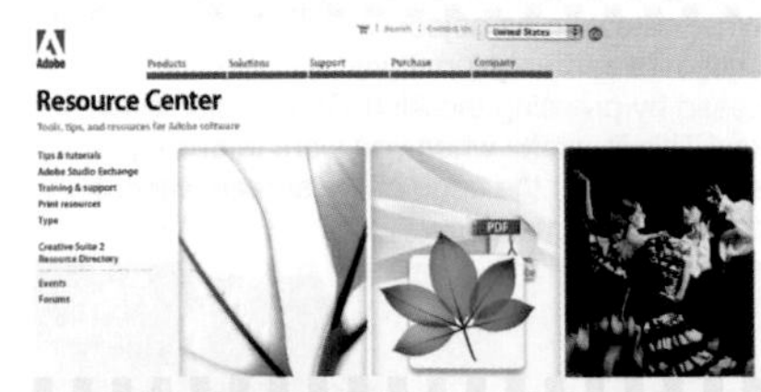

If you hit a creative or technical brick wall, ask for help. Each version of Photoshop has a comprehensive HTML database. Go to Help>Photoshop Help. Type in keywords to find assistance with your problem. There's even a link to tips in Adobe's Resource Center.

KEYBOARD SHORTCUTS Reopen dialog box

	PC	Mac
Levels with last setting	Ctrl+Alt+L	Cmd+Option+L
Curves with last setting	Ctrl+Alt+M	Cmd+Option+M
Color Balance with last setting	Ctrl+Alt+B	Cmd+Option+B
Hue/Saturation with last setting	Ctrl+Alt+U	Cmd+Option+U

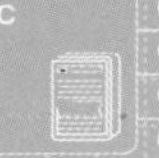

to be jumping between all the applications. How can I make sure that my colour profiles are the same in each application?
Max Carstairs

A: CS2 has been carefully designed to make all of the separate applications work together seamlessly. However it's not unusual for people to assign different colour profiles to different applications (or you may be using a shared machine in an office, making it hard to tell which application has been assigned to a particular profile). You can see which colour profile Photoshop is using by going to Edit>Color Settings. The Settings pull-down menu will give you a list of colour profile options, like Europe General Purpose 2 (which is a profile suitable for general print and screen work in Europe).

To find out if your CS applications share the same colour profile, open Adobe Bridge. Bridge is well named as it enables you to link Illustrator, Photoshop and InDesign together. You can use it to force all the Creative Suite applications to share the same colour profile, making colour handling consistent in each package. In Bridge go to Edit>Creative Suite Color Settings. The icon at the top of the Suite Color Settings dialog box will tell you if the applications in the Creative Suite are synchronised for consistent colour. If they are not, choose a suitable profile from the list of options and click Apply. The icon will change, indicating that Creative Suite is now synchronised and will handle colours consistently in each application. Just make sure that Photoshop's Color Settings dialog box

Synchronise all of your Creative Suite applications' colour profiles in an instant using Adobe Bridge's Creative Suite Color Settings dialog box

is closed before attempting to use Bridge to synch the colour profiles.

Helpful histograms?

Q: Are histograms actually of any use? How can I use them to improve any of my images?
Joe Murphy

A: Histograms are fantastic tools. They are as useful to image editors as x-rays are to doctors. A histogram gives you a visual diagnosis as to the 'health' of your picture by illustrating if your picture has a full tonal range. True blacks have a value of 0 and true whites have a value of 255. You can see if an image is over or under-exposed by looking at the way pixels are distributed

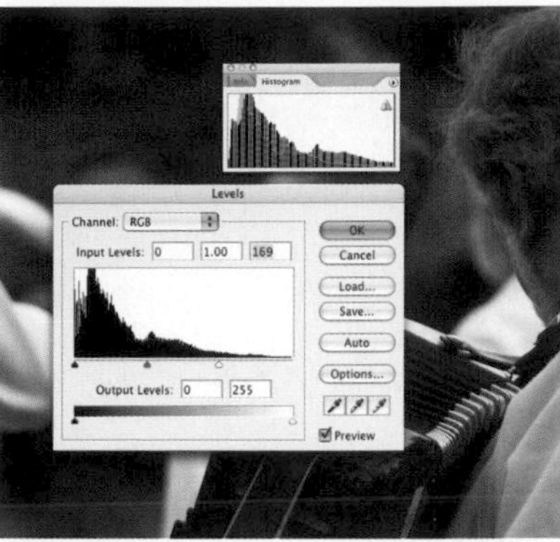

Histograms are a quick way of seeing where the problem with your images lie

across the histogram's length. Get into the habit of having the Histogram window open when you view images in Photoshop (Window>Histogram). A healthy image should have a histogram with pixels that run all the way along. The far left of the histogram shows pixels that are in the shadows. The middle of the histogram indicates the midtone pixels. The right of the histogram indicates pixels in the image's highlight range. Our example image was very under-exposed, so the initial histogram displayed more information for the shadows and midtones. There was hardly any information for the highlights. We fixed the image by going to Image>Adjustments>Levels. By dragging the white Level Input slider to the left (to 169) we re-mapped the image's lighter pixels to an Output value of 255. This brightened up the image, adding detail to the highlights without washing out the black levels.

If it feels like your Photoshop is working against you, visit the Photoshop Support site at **www.photoshopsupport.com/faq.html** for answers to queries.

To the point
Create arrowheads

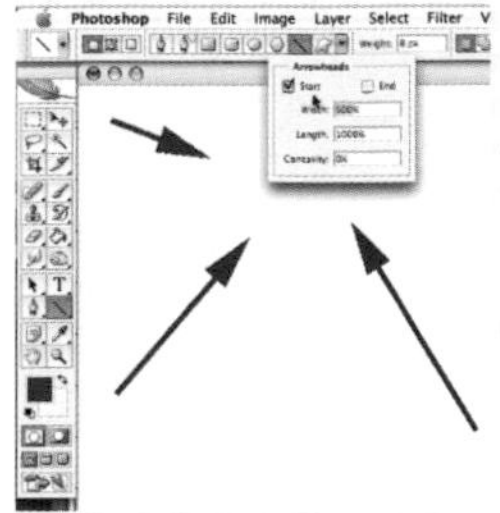

You might think that Photoshop can't create arrowheads on the end of lines, but you're wrong. It bloody can! Go to the Shape tools in the toolbar and pick the Line tool. In the Options bar, click the down-facing arrow and you'll see a dialog where you can click a checkbox to add the elusive arrowheads to your lines. You can even set how big they should be.

Back in time
Unerase edits

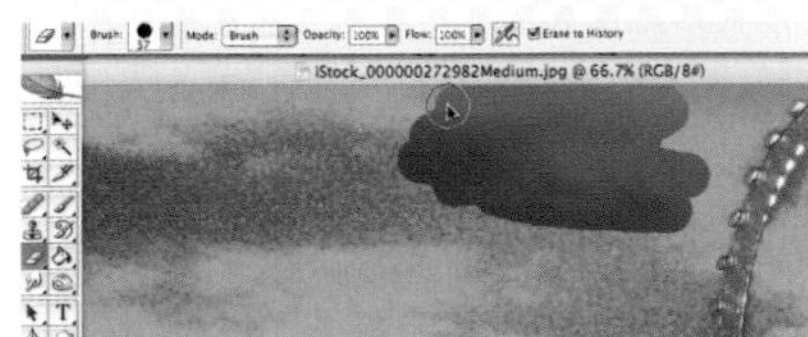

It's possible to use the History brush as a way of undoing an edit and reverting back to how an image looked before you started editing. You can do the same with the Eraser tool. Click on it and then look at the top Options bar. Check the box marked Erase to History. Instead of erasing to the background colour, the Eraser will now erase back to the original state of the image.

Curve tip
Don't guess colours

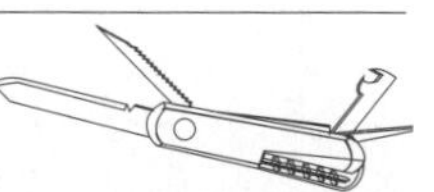

Curves are excellent for controlling the colours of an image, but how do you know where a precise colour 'lives' on the curve? It's easy – open up the Curves dialog and then Command-click (Mac) or Control-click (PC) on the colour in your image. Photoshop will then add a point on the curve which represents the colour you've just clicked on.

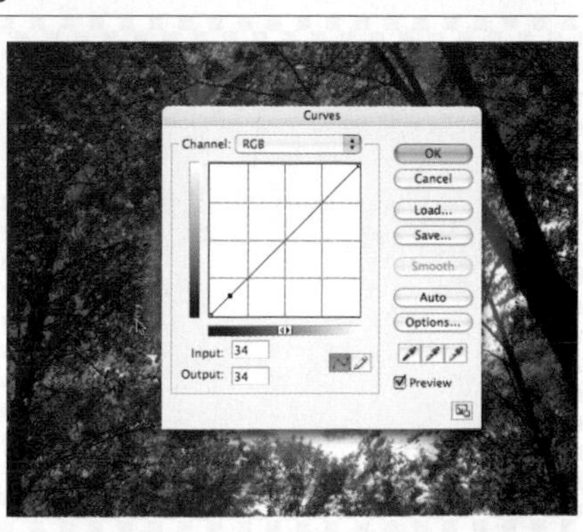

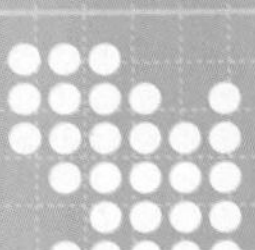

Q+A

Let us sort out your image-editing quandaries

IT'S A G-G-G-GHOST!

Haunting layer mask techniques

Q I've been experimenting with getting a ghost effect by taking a picture of a person in front of a background, then taking a photo of the background on its own and mixing the two shots together in Photoshop. However the finished result looks too clean and unconvincing. Any tips?
Dillon McPherson

A Photoshop is great for faking ghosties and ghoulies. We can augment the semi-transparent mix you mention with a layer mask and a filter to break up the ghost's layer and create a more spooky effect. Cue the *Ghostbusters* theme tune…

01 Shoot it The starting point for faking ghostly happenings is to lock the camera on a tripod and take two shots; one with the 'ghost' and one without. Set your camera to Manual exposure and focus to keep the background looking identical in both shots.

02 Mix it Place the two shots together in Photoshop. Call the shot with the figure in it 'A'. Call the background shot 'B'. Reduce the Opacity setting of shot A to 60%. This will make the background show through. This effect has been used since photography began.

03 Mask it To give the effect a unique Photoshop spin, add a layer mask to the 'ghost' layer. Target the mask and choose Filter>Render Clouds. Then choose Image>Adjustments> Equalize. This will poke misty holes in the 'ghost' layer making it look even more ephemeral.

In perspective

Q My question concerns perspective control. How do I adjust the perspective of a tall building to stop the verticals converging? In the days of film and prior to Photoshop, a photographer would have to go out and buy/hire a perspective control lens or purchase a very expensive plate camera. There is a correct and incorrect way to do it, and I was shown the correct method at a lecture I attended – but then quickly forgot! I look forward to any help you might give me.
Malcolm Lewin

Adjust a picture's pixels using a variety of techniques to correct a tall building's converging verticals

A When you shoot a tall building from below, you have to tilt up your camera to get the top of the building in shot. The building's vertical lines then converge towards a distant vanishing point. This is not necessarily a bad thing, because the converging lines can help increase the shot's sense of depth. However, if you want to display a building more faithfully you can straighten those tilting verticals in a variety of ways.

Before Photoshop was around to save the day (yes, there were indeed such dark and terrible times), photographers could avoid the problem of converging verticals by using a shift lens. This rotating wide-angle lens enabled you to shoot the building without tilting the camera upwards, thereby avoiding the converging vertical phenomenon.

Luckily we can correct our vertically-challenged building shots in the digital realm, saving us the expense and hassle of fiddling around with complicated hardware. We'll show you two ways to correct a problem shot. The first will work in any version of Photoshop. Open your photo (we worked with the picture that Malcolm sent us), and Press F to edit in Full Screen mode. This gives you a grey work area around the shot and hides any desktop clutter. Double-click the image's thumbnail in the Layers palette to unlock it. Go to Edit> Transform>Perspective (or in Elements go to Image>Transform>Perspective.) A bounding box will appear around the edge of the shot. At the corners of the box you'll spot little selection handles. Click on the top-left corner handle and drag it to the left. The right-hand corner handle will move in the opposite direction, stretching the top of the picture and making it wider at the top than the bottom. Keep dragging the handle until the sides of the building are running parallel with the edge of the frame. Hit Return to apply the changes. You might

Quick colour casts

One click is all it takes

Photoshop boasts plenty of tools to help remove colour casts caused by incorrect White balance settings on your camera, such as the Photo Filter. A lesser-known but highly effective one-click technique is lurking in the Levels dialog. Pick the Set White Point eyedropper and click on a tinted object that should be white. Photoshop will remove the colour tint instantly. Elements 4.0's new Remove Color Cast tool works in a similar way.

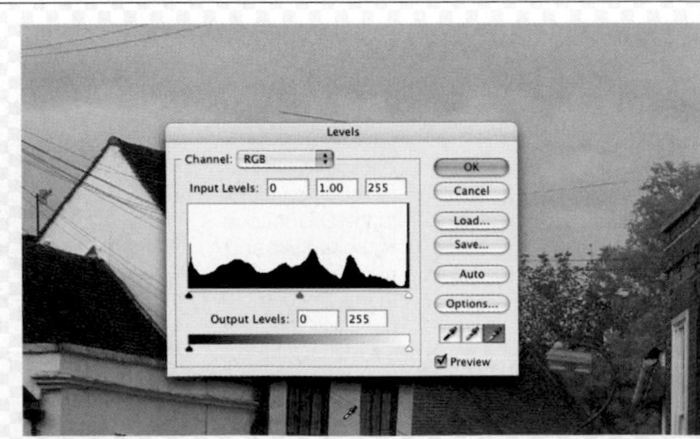

KEYBOARD SHORTCUTS Painting keys

	PC	Mac
Increase brush size	]	]
Decrease brush size	[	[
Paint or edit in straight lines	Click, Shift-click	Click, Shift-click
Erase to History	Alt+drag	Option+drag

need to go to Edit>Transform>Rotate to tweak the shot a little to get its verticals truly vertical. However, widening the top of the building to make it match the width at the bottom might cause it to look squashed. If this occurs, press Ctrl+T (PC) or Apple+T (Mac) to bring up the Free Transform tool. Use the middle selection handle at the top of the bounding box to stretch the photo's pixels upwards to restore the building to its full height.

If you're using CS2, Adobe has created a posh front-end that does a very similar job. Go to Filter>Distort>Lens Correction. This opens up the Lens Correction filter's interface, and there you'll find a Transform section. Two sliders allow you to adjust either Vertical or Horizontal perspective. To straighten out Malcolm's picture, we set the Vertical Perspective slider to -30. We also used the Angle wheel to rotate the shot a little, and slid the Scale slider to 111% to hide transparent edges that appeared at the bottom of the shot. The advantage in using the Lens Correction filter is that it has the Perspective, Scale and Rotate transformation tools under one roof.

Transform by numbers

Q I use the Transform tool to rotate layer content, and like that you can drag the tool's central origin point to make the transformed layer pivot around any point. I want to be precise about the position of the pivot, so I can rotate multiple layers from the same point. Do you have any suggestions?
Paul Crosswell

A The key to precise transformations is located in the Options bar. Press Ctrl+T (PC) or Apple+T (Mac) to activate the Free Transform tool. The tool will automatically offer to transform the layer's content from a central reference point. As Paul rightly says, you can drag that reference point to any location in the Transformation bounding box and rotate the layer content around the point's new location.

For more precise transformations, you need to do things by numbers. Near the left of the Options bar you'll see an X and a Y box. These contain the reference point's location coordinates. X defines the reference point's horizontal position and Y defines its vertical position. By typing values into the X and Y boxes you can relocate the reference point with numerical accuracy.

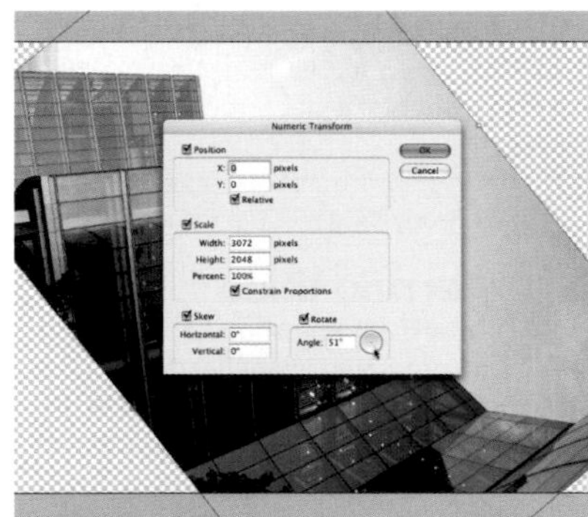

Use numbers and the X and Y axes to get some extremely accurate object rotation

Performance tip
Time for a purge

When unleashing some of Photoshop's pixel-pushing filters, the package gets hungry and hogs as much of your PC's processing power as it can get. To stop the Filter Progress bar chugging onwards, free up as much RAM as possible by going to Edit>Purge>All. This removes data floating around in the clipboard and empties the lists' History states, enabling Photoshop to focus entirely on applying your chosen filter.

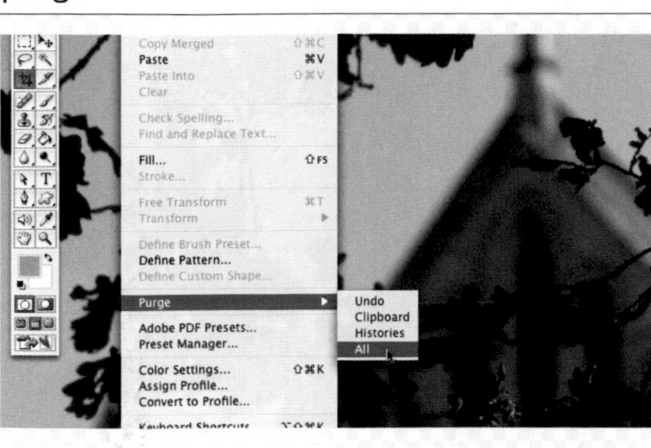

LIGHT BEAMS
Create 'god-rays' with gradients

Q Is there an easy way to create multiple beams of lights radiating from a light source such as the sun? I want to fake the effect of beams of light being broken up by tree branches.
Morris Henderson

A Directors like Ridley Scott are forever flooding their sets with smoke particles so they can capture beams of light that add texture and a sense of magic to a scene. With a quick rummage in the Gradient Editor, we can come up with a suitable digital equivalent of this attractive effect.

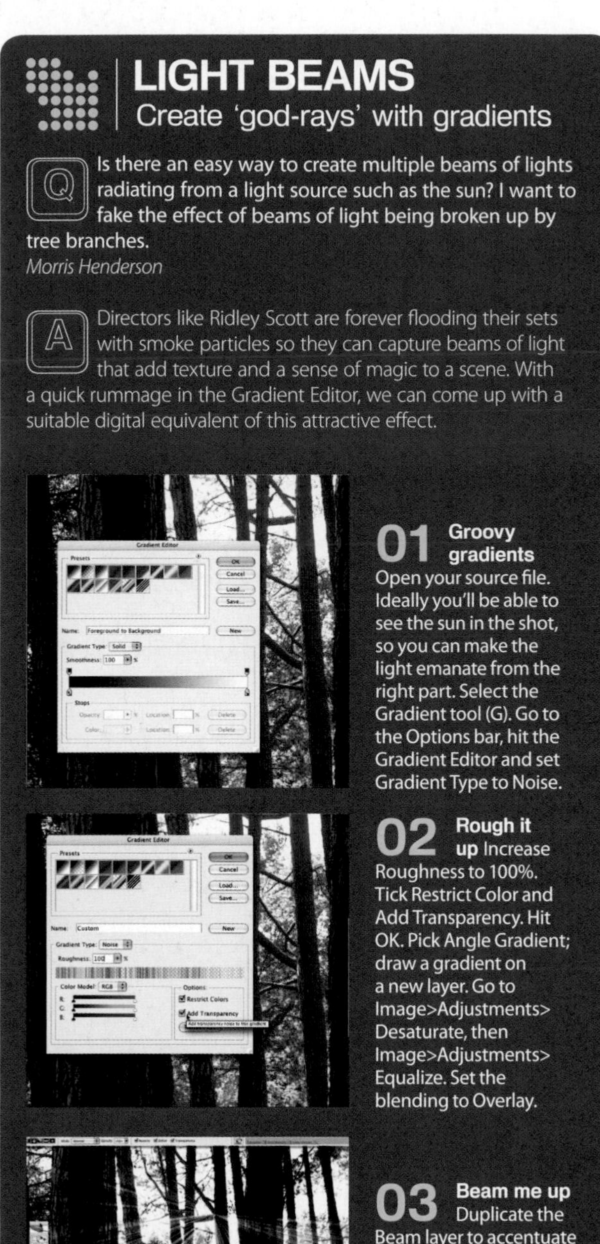

01 Groovy gradients Open your source file. Ideally you'll be able to see the sun in the shot, so you can make the light emanate from the right part. Select the Gradient tool (G). Go to the Options bar, hit the Gradient Editor and set Gradient Type to Noise.

02 Rough it up Increase Roughness to 100%. Tick Restrict Color and Add Transparency. Hit OK. Pick Angle Gradient; draw a gradient on a new layer. Go to Image>Adjustments> Desaturate, then Image>Adjustments> Equalize. Set the blending to Overlay.

03 Beam me up Duplicate the Beam layer to accentuate it. Use the Gradient Editor to restore the Gradient tool to a foreground to background gradient. Add a layer mask to each Beam layer. Draw a radial gradient on each mask, and the beams will fade out at their edges.

KEYBOARD SHORTCUTS Swift selections

	PC	Mac
Draw straight lines	Alt-click with Lasso tool	Option-click with Lasso tool
Add to selection outline	Shift+drag	Shift+drag
Hide extras	Ctrl+H	Apple+H
Reapply last filter	Ctrl+F	Apple+F

DIGITAL DELUGE

Kick up a storm

Q I'm trying to fake the effect of a person striding through a storm. Obviously this would be too tricky to shoot for real, so how can I alter a shot taken on a sunny day and make it look like something from *Wuthering Heights*?

Amy Malting

A Thanks to a combination of several Photoshop filters and some clever layer blending techniques, we can turn on the taps and give our subjects a soaking without the need to turn brollies inside out or give our friends and family pneumonia!

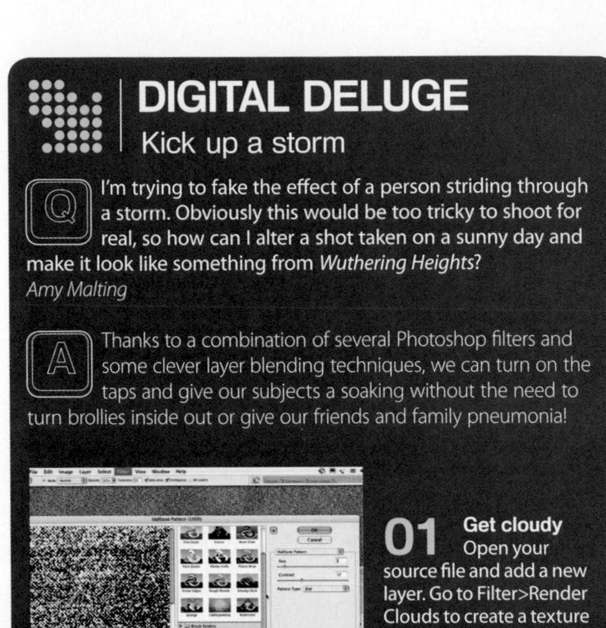

01 Get cloudy Open your source file and add a new layer. Go to Filter>Render Clouds to create a texture for the rain. Now go to Filter>Noise and set a value of 120. To add clumpier chunks of noise go to Filter>Halftone Pattern. Set Size to 2, Contrast to 17 and Pattern Type to Dot.

02 When it rains... To create sheets of driving rain go to Filter>Blur>Motion Blur. Set an Angle of 41. Set Distance to 107. To increase contrast go to Image>Adjustment> Equalize. Duplicate the Rain layer and apply Filter>Distort>Ripple to buffet the rain with wind. Set the first Rain layer's blending mode to Screen.

03 Cool things down Set the rippled Rain layer's blending mode to Overlay. Reduce the Opacity of the Rain layers to 20% to make the effect subtler. Create an overcast look via Image>Adjustments> Color Balance. Drag the Yellow/Blue slider towards the blue.

If number crunching isn't your thing, check out the little grid to the left of the X and Y boxes. This consists of nine boxes, each representing a position in the Transform tool's bounding box. Click on a box to turn it black. The Transform tool's reference point will jump to the appropriate position in the work area.

You can also use the Options bar to rotate your entire layer in precise increments. This is handy if you're creating multiple frames in an animation for example, and want to make an object rotate smoothly. An alternative (and easier) way to rotate a layer with numerical accuracy is hidden inside ImageReady. Click on the Edit in ImageReady icon at the bottom of the Toolbox. Now go to Edit>Transform>Numeric. This will open a dialog box that lets you rotate an object by dragging a little wheel or typing values into the Rotate box. The Numeric dialog box also contains boxes for you to control all the Transform values that live in the Options bar in an easier-to-use interface. You won't find the Numeric transformation box in Photoshop itself, so it's well worth making a sideways trip into ImageReady for easier transformations.

Terrific titles

Now that Photoshop CS2 has incorporated ImageReady's Animation palette into the main Photoshop interface, I use it to create title sequences for my home movies. I'm doing a spooky short and want to make the letters in the credits pulse with an eerie glow. Is there an easy way to create this animated effect?

Create an X Files-style animated title sequence for your videos by animating Photoshop's Layer Styles

Tim Dale

The fact that Photoshop CS2 can animate your files and output them to an attached camcorder is a very exciting development for video makers. As well as animating the position of an object on a layer, Photoshop can also animate a layer style. For glowing ghoulish text, first go to File>New. In the New dialog box go to Presets and choose a TV resolution preset such as PAL D1/DV, 720 x 576 (with guides). This will make sure your text fits a standard TV screen. Click OK to create a blank document. The blue guides are very handy, as they define the safe area of a TV screen.

Edit>Fill the background layer with black. Set Foreground Color to White. Select the Horizontal Type tool (T) from the Toolbox. Choose a suitable font (we went for Herculanum) and set the size to 72. Type in your chosen text.

Hide guides

When you don't need the Extra help

In the 'Terrific titles' question above, we talk about using Photoshop's blue guides to help create a title sequence. These guides are part of Photoshop's set of Extras, meaning they are there to help you with your design but they won't print out. If they distract you from your work or you want to see a clean version of the image simply press Ctrl/Apple+H.

Preference tip

Apart from the Zoom tool's magnifying glass, you can add another zooming option to your repertoire by going to Edit>Preferences> General (Photoshop> Preferences>General on a Mac) and then ticking Zoom With Scroll Wheel.

KEYBOARD SHORTCUTS Colour commands

	PC	Mac
Fill with foreground colour	Alt+backspace	Option+backspace
Fill with background colour	Ctrl+backspace	Apple+backspace
Reset default colours	D	D
Swap foreground and background colours	X	X

Go to Window>Animation to activate the Animation palette. This will contain a thumbnail of frame 1 showing the present state of the Layers palette. Go to the Add a Layer Style icon at the bottom of the Layers palette and click on the Outer Glow option. Change the colour of the glow from a default yellow to a ghostly green. Click OK to apply the Layer Style.

Now click on the Duplicates Current Frame icon at the bottom of the Animation palette. Double-click on the Outer Glow effects icon in the Layers palette to edit the text's glow attributes. Set the Spread to 20% and increase the Size to 49% to make the text glow with a vivid green. Click OK to apply the changes for frame 2. Target frame 2 in the Animation palette and click on the Tweens Animation Frames icon at the bottom of that palette. In the Tween dialog box tick the Effects parameter. Set it to Tween With Previous Frame. Add 12 Frames. Play back the animation and the glow will gently fade up around the text.

To make the glow pulse in a loop, select frame 14. Click on the Tweens Animation Frames icon and set to Tween With First Frame. The glow will now fade up and down in a loop that will cycle forever, enabling you to export it to a camcorder and then edit into a program using packages like Adobe Premiere or iMovie.

Perfect patterns

Q **I'm interested in using Photoshop to design wallpaper to liven up my PC. Is there a good source of patterns you can suggest? I've explored all the patterns available in the Pattern Overlay section of the Layer Blending Modes window. Are there any others hidden away?**
Crawford Templar

A Because patterns are designed to tile, they will fill any size or shape document you have open. A good way to get to know the patterns available is to create a selection using a Marquee tool. Then go to Edit>Fill and choose the Pattern option in the Fill dialog box. There's a Custom Pattern icon you can click on, containing a variety of default patterns. Click on the little arrow to get a pop-up menu that allows you to load in themed patterns such as Artists Surfaces or Nature Patterns. If you have CS2 there's another source of patterns hidden away. Click on the Edit in ImageReady icon at the bottom of the Toolbox to open your document in ImageReady. Pop across to the Layers palette and click on the Add a Layer Style icon. Choose Pattern Overlay. This style works the same as the Photoshop version, but is packed with dozens of new patterns. You'll be able to wallow in pattern heaven, apply your pattern to the open document and then return to Photoshop to continue editing your design.

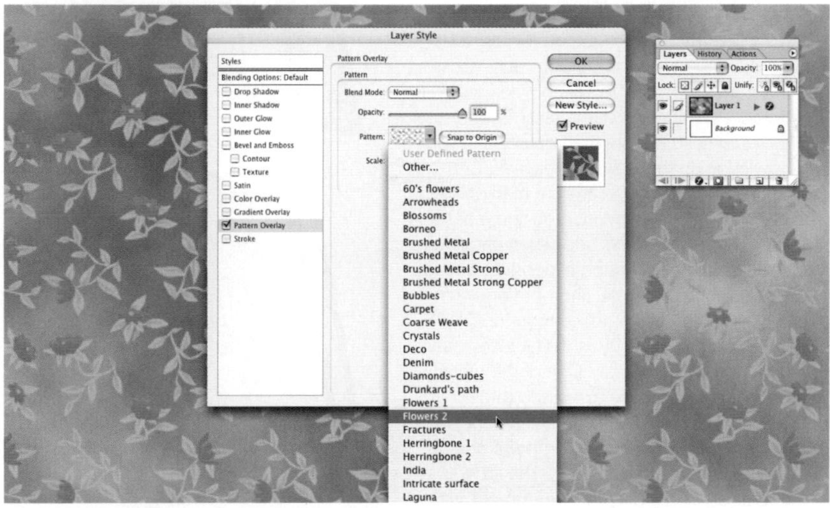

Pillage ImageReady's secret stash of patterns to create graphical content in seconds

If you are having problems hunting down the perfect photo or texture, make sure you pay a visit online. There are a host of sites offering free goodies – just do a search for 'free textures' or 'free stock photos' and Bob's your uncle!

Fine-tune selections
Adding a bit of polish

Making selections using the Marquee tools can be a fiddly business. Once you've made a selection you can move it around using the Move tool. Alternatively, move the marquee on a pixel-by-pixel basis using the arrow keys. To change the Feather value of a selection after you've drawn a marquee, right-click on it to get a pop-up menu. Choose Feather from the list of options.

Cool cropping
A few tricks of the trade

If you want to crop a shot but keep it at the same aspect ratio as all your other pictures, press F to go to Full Screen mode. This will give you a grey border around the image. Press C to activate the Crop tool and select the whole image. Then hold down Shift to constrain the aspect ratio of the Crop tool's marquee while you crop out the unwanted elements at the edge of the shot.

Creative Vision

A beautifully presented book that encourages you to be adventurous with your photographic creations and break all the rules

This book is a showcase of the endless possibilities open to you when experimenting with photographs. Catering for both those who are familiar with more traditional photographic methods and also digital image creation, *Creative Vision* provides a revealing insight into very unusual techniques. Experimentation and breaking the rules are encouraged throughout, making it a refreshing book to read. Sections such as 'Don't think, just shoot' go against the traditional methods of photography and inspire you to think outside the box. Author Jeremy Webb is a freelance photographer, digital artist and tutor in photography, so is more than qualified to share his knowledge on the subject. Webb refers to the way Photoshop can be used to manipulate photos and features information on some of the best plug-ins available. The book even encourages you to break away from using expensive cameras and equipment all the time, and opt for junk shop or toy cameras to produce more novel effects. Do not fret though, as digital techniques are still featured prominently. One of the many lessons is that a lot can be expressed through the photographic image. This is particularly evident in the chapter on images that comment on complex or controversial subjects. The artwork is extraordinary and a definite strength of the book; not the type of photography you will see very often. So if you want some more obscure suggestions for how to take your photography to the next level, you will find it within the pages of this marvellous book.

info

AUTHOR
Jeremy Webb

PRICE
£24.95

PUBLISHER
AVA Publishing

ISBN
2-88479-072-1

Picture is paramount Large images are essential to accentuate the beauty of such ground-breaking and expressive work.

Abundance of colour Learn how to use exciting techniques such as this one which was created by trapping paint between slides and then scanning it into Photoshop.

OPEN YOUR MIND

Get inventive with your Photoshop software

Learn from mistakes The book features ways to replicate supposed faults in photographs to create interesting effects.

Ray of light The key concepts of light are covered in detail, including how to get the most out of your light source and also using light to paint with.

Show off your work Presentation of work is as important as the image itself and the different methods are covered in detail, including exhibitions.

In summary One handy feature is the summaries at the end of each chapter. This helps you check that you have grasped the key concepts.

No need for a camera One interesting part of the book is the section on the cameraless photo art called Photograms.

Image

A compact guide that will both inspire and inform

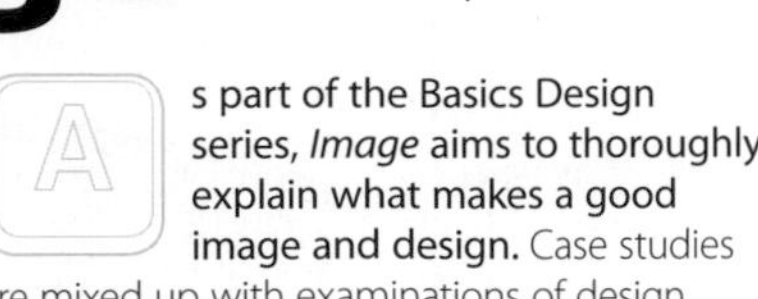

As part of the Basics Design series, *Image* aims to thoroughly explain what makes a good image and design. Case studies are mixed up with examinations of design theories, making it a very entertaining read. Alongside ogling the design examples, you will broaden your knowledge using the valuable techniques that give plenty of ideas for what to try in your own work. The chapters cover a wide range of styles, from fashion design to film poster, so there's lots on offer. But it's not just eye candy – there's plenty of practical advice for presenting your images in the best way to get them noticed. If you are a newcomer to design, *Image* is the perfect resource for learning how to introduce more innovative methods into your work to make it more exciting and cutting-edge. Even if you have an extensive grounding in design, you'll still learn something new from this book. This little gem proves that pictures do speak louder than words.

info

AUTHORS
Gavin Ambrose and Paul Harris

PRICE
£14.95

PUBLISHER
AVA Publishing

ISBN
2-88479-065-9

Not just pretty pictures With plenty of stunning artwork balanced by informative text, you have the best of both worlds.

MAKE THE IMAGE COUNT

Get the most from images

Inventive images The photomontage and collage sections are bursting with great ideas for overlaying multiple images and elements.

Variations As colour is such a major part of images, the book shows lots of experimentation with variations in both effect and hue.

Eye candy Of course we value the informative elements of the book, but it is great fun to marvel at the photography and illustration.

Exceptional examples Even the more complex terms such as juxtaposition are explained effectively and illustrated beautifully.

Adobe Photoshop CS2 A-Z

An ideal resource for succinct answers to your Photoshop function and tool queries

info

AUTHOR
Philip Andrews

PRICE
£16.99

PUBLISHER
Focal Press

ISBN
0-240-52002-5

Looking for a concise reference book for CS2? This title is the one to go for. Examining all of the features in the latest outing of Photoshop in a handy A-Z format, it is an easy to read and helpful book. A particularly useful aspect is the feature summary that lists the menu where different functions can be found. The before and after images illustrate the result of various processes within Photoshop and step-by-step instructions present the information in a clear way. Perhaps not ideal if you want an extensive or in-depth explanation, but for a concise overview this book is perfect. The Pro's Tips scattered throughout are useful for elaborating on what is written in the main text. Whether you are a beginner or an advanced user, you will find the A-Z format a handy way of getting quick answers to your queries. Although it may seem like it is not covering each area in great detail, when you look closer you realise that it is. For example, when talking about layers the book has a dedicated section to each aspect (such as Layer Styles, Layer Masks and Layer Sets). The main strength of this book is its ability to summarise the main features and leave out all the pointless information. No CD is provided but for the type of manual this is, it is not necessary.

How to Cheat in Photoshop (Third Edition)

Caplin's book presents lots of information in a light-hearted manner

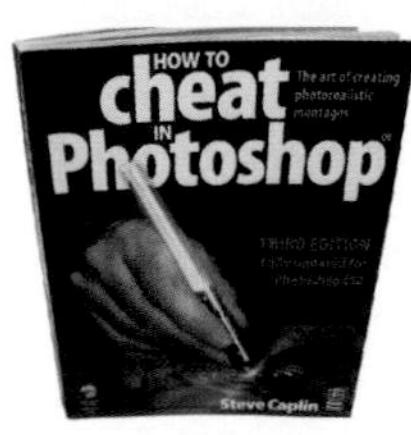

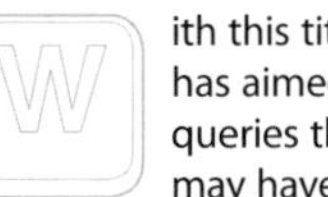

With this title, author Steve Caplin has aimed to answer everyday queries that Photoshop users may have. The book mainly features step-by-step instructions to help you achieve more realistic-looking effects in your manipulated photographs, such as vanishing points or shadow and highlights. In addition to telling you how to create effects on existing photographs, it contains sections on how to create realistic images from scratch. Examples of particularly useful features include ageing photographs authentically and adding depth to flat images. The book includes a CD so you can work through the tutorials using all the same images as Caplin, making it easier to check if you are on the right track. The CD also contains royalty-free images to use in your own projects, and there are 20 video tutorial files that are a really effective way of reinforcing the written explanations. Compared to numerous books containing large blocks of text, this is presented in a much friendlier format that places the focus on having fun with Photoshop.

info

AUTHOR
Steve Caplin

PRICE
£24.99

PUBLISHER
Focal Press

ISBN
0-240-51985-X

Colour

A proper understanding of colour will improve your designs

There's an excellent book called *Black and White*, which suggested that colour isn't always best. This book begs to differ! *Colour* is part of the Basics Design series (as was the aforementioned *Black and White*, along with an equally good title called *Image*). Having read all three, it's easy to see that this series really does broaden your understanding of the main areas in creative design, and will result in a profound improvement in your work.

Colour explores both the meaning of colour and how to use it correctly in design. Some of the colour theory covered includes the way light works and emotional reactions to colour, emphasising just how integral colour is in design. A section is dedicated to each individual colour for in-depth coverage of the topic. Examples from contemporary designers illustrate points succinctly and aid the discussions.

Printing techniques are also not ignored, including unusual ink combinations for maximum impact. *Colour* utilises case studies to great effect, combining them with technical explanations and core facts about colour. The clear layout of all the book makes it simple to follow, and being so well structured, it's easy to gain vast amounts of info.

Beginners and experts alike will enjoy this book, which stretches from basic terminology to colour manipulation. Each topic is divided into manageable chunks and includes an introductory section covering the main concepts to be discussed. The book succeeds in covering all aspects of colour, at the same time demonstrating its ability to enhance an image dramatically when used correctly.

info

AUTHORS
Gavin Ambrose and Paul Harris

PRICE
£14.95

PUBLISHER
AVA Publishing

ISBN
2-88479-066-7

Vibrant cutting-edge design As expected from the title, this book is packed with artwork where designers have utilised bold colours to great effect.

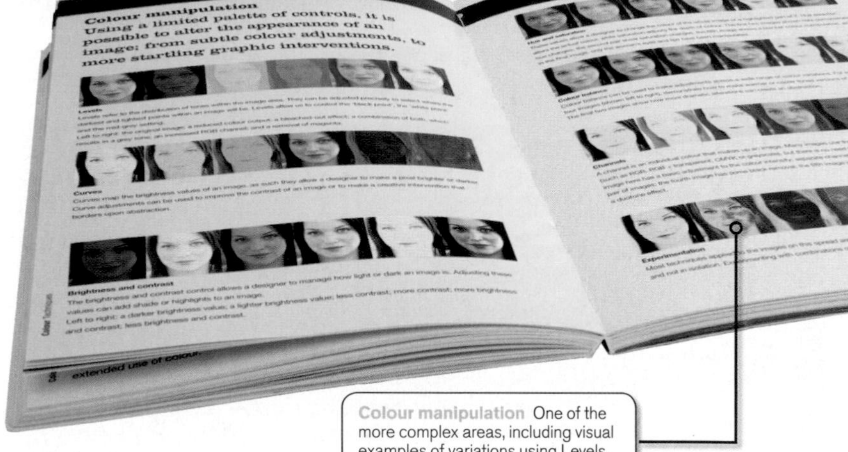

Colour manipulation One of the more complex areas, including visual examples of variations using Levels, Curves, Color Balance and more.

A BLAZE OF COLOUR

Find out how to bring your work to life with vibrant colours

Individual colour studies The book focuses on each colour individually to describe the connotations of each.

Specialist techniques Techniques such as overprinting, created by printing one element of a design over another, may interest more adventurous users.

Colour systems The info on RGB and CMYK helps you realise the importance of choosing the correct colour system for your usage.

Visualise the colour Colour theory is illustrated using the colour wheel and annotations, helping you understand the relationship between colours..

The perfect combination This guide shows how colours from various places on the wheel complement each other.

Digital Travel Photography

What makes a good shot an exceptional shot?

info

AUTHOR

Duncan Evans

PRICE

£16.95

PUBLISHER

AVA Publishing

ISBN

2-88479-082-9

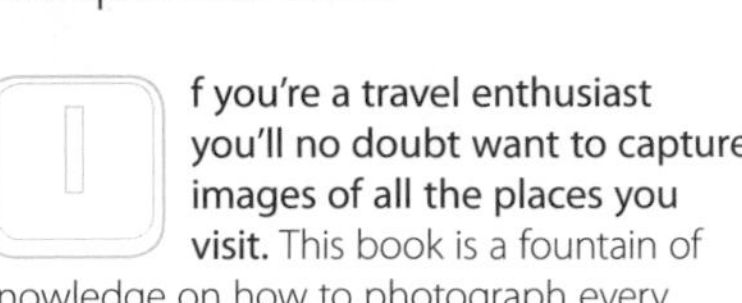

If you're a travel enthusiast you'll no doubt want to capture images of all the places you visit. This book is a fountain of knowledge on how to photograph every element of your travels, in all conditions. A particularly challenging subject is action events, but the chapter devoted to this will help you get great results. Another popular subject to photograph when on holiday is animals, and there's a chapter for this too. *Digital Travel Photography* shows the best way to get great close-ups, even underwater! All the techniques can be adapted to other areas of digital photography, and Photoshop makes a regular appearance. Most of the attention is drawn to the powerful images, with just the right amount of screen grabs and instruction – making this both a visually and intellectually stimulating book.

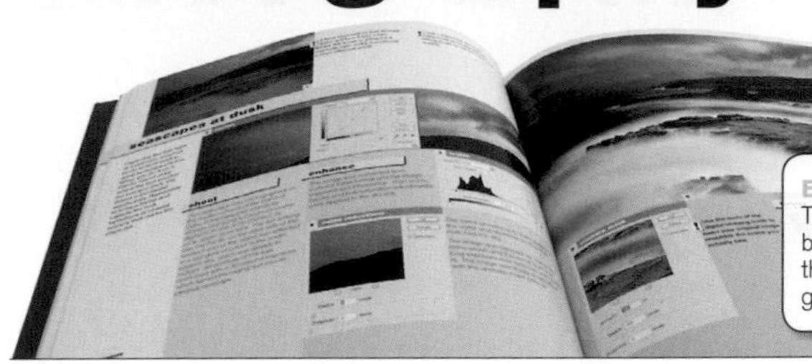

Enhance areas of landscapes The Curves feature of Photoshop has been used to bring beautiful colour to the sky and enhance the photograph, giving it a fantastical feel.

EXPERT TIPS AND TECHNIQUES

Your guide to fantastic photography

Capture all the action Follow the tips on the best way to shoot, and then enhance your photographs for dramatic shots like this.

Interior excellence Not all travel photography involves landscapes. People often want to capture astounding architecture and interiors.

Colourful creations We all want our photos to be eye-catching. With the help of a little Photoshop magic, vibrant and energetic shots are easy!

Powerful people shots When photographing the characters you meet on your travels, it's essential to also capture their traditions and culture.

The Future of Memories

info

AUTHOR

Dan Howard

PRICE

£24.99

PUBLISHER

Peachpit Press

ISBN

0-321-38399-0

Look beneath the surface and add a deeper meaning to your photography

This book not only explores the technical side of digital photography, but discusses the inspiration behind it. Heavily family-based and featuring photos of the author's wife and children, it's predominantly aimed at the home photographer. Just because you take a visually appealing shot, it doesn't mean it has significance or carries a message. This is what Dan Howard tries to convey, and from the way he writes and presents his work it's clear he has a passion for the subject. The activities and processes described are not out of reach of the home user or novice Photoshop user. Although the meaning behind images is emphasised, *The Future of Memories* doesn't ignore technical subjects such as lighting, scale, contrast and composition, and all stages of the creative process are covered. The book also details things to avoid when printing and sharing photos in order to achieve professional-looking output. There are so many ways to store and present images, it's really useful to have them laid out and fully explained. Common mistakes in digital photography occur in their composition, so doubts are cleared up with explanations and guidelines on shooting and framing everything from people to landscapes. All digital photographers will benefit from being able to enhance their work, and give it mood and meaning.

Nature

A specialist subject, but you could adapt these techniques to many other areas of design work

info

AUTHOR

Adrian Davies

PRICE

£16.99

PUBLISHER

Rotovision

ISBN

2-88046-780-2

***Nature* is the fifth book in the Digital Photographer's Handbook series.** The entire process of nature photography is covered, from creative techniques in shooting images to the best ways to output them. One section focuses on image processing, and Photoshop and Elements are discussed in detail. Info is provided on areas of the program best suited to enhancing nature photographs, but a lot of the skills can be implemented in many areas of design work and image manipulation. Common areas of nature photography are covered, such as close-up shots or animals in their habitats. However, although most nature photography occurs outdoors, the book also covers the occasions when it's only possible to shoot in a studio. A large intro section discusses types of digicam and their settings, lenses and accessories. If you're trying to make the transition from traditional nature photography into digital photography, you'll find the pages on digital images and workflow very useful. *Nature* is such a predominant area of photography that a book like this is essential.

Black and White

Packed with ways to achieve understated and beautiful black-and-white photographs

Colour isn't always best. An image can be just as powerful – sometimes more so –when it's taken in black and white. This book reinforces this to those who've forgotten the influence black-and-white photography can have in a design world that's often abundant with colour. Suitable for anyone new to this area of digital photography as well as those wanting to extend their skills, this book shows you how to push black-and-white photography to its limits.

Following recent trends in design and advertising, *Black and White* also features an interesting case study on Silhouette. Simply admiring the beautiful images will make you want to get out there and start putting the techniques into practice. Using large, impressive images, this book is highly artistically and creatively oriented.

From the selection of different types of images, Michael Freeman tries to illustrate that details in a photo can be better appreciated in monochrome. The techniques covered aren't limited to basic concepts of black-and-white images, but also converting colour to greyscale, applying effects using Photoshop, and printing and displaying your work. Also mentioned are plug-ins such as Mystical Tint, Tone and Color produced by Auto FX Software, which allow you to get even more from your image. Another very effective technique covered is hand colouring black-and-white images in Photoshop – including selective colouring, where just one element of a monochrome image is coloured and sometimes produces an even greater impact.

Many areas of this book are quite in-depth and it will delight photography enthusiasts.

info

AUTHOR
Michael Freeman

PRICE
£17.95

PUBLISHER
Ilex

ISBN
1-904705-57-X

All stages of the workflow Even the latter stages involved in producing exceptional digital monochrome images are covered, such as the best type of printer and paper to use.

Extreme contrast Case studies such as this one on silhouette, aim to show examples of the different ways that black and white can be used.

MAKE THE MOST OF MONOCHROME

Discover how black and white can work for you

In-depth discussion The book suggests various ways to approach looking at the tonal areas of your image, such as the Zone System.

Confidence with colour Don't forget colour completely. When converting to black and white, it's vital to understand colour basics and how to judge colours.

Suitable plug-ins A vast range of plug-ins is available to enhance black-and-white photography and create effects, such as adding age.

Tackling challenging areas The entire range of Photoshop's extensive features is covered, including how to get the most from the Channels.

Concepts of colour conversion The best techniques and things to avoid when converting colour images into black and white are all covered.

Adobe Photoshop CS2 One-Click Wow!

Why make design more challenging than it needs to be?

This book is a little bit different to most of the books we review here. Rather than investigating a certain Photoshop style or technique, it acts as a catalogue for the presets found on the accompanying CD. As you may have gathered from the title of the book, these allow you to achieve effects in just one click, which is great for creative sorts who are pressed for time. There is a vast range of presets on the CD for transforming text, graphics and photos. But the ones we liked the best were the Tool presets that enable you to turn an ordinary photo into different media. In addition to showing you what's on the CD, the book also demonstrates how to combine presets for even more choices.

info

AUTHOR
Jack Davis

PRICE
£21.99

PUBLISHER
Adobe Press (in association with Peachpit Press)

ISBN
0-321-24644-6

Includes Tool presets and Texture styles The brush presets (such as the Art History brush presets) save you time creating your own and can be reused to create a range of effects.

ONE-CLICK WONDER

Create that special look the quick and easy way

Simply install and you're away The professional appearance of the layer styles on the CD is impressive, and they're all easy to install.

Plentiful patterns With well over 150 patterns thrown in, you'll find that you have more than enough for all your creative projects.

Easily explained Tutorials in the book explain how to install the presets and styles, and then apply and customise them to suit your work.

Graphic presets The styles are not simply limited to photographs. There are also plenty to apply to text as well as graphics.

Photoshop CS/CS2 Breakthroughs

Succinct and sensible solutions to all your Photoshop problems

info

AUTHORS
David Blatner and Conrad Chavez

PRICE
£17.99

PUBLISHER
Peachpit

ISBN
0-321-33410-8

For quick, easy answers to difficult queries, look no further than this title. David Blatner and Conrad Chavez have tackled common problems Photoshop users encounter and skills they'd like to acquire, and compiled them into a manual of not too scary a size. Not only is it ideal for solving image-wrangling problems, but it's also a source of inspiration, suggesting techniques you may not have considered. Split into manageable sections, this book leaves no area uncovered. It's suitable for all levels of ability, tackling topics ranging from Photoshop essentials to keeping colour consistent. The to-the-point approach saves wading through pages of text to find a simple solution. The entire workflow process is covered, all the way through to the right way to print and export your images – and hundreds of solutions to common Photoshop dilemmas are offered. The layout makes it an approachable read, balancing text with visuals and handy hints. The question and answer format is ideal for covering the main areas of Photoshop, while also suggesting hypothetical situations where you may encounter them. Longer descriptions and examples are provided for more complicated topics, but the book mostly sticks to the principle that if something can be explained in a paragraph rather than a page, then why not do it?

500 More Digital Photography Hints, Tips and Techniques

Enjoyable to browse through while increasing your digital photography expertise

Keen digital photographers will enjoy this book, which is packed with hundreds of techniques to improve your digital photos. And it doesn't forget to mention Photoshop throughout. The glossy pages and vast amount of images make it a great handbook, and each tip is brief but informative. If you need ideas, simply dip into it at any point. You don't have to be a skilled photographer – it aims to widen your knowledge so you can get the most from your digicam. Techniques covered include correcting lens problems, shooting in poor weather and shooting panoramas. The basics of digital photography are explained and its advantages over traditional methods, plus terms you'll encounter when printing images. Author Philip Andrews is a pro photographer, and shares his knowledge in a highly accessible format. The tips are categorised into sections, and the book covers enhancing images using computer apps and correct printing methods.

info

AUTHOR
Philip Andrews

PRICE
£12.99

PUBLISHER
RotoVision

ISBN
2-88046-831-0

RESOURCES

Excellent tutorial sites to increase your quest for image-editing nirvana

ARTWORLD

www.artworld.si

Although this site is not limited just to Photoshop, there is a still a vast collection of over 70 tutorials dedicated to our favourite image editor. And it's not just step-by-step tutorials here – there's also a healthy selection of video tutorials. Another great thing about the site is that it features tutorials from renowned illustrators describing how they created their masterpieces. The tutorials cover the whole gamut of Photoshop, from the more specialist features such as Photomerge, to useful subjects such as managing your workspace. ArtWorld is also bursting with reviews and information on how to use Photoshop plug-ins. What more could you ask for? Well, take a look at the news for the latest happenings in the creative world and also beautiful works of art from the photographic and digital sectors in the gallery.

PHOTOSHOP LOVER

www.pslover.com

This site is a must-see if you are looking for a plentiful list of tutorials and resources on Photoshop. Most importantly this is a very diverse collection of tutorials containing hints, tips and tricks from professional graphic artists. Aiming to provide a collection of links to tutorials from all over the web, this site covers areas such as Text Effects, Colours and Special Effects. So rather than trawl through numerous sites trying to find exactly what you are looking for, let Photoshop Lover save you time by doing the searching for you.

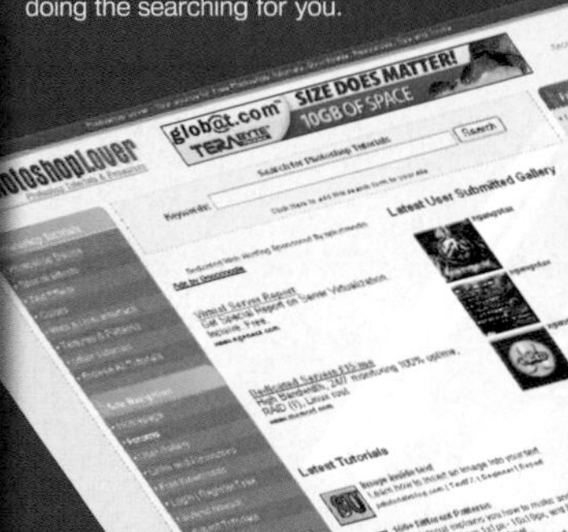

VISUAL DESIGN CORE

www.visualdesigncore.com

The tutorials listed here are more suitable for those wanting to explore the abstract design possibilities within Photoshop such as creating clouds, flowing waves or using custom light brushes. The site's Visual Core Design Forum even caters for those wanting to discuss anything design related and gives the opportunity for people to show off their amazing artwork in the Art Showcase. If you have any tutorials you wish to share you can submit them to the Visual Resources section of the forum.

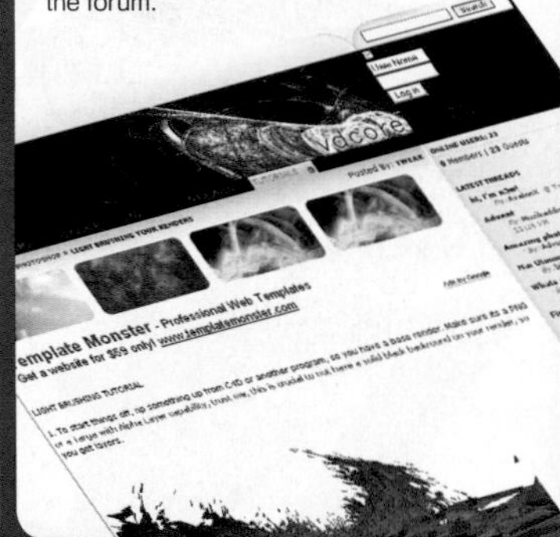

BIORUST

www.biorust.com

With some great Photoshop tutorials, this is an enjoyable interactive design resource to use. The tutorials pack in a lot of detail, with striking visuals in the gallery as an added bonus. For a more specialised list of tutorials that will have you producing realistic results, this is perfect. Plus, this site has the ideal combination of forums, galleries and tutorials. In addition to all of this Biorust has a Graphic Resources Download Centre where you can get your hands on fonts, brushes and gradients. We've included some of this content on this issue's disc.

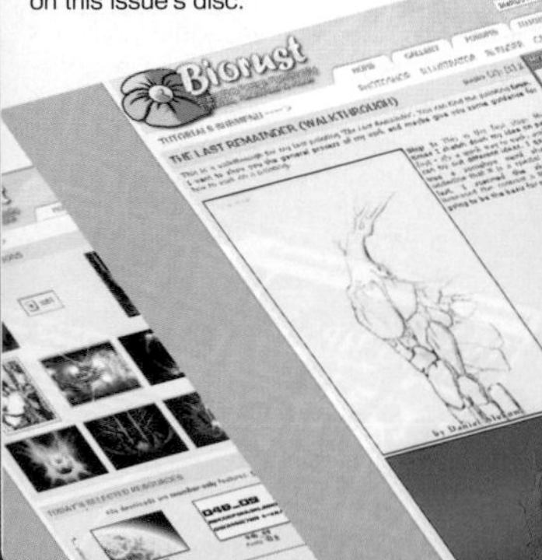

GRAPHIC ADDICTS

www.graphicaddicts.net

Graphic Addicts is essentially an art community site featuring tutorials that are not exclusively Photoshop related. However, it still does contain a considerable amount of very helpful information on the program. A couple of fairly specialised ones may not be suitable for everyone (such as how to add elf ears to a photograph) but on the whole you will find a lot of useful information and techniques listed here. Another very useful aspect of this site is the list of tutorial source files, which can be found in the Downloads section. By downloading these you can work on the same image as is featured in the tutorials. If you're feeling competitive you could even take part in a graphic battle in which artists are invited to submit their work and then visitors to the site decide which piece they like best.

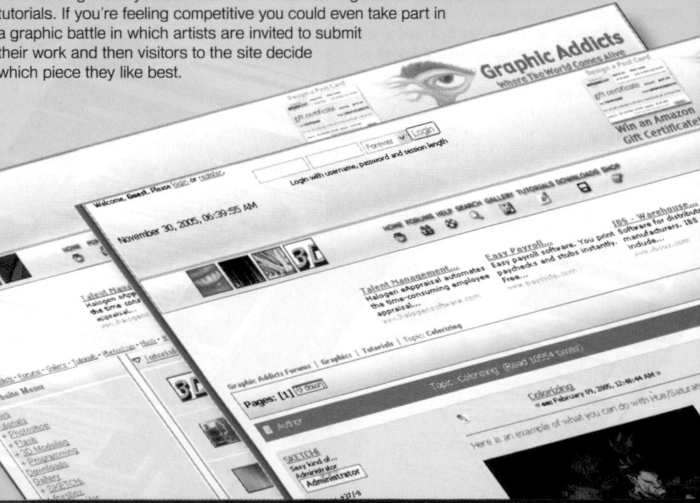

PIXEL2LIFE

www.pixel2life.com

This site is dedicated solely to tutorials and has 7,293 in the Photoshop section alone! Split into sub-categories, you can read about subjects such as Photography Tips, Pixel Art and Printed Media. Whatever you want to learn, you really are spoilt for choice, as Pixel2Life scours the web to bring you the best (and sometimes the most random) tutorials from a range of sites. It even covers the many possibilities available using Photoshop for internet-based projects. You really need to visit the site yourself to understand just how immense the list of tutorials is!

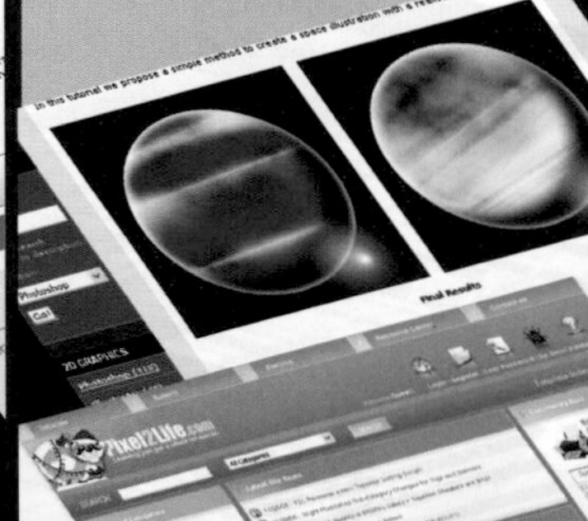

DESIGNS BY MARK

www.designsbymark.com

Designs by Mark is full of written and QuickTime Photoshop tutorials to help get you up to speed with the program. The written tutorials are in a downloadable format, which makes it easier for you to refer to as and when you need. However, the video tutorial section is the main strength of this site and provides an array of lessons on Photoshop. Of course, the great thing about video tutorials is that you can see exactly what someone is doing, which makes them an excellent learning tool. There's also a helpful collection of tips, the newest one concentrating on bringing focus to the foreground in photographs by creating more depth of field. The lessons are aimed at people of various Photoshop abilities, and the subjects range from texture and text effects to retouching photographs. Mark has kindly allowed us to include some of his video tutorials on this issue's disc, so use them now!

VOIDIX

www.voidix.com

This great site is divided up into Beginner, Intermediate and Advanced areas and features numerous tutorials dedicated to Photoshop. Topics include text effects, special effects and interface effects. Some of the tutorials seem a bit random (such as creating a Walkman) but the techniques covered will help you in other designs. For those who are new to Photoshop, Beginner's Corner is ideal for learning the software's tools. Alongside the tutorials there are images, forums and products. This site is excellent if you're interested in interactive uses for Photoshop, and is particularly useful if you want to create graphics and then use them in other programs such as Flash.

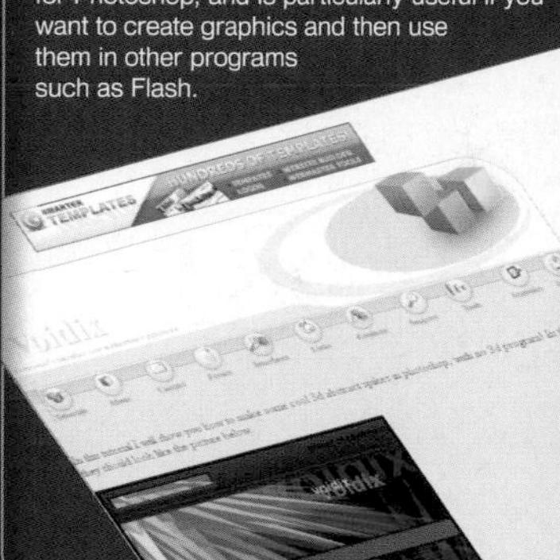

ENTHEOS

www.entheosweb.com/photoshop/

Entheos contains a delicious bevy of tutorials to create some interesting effects, including rain and torn paper. There are also more general tutorials focusing on areas such as collages and retouching photographs. The really nice thing about this site is the content isn't just limited to graphic design, because there are many handy web design tips if you are interested in creating interactive work in Photoshop. Particularly relevant are the tutorials on designing and slicing a web layout. There are plenty of design ideas you can try in your own artwork and there are also lessons dedicated to other computer software if you want to increase your knowledge even further.

EYE DIGITAL EMOTION

www.idigitalemotion.com

Learn how to create a whole range of stunning artwork relatively easily with the help of this site. Containing tutorials for Photoshop 7, CS and also ImageReady, the site covers a range of topics including airbrushing, photo manipulation and background creation. Instead of using small images to illustrate each of the steps, the tutorials contain links to separate pages showing you an enlarged image of each step, making it much easier to see exactly what you need to do.

NEW TUTORIALS

www.newtutorials.com

The New Tutorials website is split into Photoshop basics, photo manipulations, textures, backgrounds, web graphics and text effects. There are particularly interesting tutorials on areas such as photo sketch effects and creating night vision. The most popular tutorials have their own dedicated section, which you may wish to work your way through and look for design ideas to use in future projects. Rather than focusing on random tasks, useful techniques are covered, such as blending styles and colour masking. Don't neglect the section labelled 'Other' as more intriguing techniques can be found here, including how to create some heavenly wings or colour a pencil sketch. And if you fancy going for a retro look, be sure to check out the pixel art tutorial in the beginners' section.

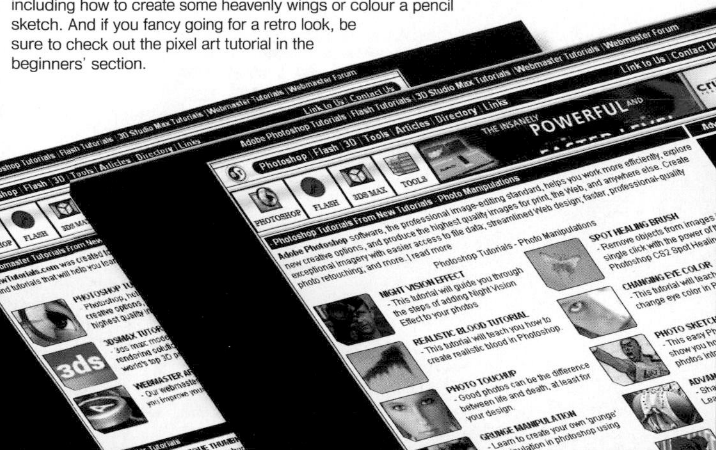

PHOTOSHOP WIRE

www.photoshopwire.tripod.com

Photoshop Wire has searched the internet for the best tutorials and brought them all together. There is a great catalogue of tutorial groups to choose from where you are bound to find the answer to your query. The topics include Animation and Interactive work, Photoshop Elements, Colour Correction, Layers and Channels, Photo Retouching and Scanning Techniques. What more could you ask for? In addition to this, Photoshop Wire lists great plug-ins available to download and even more tutorials to choose from.

On the CD

Stock photos, tutorial resource files, extra elements – discover exactly what's on your free CD

PC

Load the CD

Microsoft Windows
We support Windows XP unless otherwise stated.

The CD-ROM should autorun once placed into your disc drive. If not, follow the instructions below.

1. Browse to 'My Computer'.
2. Right-click on your CD drive and select 'Open' from the drop-down list.
3. Read the readme.txt if there's one present to find out which files you need to launch to run the interface.

Mac

Apple Macintosh
We support OS X 10.3 and higher unless otherwise stated.

This CD-ROM interface will NOT autorun when placed into your CD drive. Instead…

1. Double-click the CD icon on your Desktop.
2. Read the readme file if there's one present to find out which file you need to launch in order to run the interface.

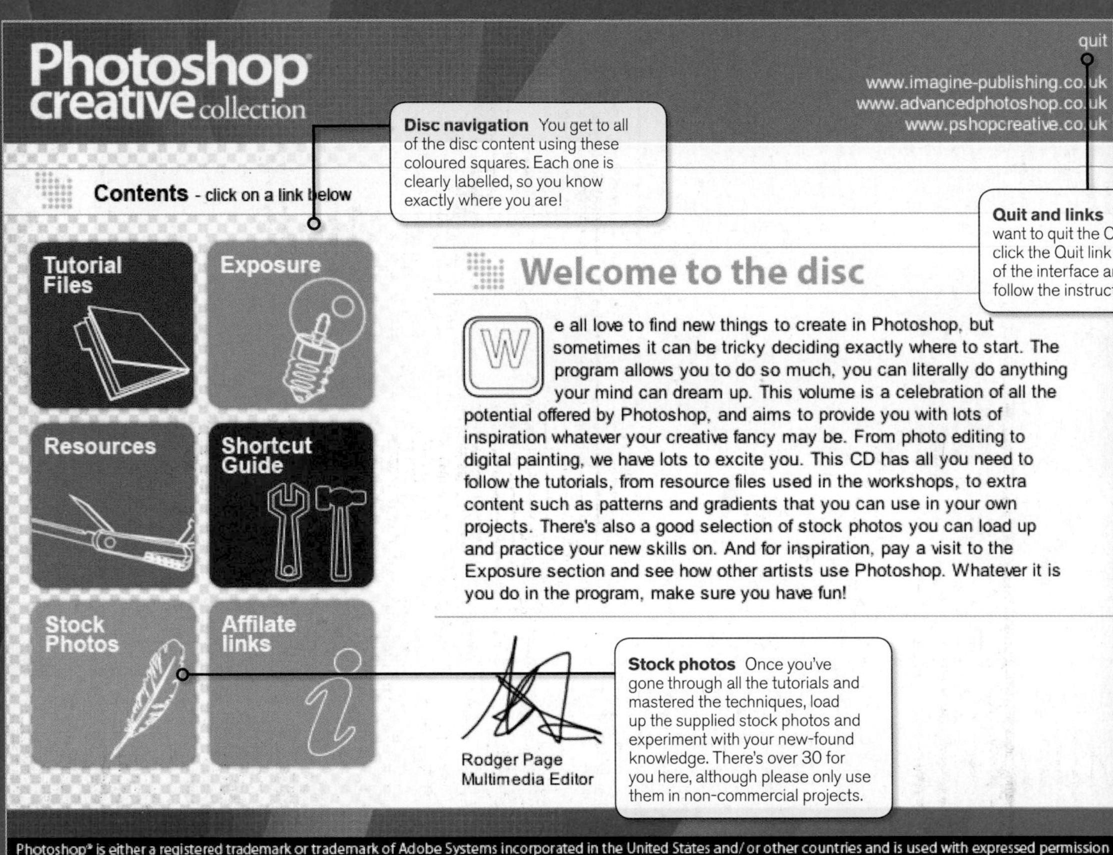

Disc navigation You get to all of the disc content using these coloured squares. Each one is clearly labelled, so you know exactly where you are!

Quit and links When you want to quit the CD, just click the Quit link at the top of the interface and then follow the instructions.

Stock photos Once you've gone through all the tutorials and mastered the techniques, load up the supplied stock photos and experiment with your new-found knowledge. There's over 30 for you here, although please only use them in non-commercial projects.

ON YOUR FREE CD

Stock photos

You can never have too many photos to hand, so we thought we'd stoke your imaging coffers some more by including over 30 high-quality photos. Covering a wide range of subject matter, you can use them however you like, as long as it's a non-commercial project. Maybe you like the idea of one of the tutorials but aren't keen on the image used. Try one of these instead! Alternatively you can use them to put what you've learnt in the tutorials to different uses, or maybe combine techniques. Of course, you may just fancy printing one out to hang up!